INTELLECTUAL
PROPERTY
RIGHTS

IN THE

GLOBAL
ECONOMY

INTELLECTUAL PROPERTY RIGHTS

IN THE

GLOBAL ECONOMY

K E I T H   E.   M A S K U S

INSTITUTE FOR INTERNATIONAL ECONOMICS
Washington, DC
August 2000

Keith E. Maskus, visiting fellow, is professor of economics and director of graduate studies at the University of Colorado, Boulder. He has been visiting economist at the Federal Reserve Bank of Kansas City and the US State Department. He is a frequent consultant to the World Bank, UNCTAD, and the World Intellectual Property Organization.

INSTITUTE FOR INTERNATIONAL ECONOMICS
11 Dupont Circle, NW
Washington, DC 20036-1207
(202) 328-9000   FAX: (202) 328-5432
http://www.iie.com

C. Fred Bergsten, *Director*
Brigitte Coulton, *Director of Publications and Web Development*
Brett Kitchen, *Marketing Director*

Typesetting by Sandra F. Watts
Printing by Kirby Lithographic Company, Inc.

Printed in the United States of America
02 01 00   5 4 3 2 1

Library of Congress Cataloging-in-Publication Data

Maskus, Keith E. (Keith Eugene)
    Intellectual property rights in the global economy / Keith E. Maskus.
        p. cm.
    Includes bibliographical references and index.
    1. Intellectual property—Economic aspects. I. Title.
    K1401.M375   2000
    338.9′26—dc21
                                        00-021475
    ISBN 0-88132-282-2

Contents

Tables

Preface

Economists and policymakers increasingly recognize that managing the powerful forces of technological change and market globalization requires establishment of legal institutions that both promote the benefits of those changes and restrain their excesses. Central to this challenge is international reform of intellectual property rights (IPRs)—patents, copyrights, trademarks, and trade secrets—which provide the foundation for building and extending markets for new technologies. Indeed, the construction of such institutional architecture is arguably becoming more important than liberalization of traditional barriers to market access, including tariffs and quotas. While this architecture ultimately could extend to issues of investment protection, competition regulation, and environmental management, IPRs are its vanguard by virtue of their already having been included in the core agreements defining the World Trade Organization (WTO) and the global trading system.

The research program of the Institute for International Economics has already addressed a number of aspects of this microeconomic structure. Edward M. Graham's *Global Corporations and National Governments* (1996) and *Fighting the Wrong Enemy: Antiglobal Activists and Multinational Enterprises* (2000), and Theodore H. Moran's *Foreign Direct Investment and Development: The New Policy Agenda for Developing Countries and Economies in Transition* (1998) analyze the role of foreign direct investment (FDI). Edward M. Graham and J. David Richardson's *Competition Policies for the Global Economy* (1997) and *Global Competition Policy* (1997) edited by Edward M. Graham and J. David Richardson covered that set of issues. Sector-specific studies have included Ben Petrazzini's *Global Telecom Talks: A Trillion Dollar Deal* (1996) and *Unfinished Business: Telecommunications after the Uruguay Round* (1997), edited by Gary Clyde Hufbauer and Erika Wada, Wendy Dobson and Pierre Jacquet's *Financial Services Liberalization in the WTO* (1998), *Flying High: Liberalizing Civil Aviation in the Asia Pacific* (1996), edited by Gary Clyde Hufbauer and Christopher Findlay. Catherine L. Mann, Sue E. Eckert and Sarah Cleeland Knight's *Global Electronic Commerce: A Policy Primer* (2000), link all of these issues together in the context of the Internet and electronic commerce.

In this new study, Keith Maskus addresses the difficult and complex issue of IPRs and their relation to international trade, investment, technology transfer, innovation, and growth. This is the first comprehensive study of the international economics of intellectual property protection, a critically important policy issue that remains intensely controversial. Maskus first explains the nature of IPRs and why they are becoming increasingly important for global commerce. The success of entire industries—ranging from pharmaceuticals and biotechnology to computer software, recorded entertainment, and electronic commerce—depends on the specification and enforcement of private rights to market their products. In an era in which technological change is expanding dramatically, and the costs of copying digital products and new technologies are falling drastically, the search for appropriate and equitable systems of protection takes on great urgency.

That IPRs are globally controversial stems from their remarkably unequal distribution across countries. The United States, Japan, and a few countries in Western Europe are home to the firms that produce the vast bulk of internationally marketable technologies and goods. Policymakers in these countries are interested in strong global protection and argue that a firm regime would result in a considerable flowering of innovation and growth, with beneficial spillovers to poor countries. For their part, policymakers, consumers, and competing firms in countries that must import technologies worry that a strengthened system would raise the costs of medicines and critical agricultural inputs, and reduce their access to new information products. This conflict is at the center of the increasingly harsh debate about institutional reform in the WTO.

In this environment, Maskus provides a detailed analysis of the implications of stronger IPR protection for the world economy. He reviews recent evidence on how patent rights affect international trade, FDI, licensing, and growth. His conclusion is that, while there are reasons to be concerned about potential exercise of market power by firms endowed with greater intellectual property protection, the balance of evidence strongly suggests that IPRs provide an important foundation for promoting technology transfer, local innovation, and economic growth in the long run. This finding points to the importance of implementing systems that are appropriate to the development needs of each country, yet consistent with minimum global norms. Maskus presents quantitative calculations of the potential gains in technology acquisition and growth for many countries, results that should assuage concerns that the new global system will damage the growth prospects of developing countries.

Nonetheless, the study clearly demonstrates that stronger IPRs alone are not enough to promote growth. To realize the long-term benefits from IPRs reforms, developing countries should adopt important complementary policies such as educational reform, market liberalization, and competition enforcement. To secure the economic gains from improved international protection, developed countries should stand ready to provide adequate technical and financial assistance to promote these broad reforms. There are also policy areas in which multilateral coordination of IPRs may be required to promote global well-being. Thus, continuous and dynamic reforms of the evolving system will be the watchword for the future.

The Institute for International Economics is a private nonprofit institution for the study and discussion of international economic policy. Its purpose is to analyze important issues in that area and develop and communicate practical new approaches for dealing with them. The Institute is completely nonpartisan.

The Institute is funded largely by philanthropic foundations. Major institutional grants are now being received from the William M. Keck, Jr. Foundation and the Starr Foundation. A number of other foundations and private corporations contribute to the highly diversified financial resources of the Institute. About 26 percent of the Institute's resources in our latest fiscal year were provided by contributors outside the United States, including about 11 percent from Japan.

The Board of Directors bears overall responsibility for the Institute and gives general guidance and approval to its research program—including the identification of topics that are likely to become important over the medium run (one to three years), and which should be addressed by the Institute. The Director, working closely with the staff and outside Advisory Committee, is responsible for the development of particular projects and makes the final decision to publish an individual study.

The Institute hopes that its studies and other activities will contribute to building a stronger foundation for international economic policy around the world. We invite readers of these publications to let us know how they think we can best accomplish this objective.

C. FRED BERGSTEN
Director
July 2000

Acknowledgments

The publication of this book marks the culmination of a long journey. Since 1989 I have devoted the lion's share of my research effort to an attempt to understand the international trade aspects of intellectual property rights. At that time, there were no serious analytical studies by economists of the practical implications of differential levels of intellectual property protection around the world on trade, investment, and technology transfer. This struck me as a significant gap in our body of knowledge, made all the more serious by the ongoing global negotiations on intellectual property in the Uruguay Round.

Those negotiations proceeded apace with virtually no empirical evidence on which to assess competing claims. Perhaps that is typical for trade negotiators, but economists should be able to inform such serious discussions better than we often do. After all, while trade specialists are outstanding at simulating the effects of tariff cuts, we have made little real progress in predicting the impacts of fundamental regulatory change, like that required by the Agreement on Trade-Related Aspects of Intellectual Property Rights (TRIPs). Arguably, the regulatory reforms are more influential than the tariff cuts.

In a series of theoretical and empirical studies I, along with many other colleagues, have tried in the last decade to provide more analytical structure. Indeed, the international economics of intellectual property rights may now legitimately claim to be an important literature in trade and development. This volume reflects the current state of the knowledge gleaned from that work. Though we have made considerable progress in putting these issues on firmer analytical ground, much work remains to be done. I hope the book will be a roadmap for those interested in moving the work forward.

This volume is devoted to a comprehensive analysis of policy reform issues that arise with the global strengthening of protection for intellectual

property. The chapters devoted to such reforms are necessarily more speculative and qualitative than other chapters. However, the policy discussion
is informed by current economic reasoning. I hope that readers will find
the discussion balanced and informative, if not always to their liking.

It is impossible to travel such a long distance without the invaluable
guidance and assistance of numerous colleagues and friends. I wish first to
thank Professor Robert Baldwin of the University of Wisconsin, who originally suggested to me that I study this new (to trade economists) subject
being negotiated in Geneva called intellectual property rights. What I thought
would be one simple paper has grown into a deep body of work. I thank
also Gregory Schoepfle of the International Labor Affairs Bureau of the US
Department of Labor, who provided research funding at an early stage, and
colleagues at the European Commission, the World Bank, the Asia Foundation, the National Bureau of Asian Research, and UNCTAD, all of which
have provided support for my work. I am particularly grateful to Pedro
Roffe and Assad Omer of UNCTAD for opening my eyes to difficult intellectual property issues facing developing countries. I am also indebted to
Sean Dougherty, Andrew Mertha, Gavin Tritt, and especially my great friend
Lisa Zhang for their assistance and wisdom in China.

My work has been immeasurably assisted by colleagues at the University of Colorado in Boulder who have graciously read manuscripts, listened
to seminars, and agreed to write papers with me. I wish to thank particularly James Alm, Ann Carlos, Yongmin Chen, James Markusen, and Thomas
Rutherford. I owe a great debt of gratitude to a number of outstanding
graduate students, whom it has been my pleasure to supervise and with
whom I have written many papers on intellectual property rights. These
include Denise Eby-Konan, Juan Blyde, Mohan Penubarti, Jill Holman,
Guifang Yang, Christine McDaniel, Roger Mahler, Mark Baker, Manaswini
Sahu, David Carr, and Michael Nicholson.

Numerous colleagues at other institutions have been supportive and
gracious over the years. They include Jonathan Aronson, Kym Anderson,
Claude Barfield, Bijit Bora, Alan Deardorff, Michael Ferrantino, Carsten
Fink, Amy Glass, Richard Harris, Bernard Hoekman, Edwin Lai, Will Mar-
tin, Jack Mutti, Walter Park, Carlos Primo Braga, Dani Rodrik, Kamal Saggi,
Pamela Smith, and Robert Stern. I am grateful to all of them. I also thank the
School of Economics at the University of Adelaide for funding a sabbatical
in 1997, during which some of this work was undertaken.

The fact that relatively few economists work in this area does not mean
that I had little literature to work with. Many talented legal scholars write
extensively, persuasively, and with insight about the international legal
structures of intellectual property rights. I have learned a great deal from
reading their work. Among these lawyers I would mention particularly
Frederick Abbott, John Barton, Carlos Correa, Paul Geller, Hans Ullrich,
and Zheng Shi.

Above all, I owe an immense debt of gratitude to Jerome Reichman, one
of the world's greatest legal authorities on intellectual property. He has

been patient, kind, and thoughtful in listening to my half-baked ideas and econometric findings. He has taught me most of what I know about the complex legal issues in intellectual property and made me aware of the significant economic implications of small changes in regulations. I consider him a mentor and friend.

I am grateful to many colleagues at the Institute for International Economics, both for their wisdom and insights and for their patience in waiting for this manuscript. I particularly thank Fred Bergsten, Kim Elliott, Ellen Frost, Monty Graham, Catherine Mann, David Richardson, Daniel Rosen, and Jeff Schott. I am most indebted to Jayashree Watal, a brilliant attorney, economist, and former trade negotiator for India, who read this manuscript carefully. Her many corrections of my weak understanding of the law of intellectual property are greatly appreciated, as are her comments on my interpretations of evidence. This book is much better for her generous contribution.

Finally, I am indebted to Susan Rehak for again displaying great enthusiasm and extreme patience during this project. A trade economist should plunge into the thickets of intellectual property rights only if he or she has an understanding companion.

1

Introduction: The Issue Is Deeper than American Movies

In 1984, the United States designated inadequate protection of patents, trademarks, and copyrights as an unfair trade practice that could invoke retaliation under Section 301 of the Trade Act of 1974. In the ensuing 16 years, intellectual property rights (IPRs) have moved from an arcane area of legal analysis and a policy backwater to the forefront of global economic policymaking. Indeed, the world is witnessing the greatest expansion ever in the international scope of intellectual property rights. In the 1990s, dozens of countries strengthened their intellectual property laws and regulations (often under pressure from the United States); many others are poised to do likewise. Numerous regional trade and investment agreements, such as the North American Free Trade Agreement (NAFTA) and bilateral accords between the European Union and countries in the Middle East and North Africa, have protection of intellectual property at their core. At the multilateral level, the successful conclusion of the Agreement on Trade-Related Aspects of Intellectual Property Rights (TRIPs) as a founding component of the World Trade Organization (WTO) elevates recognition and enforcement of IPRs to the level of inviolable international commitment. International efforts are also under way to enlarge intellectual property protection for critical new technologies, such as electronic commerce.

As such agreements are implemented, global protection for creative invention and expression will markedly increase, as will the gradual harmonization of national IPRs policies. Indeed, the TRIPs agreement represents a major turning point in the global protection of intellectual property. As I will discuss in detail in this book, the agreement sets strong minimum standards in each of the areas commonly associated with IPRs, including patents, copyrights, trademarks, *sui generis* methods for protecting new forms of technology, and trade secrets. Moreover, it mandates that countries set up mechanisms for enforcing these stronger rights. On a sectoral level, international rights protecting pharmaceutical goods, biotechnological inventions, plant varieties, computer software, entertainment products, and electronic databases will be markedly stronger.

The TRIPs agreement is important beyond its strengthening of IPRs. It is the first multilateral trade accord that aims at achieving partial harmonization in an extensive area of business regulation. Undoubtedly, it forms the vanguard of efforts to establish deep integration of domestic regulatory policies among countries.

The only previous period of comparable activity in IPRs came at the end of the 19th century with the negotiation of the Paris Convention (1883) covering various industrial property rights and the Berne Convention (1886) covering copyrights. These conventions were concluded by a small number of countries and are far less comprehensive in coverage, scope, and enforceability than is the TRIPs agreement. It is interesting that the Paris Convention was adopted during the extensive industrialization of that era, suggesting that patents were in demand as a significant component of public support for appropriating the returns to invention in the manufacturing age.

Today's even greater advances in protection anticipate the importance of IPRs in supporting the high-technology, information-based economy of the new century. The world is increasingly characterized by the international exchange of information, technologies, and creative goods and services. As detailed in chapter 3, the scope of such exchanges is huge and continues to grow rapidly through foreign direct investment (FDI) of various forms and through inter- and intrafirm trade in goods and professional services. Also important is licensing of knowledge-based assets, including technical advantages, know-how, management skills, and reputation.

In this environment, the economic value of products, services, and technologies is primarily a function of the creativity that goes into them and how they apply to market needs. However, whether such value is appropriated by original creators or by others depends on the market and policy mechanisms that protect it. Many inventions have long market lead times that give enough protection for the inventor to realize the returns to her work without public intervention. Many others suffer from low-cost appropriation by second comers through copying or imitation.

The ongoing process of economic globalization is a result of technical change, reduced transport and communication costs, and market integration through reduction of impediments to investment and trade. Firms increasingly look to international markets as these changes raise local demand and expand market access. A crucial component of this process is that, while the focus of competition shifts increasingly toward invention and innovation, the costs of many creative activities rise even as it is becoming much easier to copy them. Examples include pharmaceutical products, biotechnological inventions, operating software, and theatrical films, which are costly to produce and subject to considerable uncertainty in costs and demand but are often straightforward to reproduce in bulk. In consequence, firms are interested in international policies for protecting their proprietary information and trademarks.

The use of intellectual property rights in international commerce is nearly universal. Virtually any traded product or service carries some form of trademark or trade name. Computer software is a key input into nearly all production processes. Recorded entertainment constitutes one of the most dynamic sectors of the global economy. Advanced technologies provide the main stimulus to FDI in many industries. In this context, the international protection of IPRs forms a core component of the advancing global regulatory framework.

The Evolving Global System

By tradition, policy choices in IPRs are a matter of national discretion because intellectual property law applies solely within designated territories. A country's system of intellectual property rights encompasses the *standards* it enacts to establish a creator's rights to exclude others from exploiting the economic value of her inventions or artistic expressions, *limitations* imposed on those rights for purposes of domestic economic and social policy, and *enforcement* of the rights. Standards define the scope of patents, trademarks, copyrights, and related rights, including recognition of trade secrets. Limitations may include, among many other elements, compelled licensing of technologies to ensure their use, fair use of copyrighted material for educational and scientific advancement, and antimonopoly rules to maintain adequate competition. Enforcement entails administrative and judicial actions by public authorities to safeguard the rights granted.

With this many policy components, no two countries outside the European Union have identical IPRs protection.[1] Indeed, there remain substantial differences in IPRs systems, even among developed economies. For example, the United States and the EU differ in their treatment of geographical indications, biotechnology patents, fair-use exceptions in patents and copyrights, parallel trade, and misappropriation of trademarks, among other issues. Furthermore, there are substantive and controversial disagreements within countries about the appropriate scope of some rights and even the wisdom of granting them.

---

1. For example, the EU is moving toward an EU-wide patent. However, even within the EU there are significant differences in certain national practices.

The largest policy divergences run along North-South lines, with some developing countries maintaining weak standards and limited enforcement for IPRs. In the view of industrialized—and increasingly of industrializing—economies, several primary shortcomings that existed before TRIPs remain during the implementation period. Inadequate copyright and trademark protection promotes copying of software and entertainment products and misappropriation of well-known trademarks. Pharmaceutical drugs and agricultural chemicals are widely considered not patentable; so are biotechnological inventions. Many countries do not protect new plant varieties. Rules protecting trade secrets are absent or weak. Perhaps most significantly, procedures and resources for enforcement of IPRs are often inadequate to protect rights under even the existing weak standards.

In recent years, this system of highly variable national rights has become increasingly incompatible with the globalization of markets, where firms must exploit their technical and product advantages on an international scale. Governments met with intense pressure for reform from multinational enterprises (MNEs) in industries like pharmaceuticals, software, and recorded entertainment that are particularly attuned to multinational activity and vulnerable to imitation. These sectors are important net exporters in the American economy, which may explain their extraordinary ability to induce a massive shift in emphasis in US trade policy toward encouraging and forcing reform in IPRs in key developing economies (Ryan 1998).

Pressure from the United States and the European Union certainly played a critical role in pushing forward a global reform agenda. Widely publicized American negotiations and threats in the 1980s and 1990s helped usher in stronger IPRs legislation in South Korea, Argentina, Brazil, Thailand, Taiwan, and China, often using Section 301 authority. European Union negotiations and assistance advanced IPRs in Egypt and Turkey.

External trade pressure, however, only partially accounts for the upgrading in the 1990s of IPRs regimes by so many developing countries and countries in transition. Business interests inside rapidly developing economies also are mounting effective campaigns for stronger protection, recognizing that their own innovative efforts are disadvantaged by weak systems (Maskus 1998a; Sherwood 1997). More generally, in advanced developing countries, governments are increasingly convinced that (1) greater linkages to globalization processes through access to technology and information are critical for growth and (2) stronger IPRs can play an important role in providing that access. Whether this view is accurate or is wishful thinking depends on a wide set of factors in each country, a point that I will develop considerably in chapter 6. It is questionable whether regime changes are sustainable in poor economies that may lack domestic economic interests to support them.

Unilateral improvements in IPRs laws contribute to the new global system, but equally important are regional trade agreements with commitments on intellectual property. The process began in the 1980s when the United States began negotiating a series of bilateral investment treaties (BITs). A key component of BITs is a commitment on the part of the partner country to establish IPRs that are adequate for protecting proprietary technologies inherent in FDI. Intellectual property rights became a core element of broader trade agreements with the negotiation of chapter 17 in NAFTA. Chapter 17 commits all three member countries to standards of protection that are stronger in some cases than those in TRIPs (Maskus 1997a). In particular, it requires Mexico and Canada to enforce IPRs that go beyond those each had adopted earlier.

Regional agreements aim at one of four levels of coordination on IPRs:

1. The most extreme form is full policy harmonization, in which all members adopt the same standards. This is the stated goal of the European Union in IPRs, toward which considerable progress has been made.

2. Second is to commit to high minimum standards, which may exceed the standards set out in TRIPs, but not to achieve harmonization. NAFTA is an example of this approach.

3. Third is to adopt somewhat lower standards that are consistent with TRIPs but again allow for policy divergence. Often this approach consists simply of nations committing to adopt TRIPs standards. Examples here include IPRs in Mercosur and the series of bilateral agreements under negotiation between the European Union and nations in Central and Eastern Europe, North Africa, and the Middle East.

4. Finally, there is the approach based on mutual exhortation to proceed as is appropriate to each nation, without formal negotiations on IPRs. This characterizes the procedure to date in the Asia Pacific Economic Cooperation Forum (APEC).

Each approach has achieved some regional strengthening of standards.

The overarching international agreement is TRIPs, which I discuss at length in chapters 2 and 6. All WTO members must bring their IPRs standards and enforcement procedures into conformity with TRIPs requirements within designated times. Because TRIPs sets out minimum standards that countries are free to exceed, it does not aim at complete harmonization. However, many developing countries are required to maintain high standards for the protection of software copyrights, pharmaceutical patents, and plant varieties, and to ensure effective enforcement and administration of the agreement.

TRIPs also brings intellectual property rights into the realm of WTO dispute resolution procedures, which represents a major strengthening of the global system over the previously unenforceable conventions supervised by the World Intellectual Property Organization (WIPO). As additional countries join the WTO, they must adhere to TRIPs, meaning that its disciplines ultimately will extend as far as China and Russia. Indeed, China has upgraded its intellectual property laws to be virtually consistent with TRIPs in anticipation of WTO membership.

The TRIPs agreement is the first comprehensive and enforceable global set of rules covering IPRs. However, its implementation in many countries is not complete; controversies could emerge over perceived weakness in implementing legislation. Moreover, TRIPs remains a work in progress, subject to revision and updating both within its own procedures and in any new round of trade negotiations (Maskus 1998c; Watal 2000b). Questions of particular interest include further protection for biotechnological products, the relationship of competition policy to IPRs, and whether there should be global rules on the treatment of parallel imports.

Furthermore, dynamic technologies and markets already render TRIPs coverage incomplete. Thorny issues surrounding copyright protection for electronic commerce were not addressed explicitly in TRIPs, requiring the negotiation in 1996 of the Copyright Treaty and the Performances and Phonograms Treaty under the auspices of WIPO. These treaties build on but go beyond the Berne Convention and TRIPs. Clearly, the world has not seen the end of IPRs negotiations and policy reform.

Economic Issues

Massive policy shifts inevitably entail considerable controversy. In the case of IPRs, the greatest requirements for change are placed on developing countries, which are decided net importers of new technologies and high-technology products. The international strengthening of IPRs raises concerns that it will reduce the ability of poorer countries to imitate foreign products and technologies, which would be available only at higher costs, deteriorating their terms of trade. There are particular worries about potentially higher prices of patented pharmaceuticals and biotechnological inventions and for protected seeds from new plant varieties. Such impacts would raise costs for health care providers and farmers. Similar concerns extend to information and technology users in developed countries as well, with significant reservations expressed about the emergence of patents in biotechnology and software and about limitations on fair use of copyrighted Internet materials.

The potential for such costs is real, as I discuss later. However, there could also be significant potential benefits from extended IPRs. Clearly, stronger rights will provide competitive advantages for innovative firms, allowing them to appropriate larger returns from creative activity and generating incentives for additional invention. By reducing contracting costs through greater business and legal certainty, stronger IPRs should expand investment and technology flows to developing countries, raising hopes that they will enjoy closer integration with global sources of technology. It is likely that some developing nations will become greater sources of innovation themselves.

Few international economic policy questions are so important and so starkly framed as the potential distribution of benefits and costs that could emerge under a stronger global system of IPRs. Distribution effects will emerge in a static sense both within countries and between countries. Perhaps more important are the potential dynamic responses of innovation, imitation, and diffusion to globally strengthened IPRs, suggesting that there are intergenerational issues as well. Such possibilities evoke considerable passion and exaggerated claims from both advocates and opponents of stronger property rights in information. In turn, in the absence of systematic economic evidence, these claims tend to drive policymaking.

Objectives of the Study

A central objective of this book is to shed light on these competing claims through a comprehensive analysis of the economic impacts of extended international protection and partial harmonization of IPRs. To do this, I bring together recent studies of aspects of the issue as well as performing new quantitative and qualitative inquiry. Though there are extensive treatises on the subject by legal scholars and international relations specialists,[2] they tend to take the basic economic impacts for granted rather than analyze their subtleties and test them with empirical evidence. To date no one has gathered together in one volume the variety of economic approaches that assess the effects of strong international IPRs.

In the chapters that follow, I pose several questions that may be addressed with theoretical and empirical economic inquiry. The data available for answering many of them are scarce, so the results should be treated with caution. Taken together, however, they paint a comprehensive picture of the international economics of intellectual property protection, an area that is vastly understudied by economists. The questions are:

- What determines the international strength of IPRs and what factors explain the decisions of countries to improve their protection?

- What recent trends in international transactions in IPR-sensitive goods, services, and information help explain the rising equilibrium level of global protection?

---

2. See, for example, Reichman (1995) and Ryan (1998).

- What are the recent trends in international use of IPRs, as indicated by patent and trademark statistics? Are there systematic differences among countries? Are firms in developing countries making greater use of their own IPRs?

- To what extent does stronger protection support monopoly prices and what circumstances affect pricing decisions?

- How well do international variations in IPRs explain international trade, FDI, and licensing transactions? On what other key economic characteristics do these flows depend and how do these characteristics interact with IPRs?

- What are the major mechanisms by which technical information is diffused across borders? Would strengthening IPRs help or hinder this process of learning?

- What are the relationships between IPRs, innovation, and economic growth? Under what circumstances do IPRs contribute to dynamic growth rather than restrict dynamic competition?

A second fundamental objective of the study is to relate the economic analysis to the numerous policy questions that arise. Having given qualitative and quantitative answers to the previous questions, I apply those results to the following problems:

- What will be the balance of global benefits and costs from the TRIPs agreement? If TRIPs should be detrimental to some countries, what forms of compensation might be required to promote their adherence?

- Given the underlying desire that stronger IPRs contribute to a dynamically procompetitive economic environment, what implementation strategies for TRIPs might be recommended to economies at varying development levels?

- What can economic analysis contribute to the design of policies for social or noneconomic regulation of IPRs?

- How should stronger IPRs fit into broader policy packages in various countries in order to maximize the net dynamic gains?

A third set of questions relates to systemic reform. TRIPs makes many fundamental changes in global norms for IPRs but does not address some important questions that can only be answered in qualitative terms at this time. However, such analysis will inform attempts to extend TRIPs in future trade negotiations. For instance:

- How desirable is a global proscription against parallel imports of goods protected by IPRs?

- Given that the regulation of IPRs entails use of competition rules, how important is the specification of such rules in countries where they are weak or absent?

Organization of the Volume and Summary of Findings

In chapter 2, I describe in detail the structure of minimum IPRs standards that TRIPs requires so that readers will have a specific policy context within which to think about the economic analysis that follows. I highlight the changes in standards that are most significant from the perspective of economic development and technology policy. An important general conclusion is that TRIPs represents the first fully multilateral agreement aimed at setting comprehensive rules covering the commercial regulatory environment, as opposed to disciplines on literal trade distortions, such as border taxes, nontariff trade barriers, and trade subsidies. Thus, TRIPs is a critical landmark in the evolution of global trade regulation.

In chapter 3, I explain the basic nature and economics of IPRs. My first task is to analyze the economic justifications for protecting rights to exclusive use of information, with emphasis on issues emerging in open economies. There is a sound public interest in defining and sustaining such rights in order to overcome the natural failure of markets to encourage investment in new technologies and artistic works. There is also justification for distributing the fruits of such invention and creation widely to consumers at relatively low cost. IPRs must strike a balance between these fundamentally conflicting objectives. Interests in establishing either strong or weak protection vary between producer and user groups within nations and, even more starkly, between information-exporting countries and information-importing countries.

Later in chapter 3, I point out important and subtle distinctions in how different IPRs affect incentives for creative activity. As rewards for industrial invention, patents are provided on the condition that the patent owner add her information to society's technology base. Copyrights protect exclusive rights to duplicate the particular expression of an idea, such as a book, film, or computer program. Trademarks offer guarantees to consumers about the ultimate origin of a product, thereby lowering the costs of searching for preferred alternatives and encouraging firms to establish reputations for quality. Trade secrets exist to protect confidential, unpatented information from unfair or dishonest disclosure by competitive rivals. Various newer forms of technology are protected with special regulatory regimes that combine attributes of these classic devices.

I also discuss in detail the economics of IPRs in particular sectors. An identifiable "patent complex" comprises pharmaceuticals, biotechnology, and plant genetics. These industries combine significant fixed costs of inventing and marketing new products but are vulnerable to straightforward learning of their technologies through reverse engineering. A "copyright complex" covers recorded entertainment, software, electronic databases, and internet content providers. These sectors are based intimately on the application of information technology to particular market needs. Information technologies are clear examples of high fixed-cost, low marginal-cost activities, making them vulnerable to rapid entry and cheap copying. The nature of these goods and services raises difficult questions about the protection of intellectual property. Trademarks and trade secrets are used extensively in all industries, though some forms of goods and services are more prone to their application. For example, producers of wines and alcoholic spirits claim that policymakers must recognize exclusive geographical indications as guarantors of product origin.

In the final section of chapter 3, I present data showing that the global use of IPRs, through the registration of patents and trademarks and through the demand for information technologies, is rising rapidly at virtually all levels of development. Further, there is growing exchange of technology and information across borders through trade, FDI, and licensing activity. I conclude the chapter with an explanation of why demands for greater international protection of intellectual property have become so strong: As enterprises rapidly exploit their intellectual property on a global scale, the technical ease of copying and imitating new information has also increased dramatically. There is also the complex and evolving nature of intellectual property protection in newer technologies.

In succeeding chapters, I put forward the primary analytical contributions of the book, presenting theory and evidence regarding my first set of questions, such as the international determinants of IPRs and the impact of differing standards on trade and FDI. In chapter 4, the evidence clearly supports the view that the strength of IPRs rises endogenously with economic development, in interesting ways. For example, low-income countries might choose to reduce the strength and scope of their patent rights as they acquire better abilities to imitate technical information and establish production facilities based on that imitation. Middle-income countries find a growing interest in improving protection as their markets deepen and their capacities to innovate become stronger. Protection seems to accelerate rapidly at even higher income levels. The computations suggest that many developing countries are a long way from income levels that would encourage them to adopt stronger patent rights as a matter of course. This disparity points to potential difficulties in effective implementation of TRIPs and enforcement of new policy regimes.

Of more fundamental concern for this volume, I report extensive economic theory and econometric evidence about the implications of varying international levels of protection for IPRs. Theoretical approaches cannot unambiguously determine how intellectual property owners would react to different patent and copyright regimes. Other things being equal, international trade flows could be higher or lower for a country with strong IPRs than for one with weak IPRs. The same is true for FDI and technology licensing. This inability to make strong qualitative theoretical predictions stems from the interplay of market power, free riding, contracting uncertainties, and other features of international markets for information.

Thus, while theoretical models help considerably in understanding the mechanisms through which IPRs affect commerce, extensive empirical analysis is required to arrive at practical answers. In chapter 4, I discuss empirical studies that academic economists have undertaken. The results strongly support the view that international trade, FDI, and technology licensing react positively, and in some cases elastically, to the strength of patent protection across countries.

These findings deserve some qualification. For example, small, poor countries might experience losses from the exercise of additional market power by firms awarded stronger patents. Nonetheless, the overall impacts are strikingly positive. Moreover, these rising flows of trade, investment, and technology transfer would in turn provide potential spillover benefits in the form of faster growth. I put forward simple calculations of these growth benefits, finding them to be potentially significant. However, the growth impacts depend critically on other economic variables, including economic openness. Thus, there are potential long-term gains from the stronger global regime for those countries that choose an appropriate mix of policies. Indeed, this is the central message of the book.

In chapter 5, I analyze the relationships between IPRs and economic development. While there is some empirical evidence, the analysis is more qualitative and less amenable to systematic econometric approaches. The channels of causation between intellectual property protection and development flow in both directions. Rising income levels generate stronger incentives for upgrading protection of IPRs, which in turn lays a foundation for further growth if the protection is embedded in an appropriate system of regulation and incentives.

IPRs could have both positive and negative impacts on processes of economic development. On the positive side, survey evidence suggests that certain IPRs can stimulate innovative activity even at low levels of economic development. For example, trademarks can be instrumental in permitting domestic enterprises to achieve economies of scale in national marketing. Further, protection for incremental innovation is important in promoting learning and diffusion of technical information. Improved and more effective IPRs systems could encourage innovative enterprises to focus R&D work on the market needs of developing countries.

Negative aspects of a strengthened intellectual property regime could emerge as well. Firms that are pirating or counterfeiting must shut down, perhaps raising transitional unemployment problems. Stronger IPRs could under some circumstances invite monopoly pricing, though available evidence suggests that the impacts could be moderate. Rights holders might attempt to extend the scope of their protection through restrictive licensing clauses. To the extent that such practices could emerge, policy authorities should remain vigilant to the need for maintaining effective competition.

This analytical framework permits a series of conclusions about policy design that I apply to the TRIPs agreement in chapter 6. That chapter begins with an extensive review of actual policy changes that must be undertaken in association with multilateral initiatives in IPRs. It attempts to characterize the extent of policy strengthening and harmonization that the new system will entail. I discuss the extensive flexibility that TRIPs provides in selecting standards of protection. The agreement requires comprehensive minimum standards but permits countries to exceed these levels and also, with adequate justification, to limit the scope of protection. For example, standards may be selected that promote economic development by encouraging technology-follower firms to compete fairly, rather than to engage in simple copying or imitation.

Considering the various TRIPs requirements and the likely strength of their implementation, it is possible to use the econometric results from prior chapters for rough calculations of potential impact on international transactions in intellectual property. The major short-term impact is a transfer of economic benefits from technology-importing to technology-exporting nations, with the largest gains accruing to the United States. Over time, however, additional cross-border activity would be generated by the incentives implicit in stronger IPRs. The analysis points out the important interactions between IPRs reform and market liberalization that should be taken into account in designing policy. In particular, there is evidence that stronger IPRs encourage growth in economies that are open to international trade and investment. One reason is that IPRs help safeguard returns on the investments in technology and productivity that are required to compete in open systems. In developing countries, these processes apply similarly to adaptive investments that ensure effective acquisition of foreign technology.

An important question is whether TRIPs moves the world closer to a global economic optimum: Does it strike the best balance between dynamic incentives and static market needs and ensure an acceptable distribution of benefits across countries? No such optimum may be defined analytically, but I discuss in qualitative terms the potential for innovation to emerge. Because this potential is significant in important sectors, TRIPs should achieve dynamic net gains for the global economy over the long run. However, the problematic international distributive consequences have not yet received sufficient policy attention.

In chapter 7, I broaden the analysis to place intellectual property rights into proper context. Taken alone, stronger IPRs may not behave as suggested by economic theory and may not have the benefits advocates ascribe to them. Rather, they must be embedded in complementary policies and regulatory approaches that optimize the potential for dynamic competition. For example, there are subtle but important relationships between IPRs reform and liberalization of foreign trade and investment restrictions. Similarly, IPRs are complementary with human skills in encouraging technology acquisition and innovation, pointing to the importance of building human capital.

Equally significant are policies for supporting competition through antimonopoly practices in licensing and distribution. A particular issue to which I devote considerable attention is how parallel imports encourage price competition while limiting marketing incentives. Parallel imports are governed by each country's policy on the territorial exhaustion of distribution rights associated with IPRs. Once again, economic theory and limited empirical evidence reveal that parallel imports arise from a multitude of causes and have complex impacts on economic behavior and welfare. I conclude that it is inadvisable at this time to consider a global policy banning parallel imports. Additional complications in the international distribution and regulation of pharmaceuticals and vaccines, however, could support restrictions on parallel exports.

Regulating the use of IPRs in order to meet social objectives—such as affordable medicines, accessible biotechnological inventions and seed varieties, and sustainable biodiversity—is even more complex. These are among the most controversial aspects of the new global protection regime. There are critics of strong property rights in developed as well as in developing economies. Thus, I review the essential economics of social regulation in this area, noting the inevitable conflicts that emerge between longer-term needs for innovation and product development and intermediate-term needs for affordable therapies and technologies.

The final inquiry in chapter 7 is on the need for further international initiatives in intellectual property rights, both within the WTO and beyond. Within the WTO, I argue, enthusiasm for TRIPs in the developing countries would rise if the developed countries made efforts to meet their voluntary commitments to expand technical assistance and technology transfer. Further, there is scope for using TRIPs as a springboard for a limited future agreement on regulating competition. Finally, I believe it sensible to incorporate into TRIPs the Copyright and the Performances and Phonograms treaties recently concluded under the auspices of WIPO.

Beyond TRIPs, it is desirable to provide further incentives for firms to develop new vaccines for the diseases of poverty and to transfer those vaccines at low cost to poor countries, though the subtle economic questions implied in this approach require further analysis. I also briefly discuss mechanisms for managing the extraction of genetic resources, encouraging sustainable biodiversity, and promoting other environmental goals within a regime of effective intellectual property protection. Compromise and coordination will clearly be important in such initiatives.

No specific set of optimal regulations can deal with the complexities of the national and international regulation of intellectual property in all circumstances, but it is important to understand the stakes they raise for policymakers as the global IPRs system continues to strengthen.

In chapter 8, I provide conclusions and policy recommendations. The initial questions surround the TRIPs implementation decisions being taken by developing countries throughout the world. The analysis helps inform the levels at which countries may choose to implement TRIPs standards in order to enhance competition and achieve certain noneconomic objectives. Over the medium term, critical IPRs issues arise in relation to any future round of trade negotiations. These include the suitability of a global ban on parallel trade in IPR-protected goods and whether competition rules covering IPRs should be introduced into the WTO.

The protection of intellectual property rights is at the forefront of controversies over the impacts of globalization. The frustrations of some developing countries about the potential implications of TRIPs and the concerns of nongovernmental organizations about its environmental aspects have made it a focus of contention about the future of the WTO. I argue that there are legitimate reasons for including IPRs in the WTO ambit and that developing countries could gain in the long run from greater rationalization of dynamic economic incentives as a result of the new global regime. However, achieving those gains will not be costless.

This book will not satisfy all readers, precisely because there are so many divergent views on the international protection of intellectual property. Moreover, the empirical evidence put forward, though intriguing, is not definitive; it would benefit from further study. However, I hope that by setting out the arguments and evidence in a consistent economic framework, the book will stimulate more thinking and ideas that may be applied to the resolution of key policy questions. If it stimulates further discussion of these controversial questions, the volume will have served its primary purpose.

2

A Road Map for the TRIPs Ahead

Before the Uruguay Round began at Punta del Este in 1986, intellectual property developers in the United States made plain their dissatisfaction with the prevailing international system of IPRs. That system consisted first of highly variable laws and enforcement across countries and regions, with the weaker regimes responsible for tens of billions of dollars in lost sales annually, according to surveys conducted by the United States International Trade Commission (1984; 1988). Most complaints in both surveys related to straightforward counterfeiting of American trademarks and copyrights, though the later survey noted perceived damages from weak patent laws. Whatever the validity of the complaints, they did reflect considerable irritation with piracy, which was increasing rapidly because of the proliferation of low-cost means of copying.

The second feature of the system was a series of international treaties, managed primarily by WIPO, purporting to set minimum standards for IPRs as guidelines for member countries. The major treaties—the Paris Convention for the protection of industrial property and the Berne Convention for the protection of artistic and literary property—enjoyed widespread international adherence.

Perceived problems with these treaties were threefold:

1. Some standards were weak and vaguely specified. The Paris Convention, for example, essentially required only national treatment in each member's patent laws and grant of priority rights.

2. They provided no effective procedures for settling IPRs disputes and were therefore only statements of intention on the part of signatory

nations. Departures from the Paris Convention guidelines covering compulsory license issuance, for example, were common in national laws.

3. It was difficult to renegotiate the conventions rapidly and flexibly enough to handle new technologies, such as integrated circuits, software, and electronic databases, which were straining classical conceptions of intellectual property protection.[1] Among many developed economies these technical advances were pushing forward changes in IPRs, which evolve dynamically in any event, but the WIPO conventions were seen as hidebound.

In the 1980s, the accelerating globalization of intellectual property use through international trade, FDI, and licensing inevitably came into conflict with these regimes, a conflict that would only worsen in the 1990s. That is, the rising need to sell intellectual property on an *international* scale became increasingly at odds with existing IPRs based strictly on *national* or *territorial* laws and regulations. The United States first pushed for an international code on counterfeiting, introducing it at the 1982 trade ministerial meeting, but there was little enthusiasm for the initiative. Four years later, however, at the Uruguay Round meeting in Punta del Este, American negotiators, joined by representatives of the European Union and Japan, successfully introduced IPRs into the deliberations on global trade rules.

The TRIPs accord was fashioned against a backdrop of diplomatic efforts to upgrade global IPRs protection. The United States aggressively pursued improvements in numerous developing countries, ranging from South Korea and Taiwan in the late 1980s to China and Brazil in the mid-1990s. Regional trade agreements negotiated in this decade routinely contain language governing IPRs standards. This process began with NAFTA and the extensive obligations it required of Mexico, but it has been extended through partnership agreements of developing countries with the EU and through regional trade arrangements, including Mercosur, the Andean Pact, and APEC. Finally, new treaties now aim to protect copyrights in cyberspace.

The TRIPs agreement constitutes the most significant strengthening ever of global norms in the intellectual property area. Enforcement of TRIPs obligations amounts to a marked movement toward international harmonization of standards and a definite solidification of the international regime.

The negotiating history of the TRIPs agreement and its role in the establishment of the WTO, though fascinating, lies outside the scope of

---

1. One possible exception was the 1989 Washington Treaty, which set out standards for protecting integrated circuits. However, the treaty was considered too weak by computer chip designers in major countries, particularly Japan and the United States, and did not attract many national accessions.

the discussion here.[2] Rather, I discuss the provisions of TRIPs that require significant changes in norms of protection, along with limitations of those norms. This is useful for assessing the degree of policy change and effective harmonization that TRIPs represents. The discussion is not a close legal reading of the text, but rather an interpretation of its broad requirements that could affect economic processes as they are implemented and strengthened.[3] The treatment here presumes that readers have some familiarity with IPRs. In chapter 3, I provide fuller explanations of what these rights are and why they exist.

General Obligations

The TRIPs agreement consists of seven parts and 73 articles covering all aspects of IPRs, their enforcement, and institutional arrangements. The key provisions are listed in table 2.1, adapted from Maskus (1997a). TRIPs Part I, Article 3 provides for general obligations, including nondiscrimination in the form of national treatment and use of the most favored nation (MFN) principle. National treatment applies to persons or legal entities, rather than goods, as is the case under the GATT. This represents an important extension of standards-based legal doctrine into the WTO. The MFN obligation, placed for the first time into international intellectual property law, recognizes certain exemptions for regional trade agreements with IPRs accords and from reciprocity relations in copyright established under the Berne and Rome conventions.

Transparency is also established as a basic principle in Article 63: countries must publish laws and regulations, including judicial decisions and administrative findings that bear on the treatment of intellectual property.

Copyrights

The agreement then goes on in part II to set minimum standards in all functional IPRs areas. In copyrights, TRIPs incorporates the standards of the Berne Convention by reference, so that all WTO members must observe those rules at a minimum. However, at the insistence of the United States, TRIPs does not require the provision of moral rights as specified in the Berne Convention (Article 6bis). Extension of the Berne Convention to countries that were not previously members thereby establishes a

---

2. Bradley (1987) discusses the early history; Ross and Wasserman (1993) and Watal (2000b) undertake extensive interpretations.

3. See also Primo Braga (1996), UNCTAD (1996), and Beier and Schricker (1996). Watal (2000) provides a comprehensive and detailed legal interpretation, with excellent commentary on many of the potential economic implications for developing nations.

Table 2.1 Substantive requirements of the TRIPs agreement in the WTO

General Obligations	Comments
1. National treatment	Applied for persons
2. Most favored nation	Reciprocity exemptions for copyright; prior regionals/bilaterals allowed
3. Transparency	
Copyright and related rights	
4. Observes Berne Convention	Does not require moral rights
5. Minimum 50-year term	Clarifies corporate copyrights
6. Programs protected as literary works	A significant change in global norms
7. Data compilations protected similarly	
8. Neighboring rights protection for phonogram producers, performers	
9. Rental rights	A significant change in global norms
Trademarks and related marks	
10. Confirms and clarifies Paris Convention	
11. Strengthens protection of well-known marks	Deters use of confusing marks and speculative registration
12. Clarifies nonuse	Deters use of collateral restrictions to invalidate marks
13. Prohibits compulsory licensing	
14. Geographical indications	Additional protection for wines and spirits
Patents	
15. Subject matter coverage	Patents provided for products and processes in all fields of technology
16. Biotechnology	Must be covered but exceptions allowed for plants and animals developed by traditional methods
17. Plant breeders' rights	Patents or effective *sui generis* system required
18. Exclusive right of importation	
19. Severe restrictions on compulsory licenses	Domestic production can no longer be required; nonexclusive licenses with adequate compensation
20. Minimum 20-year patent length from filing date	
21. Reversal of burden of proof in process patents	
22. Industrial designs	Minimum term of protection: 10 years
Integrated circuits designs	
23. Protection extended to articles incorporating infringed design	Significant change in global norms
24. Minimum 10 years protection	
Undisclosed information	
25. Trade secrets protected against unfair methods of disclosure	New in many developing countries
Abuse of IPRs	
26. Wide latitude for competition policy to control competitive abuses	Cannot contradict remainder of WTO agreement

(table continued next page)

Table 2.1 (*continued*)

General Obligations	Comments
Enforcement measures	
27. Requires civil, criminal measures and border enforcement	Will be costly for developing countries
Transitional arrangements	
28. Transition periods	5 years for developing and transition economies; 11 for poorest countries
29. Pipeline protection for pharmaceuticals	Not required but a provision for maintaining novelty and exclusive marketing rights
Institutional arrangements	
30. TRIPs Council	Agreement to be monitored and reviewed
31. Dispute settlement	Standard approach with 5-year moratorium in some cases

Source: Maskus (1997a).

global standard that copyrights shall extend for the life of the author plus 50 years. However, TRIPs expands the Berne Convention by clarifying that copyrights owned by corporations shall extend a minimum of 50 years. A further noteworthy extension of international copyright law was the introduction into TRIPs of a requirement to provide rental rights for computer programs, audio recordings, and, to a limited extent, cinematographic films.

More significant change comes in TRIPs Article 10, which mandates that both computer software and data compilations are to be protected by copyright as literary works under terms of the Berne Convention. TRIPs does not require that programs be protected by patents if they meet conditions for patentability, as is the case in the United States, but it does not preclude that option. When TRIPs entered into force in 1995, numerous developing countries did not recognize computer programs and databases as copyrightable. Thus, this provision requires extensive legal reform. In the area of neighboring rights, TRIPs mandates a 50-year minimum term of protection for performers and producers of recorded music, which extends the protection of the Rome Convention.

Trademarks and Indications

TRIPs specifies that procedures for registering trademarks should be both transparent and independent of the characteristics of the goods and services for which protection is sought. An important requirement is that countries must extend protection to internationally well known trademarks in order to head off speculative registration and fraudulent use of those marks. Equally significant is that countries may no longer put use requirements onto trademark registrations. A typical example is the practice of requiring that a product be present on the market in order to maintain registered rights but preventing importation, as a means of accomplishing this presence, via a trade restriction, thereby invalidating the trademark. Such practices are no longer permissible for WTO members.

While TRIPs Article 21 permits authorities to regulate the licensing and sale of trademarks, it prohibits their compulsory licensing. It should be noted that compulsory licensing in the trademark area was in any event rarely used in the developing world.

Certain EU member states and Switzerland were eager to establish an agreement protecting geographical indications. What emerged, in Article 23, was additional protection for the place names used in identifying wines and spirits, even if products made outside the legitimate region are modified by words such as "type" or "imitation." However, Article 24 set significant limitations and an agreement was reached whereby members would work toward a new solution. Those negotiations have not begun, though many countries have lists of geographical names they wish to see protected and have submitted proposals on how to go about such negotiations.

Patents

The most significant changes came in the area of patents, which is not surprising given the controversy over technology protection. Article 27 requires a broad definition of protectable subject matter. Specifically, "patents shall be available for any inventions, whether products or processes, in all fields of technology, provided that they are new, involve an inventive step, and are capable of industrial application." Thus, many countries must extend patent protection to such important areas of technology as chemical products and processes, pharmaceutical products and processes, and food products. Broad exemptions from patentability remain, to protect public order or morality, prevent environmental deterioration, and protect animal, human, or plant life. However, these exemptions are limited by the stipulation that any inventions so excluded not be commercially exploited within a country. Exemptions are also allowed for diagnostic, therapeutic, and surgical methods, as is the standard in most nations.

Most controversial is the exemption in Article 27.3.b for biotechnological inventions. In principle, such inventions are subject to patents, and patents must be provided for microorganisms and microbiological processes. However, unlike the strongly protective American approach,

TRIPs permits exclusions from patentability for traditional breeding ("essentially biological") methods and higher life organisms (plants and animals). Yet all countries must adopt either patents or an effective *sui generis* system of protection for plant varieties. Thus, countries cannot escape the obligation to provide plant breeders' rights. This delicate compromise was not altogether appealing to biotechnological firms and TRIPs calls for a review of Article 27, beginning in 1999. That review is progressing slowly within the TRIPs Council but no report has been issued to date.

In addition to extending the required coverage of patents, TRIPs strengthens the scope of patent rights. It recognizes an exclusive right of importation in Article 28.1.a., though many legal scholars argue that this right was implicit in the right to sell. Article 27.1 establishes that importation is sufficient to meet working requirements. Because obligations to work patents through domestic production are no longer valid, they may not be used to justify compulsory licenses. However, the importation right is explicitly limited by Article 6, which specifies that each country may adopt its own regulation regarding whether the first international sale of a good would exhaust distribution rights.

This interpretation of TRIPs is not uniformly accepted: Some observers consider that Article 6 only removes parallel imports from the dispute settlement process but is otherwise governed by substantive requirements in functional IPRs areas (Cottier 1998). However, Abbott (1998) is persuasive that the importation right is attenuated by the prospect of parallel imports. This controversial question is discussed in chapter 7.

TRIPs recognizes the legitimacy of using compulsory licenses to achieve goals related to health and nutrition or other social purposes and to discipline competitive abuses of patent rights, but it significantly restricts their use.[4] Governments must negotiate beforehand with patent owners, can issue only nonexclusive, temporary (in principle) licenses meant primarily for the domestic market only, and must rescind the licenses when the conditions that triggered their use disappear. Adequate, market-based remuneration of patent holders is required of compulsory licensees. Authorities may issue compulsory licenses to permit the use of dependent patents—grants for which exploitation is tied to access to a technology protected by a prior patent. However, such licenses are permissible only when the later patent covers "an important technical advance of considerable economic significance" beyond the prior patent.

TRIPs affects harmonization of patent length by requiring a minimum term of protection of 20 years from date of filing. Moreover, it mandates that in adjudicating process patent infringement cases the burden of proof is reversed, being placed on the defendant under certain conditions. That

---

4. Watal (2000b) argues that these conditions are not overly restrictive and allow considerable flexibility for authorities to employ compulsory licenses.

is, the defendant must demonstrate that his process does *not* infringe the plaintiff's patent. This procedure recently became the norm in many industrialized countries, where it is recognized that proving process infringement is quite difficult, though the procedure requires a change in patent laws in many developing and some developed nations. The agreement also protects industrial designs for a minimum of 10 years.

Integrated Circuits

Original designs of integrated circuits are protected for a minimum of 10 years from filing. Protection covers the layout design, chips on which it is masked, and products that incorporate the chip. Thus, articles that contain an infringing design are themselves deemed to infringe the protected design, whether wittingly or unwittingly, and may be prevented from entering commerce. Though TRIPs limits the use of compulsory licenses in integrated circuits, it specifically permits reverse engineering.

Trade Secrets

TRIPs requires, for the first time in the global economy, that countries provide effective protection of trade secrets, which are confidential business information. Trade secrets have long been considered problematic in many developing nations under the logic that protecting them without requiring disclosure of technical information failed to achieve the benefits of technology diffusion. As discussed in chapter 3, however, trade secrets constitute a potentially beneficial supplement to the patent system, particularly in technology follower countries, as they do not prevent independent discovery by honest means.

The TRIPs approach is to recognize undisclosed information as a form of intellectual property but to require its protection by actions against unfair competition as identified in Article 10bis of the Paris Convention. In this sense, actions that are "contrary to honest commercial practices" constitute infringement only when those actions are aimed at learning trade secrets maintained with sufficient care. Illegal practices include making fraudulent and confusing claims about the quality, characteristics, and origin of goods produced by competitors, making false and misleading claims about products sold by firms themselves, and the misappropriation of trade secrets or confidential information. The last term includes breach of contract, inducement of others to breach contracts, and the acquisition by third parties of information known to be disclosed dishonestly (or when failure to know the disclosure was dishonest would constitute gross negligence). Note in particular that reverse engineering was not mentioned by the Paris Convention, meaning that it is considered a legitimate form of learning technical secrets.

With some limitations, Article 39.3 of the TRIPs accord also requires governments to protect against unfair commercial use of confidential test data submitted in the process of securing regulatory and marketing approval of new pharmaceutical products and agricultural chemical products. This is significant. No international law before TRIPs had any specific requirement for the protection of test data.

The essential issue is what constitutes unfair commercial use. While disclosure may be permitted in order to safeguard public health, release of such data to potential competitors solely to grant a market advantage is widely seen as unfair. Indeed, US pharmaceutical firms complain about the leakage of confidential information into competitive commerce through this channel.

The more substantive question is whether there should be a period during which governments may not use test data submitted by a first applicant in its approval procedures for second applicants presenting generic copies or similar products with closely similar therapeutic qualities. For example, the United States generally provides a protection period of five years, a standard that was adopted in NAFTA. Failing to provide such a period of exclusivity could absolve second comers of the costs of undertaking clinical trials, providing them with a competitive advantage.

At the same time, generic drug producers denied access to the previous test data would be forced to wait for the duration of the exclusivity period before receiving approval unless they also undertook costly testing. Moreover, such duplicative testing could be socially wasteful when performed on bioequivalent products. Some observers therefore regard proposals for such a period as an effective extension of patent protection beyond the period of patent expiry, an issue of great concern in many countries, developing and developed.

TRIPs sets no clear requirement to avoid relying on prior test data for subsequent applications; nor does it mandate a fixed period of market exclusivity. This situation has resulted in two interpretations among legal scholars (Watal 2000b). First, some argue that authorities must keep test data secret, except where disclosure is required for public health purposes, but may use the data for subsequent approval of bioequivalent generic substitutes. Argentina has implemented such a law, which may become the standard approach among developing countries. Second, some scholars believe that the provision requires an exclusivity period of at least five years during which competitors may not be allowed to rely on prior test data, either directly or indirectly through official use. The United States and the European Union have rules of this kind, and similar laws have been implemented in New Zealand and Australia.

Control of Anticompetitive Practices

In negotiating TRIPs, representatives of key developing countries consistently voiced the concern that stronger patents, trademarks, and trade secrets protection could permit rights holders to impose abusive licensing conditions, thereby inhibiting the effective transfer of technology. This has been a frontal concern of developing countries for decades, and underlay the attempt in the 1980s to fashion international codes of conduct governing restrictive business practices and transfer of technology (Sell 1998).

Article 40 of TRIPs thus anticipates that the exercise of IPRs may have anticompetitive effects that may be controlled by competition regulations. The agreement lists three examples of anticompetitive practices: exclusive grantback conditions, conditions preventing challenges to validity, and coercive package licensing. Though there is debate among scholars whether these conditions are exhaustive, the list seems strictly illustrative. The agreement further provides considerable latitude for member states in setting such regulations. However, competition rules used for this purpose cannot be inconsistent with other provisions of TRIPs and the agreement calls for opportunities for consultation. One observer (Primo Braga 1996) wrote that the vague language of Article 40 is likely to generate disputes over competition regulation in IPRs without effectively disciplining abuses. Competition policy in the regulation of intellectual property rights is an area I address in a later chapter.

Enforcement

The TRIPs agreement in part III requires standards for effective enforcement of IPRs. Enforcement measures must provide for border controls, civil and criminal sanctions in some cases, and expedited procedures for disciplining infringement, including preliminary injunctions and seizure and destruction of counterfeit goods. Further, access of complainants to such measures should be fair and equitable, available to both domestic and foreign rights holders, and not overly expensive and complex. Decisions should be subject to judicial review, though TRIPs does not require that a separate arm of the judiciary be established for IPRs. At the same time, enforcement measures should not be so stringent as to constitute barriers to legitimate trade.

These comprehensive requirements will, in principle, require many developing nations to implement new legal obligations and to devote considerable resources to the enforcement of IPRs. It is noteworthy that TRIPs is the first multilateral trade agreement that sets out detailed obligations for the legal enforcement of rules and disciplines. In itself, this commitment to enhanced enforcement represents a signal victory for intellectual property developers in industrial nations. The most visible and pervasive aspects of IPRs infringement continue to be unauthorized copying of recorded entertainment and software and counterfeiting of trademarks. Stronger prohibitions against these activities may potentially raise the global demand for legitimate goods by significant, but unknown, amounts.

Transition Periods

Countries are now well into the transition periods specified in TRIPs. Establishment of national treatment and the MFN principle was an immediate obligation of all countries, while a standstill provision prevents the introduction of weaker standards than those required by TRIPs during the transition years. Developed economies were given one year from the entry into force of the WTO, until January 1, 1996, to comply with all TRIPs requirements. Developing economies and economies in transition were given five years, until January 1, 2000. Many such countries have just finished implementing new laws, while others have not yet been able to comply.

Finally, the least-developed countries were allowed an 11-year period, until January 1, 2006, to assume their TRIPs obligations. These countries are also permitted to request open-ended extensions, suggesting that they have a quasi-permanent "opt-out" privilege. However, such an approach would frustrate the intent of TRIPs and could lead to long-term technological isolation of countries that invoke it.

Developing nations have ten years to provide patents for areas of technology that were not previously covered in developing countries, namely pharmaceutical products, agricultural and other chemicals, food products, and microorganisms. Pipeline protection of drugs and chemicals on patent elsewhere but not yet marketed in these countries is not required, thereby permitting local pharmaceutical firms to continue producing imitations. As partial compensation, however, authorities must establish a "mailbox" procedure, whereby they accept applications for patents during the transition period, providing a priority claim when such applications are ultimately examined. Moreover, if marketing approval is provided to drugs in the mailbox, authorities must provide exclusive marketing rights for the shorter of five years or the period until the patent grant is decided.

Administration of TRIPs

The final part of the agreement establishes a TRIPs Council to monitor its operation. The language also calls for developed countries to provide technical and financial assistance to countries adopting the new standards, on mutually agreed terms. It also sets up conditions for review and modification of the agreement. Indeed, in 2000, TRIPs is scheduled for review, which has not yet begun, and every two years thereafter.

An important component of TRIPs is that it folds disputes over IPRs into the integrated dispute settlement mechanism that lies at the heart of the WTO. The agreement stipulated a five-year moratorium on the use of dispute settlement against indirect violations of TRIPs, allowing countries to select implementation strategies without this kind of interference. In systemic terms, one of the primary achievements of TRIPs in establishing a broad set of multilateral disciplines over IPRs is that future conflicts will be handled in a recognized forum. These conflicts surely will grow in number as global integration increases and the importance of IP-sensitive goods and services in international commerce grows.

Summary

The TRIPs agreement sets out substantive minimum standards in virtually all areas of intellectual property protection. Particularly significant are changes in patent eligibility, requirements for protection for plant varieties, copyrights for computer software and electronic transmissions, protection for well-known trademarks, and effective measures to safeguard confidential information. The agreement further calls for adequate administration and enforcement and incorporates intellectual property into the dispute settlement mechanism of the WTO.

Thus, TRIPs is the most significant international undertaking on IPRs in history. Because it tilts the global balance toward stronger rights for information developers, it promises to effect a short-term distribution of income in their favor from information users, in both developed and developing countries. Over the longer term, because TRIPs fundamentally alters incentives for international commerce, imitation, and innovation, it should generate dynamic benefits with a broader scope of winners. To the extent that additional social costs could emerge, it will be important to develop policies to manage such costs. These are themes that I develop in later chapters.

3

Globalization and the Economics of Intellectual Property Rights: Dancing the Dual Distortion

Human thought is astonishingly creative in finding solutions to applied technical and scientific problems, in communicating the existence and quality of products and persuading consumers to buy them, and in expressing images and ideas. These intellectual efforts create new technologies, products, and services, describe new ways of doing things, and expand the cultural richness of society. They result in intellectual assets, pieces of information that may have economic value if put into use in the marketplace. To the extent that their ownership is recognized, such assets are called intellectual property. The economic returns on them depend on the costs of their creation, their desirability to potential users, the structure of markets in which they are sold, and the legal rights that permit their owners to control their use. The legal devices that provide such control are called intellectual property rights.

Three distinct philosophies about the nature of intellectual property and its protection may be discerned from history:

- The *natural rights* view, stemming from some European traditions, assigns ownership of mental creations to their inventors under the precept that failure to do so constitutes theft of the fruits of their effort and inspiration. Moreover, creators should have the right to control any reworking of their ideas and expressions. This moral view of IPRs exists independently of any thoughts about the incentive effects or economic costs and benefits of regulation. This approach is evidenced today in strong protection for artists' moral rights in European law.

- In contrast, under what might be called the *public rights* view, it is inappropriate to assign private property rights in intellectual creations.

Information belongs in the public domain because free access to information is central to social cohesion and learning. This approach found its strongest application in socialist systems, which did not recognize the notion of private ownership of intellectual assets. The task of generating knowledge fell to the state; the fruits of its invention were provided widely to potential users (at least in principle). This precept still underlies conceptions of the nature of information in some developing countries.

■ There is much room between these extreme positions for recognizing that IPRs may be assigned and regulated for purposes of social and economic policy. Most legal systems adopt a *utilitarian* view, in which IPRs strike a balance between needs for invention and creation, on the one hand, and needs for diffusion and access, on the other. Private property rights in information bear both benefits and costs, suggesting that they may be designed with incentives and trade-offs in mind. This is the point of departure taken by economic analysis of IPRs.

Economics of Intellectual Property Rights

Designing an effective and appropriate system of IPRs is complex for any country. The mechanisms by which IPRs operate vary across functional areas (patents, trademarks, copyrights, *sui generis* forms of protection, and rules against disclosure of trade secrets) and their importance differs across sectors. Indeed, as discussed below, the nature and purposes of these mechanisms are distinctive, although they share certain fundamental characteristics that bring them under the IPRs umbrella. The strength of IPRs depends on demand characteristics, market structure, and other forms of business and competition regulation. However, the essential economic processes may be described simply.

Static and Dynamic Failures in Markets for Information

Because intellectual property is based on information, it bears traits of a public good in two separate but important ways. First, it is *nonrivalrous*: one person's use of it does not diminish another's use. Consider a new means of production, a musical composition, a brand name, or a computer program. All may be used or enjoyed by multiple individuals. In this context, it is optimal in a static sense to permit wide access to intellectual property. Indeed, the public interest is extreme in that the marginal cost of providing another blueprint, diskette, or videotape to an additional user may be low or zero. Unlike the case of physical property, a multiplicity of users does not raise congestion costs in the exploitation of intellectual property.

The second characteristic is that intellectual property may be *nonexcludable* through private means: it may not be possible to prevent others from using the information without authorization. If an intellectual effort is potentially valuable but easily copied or used by others, there will be free riding by second comers. In turn, there may be no incentive to incur the costs of creating intellectual property. Society has a dynamic interest in avoiding this outcome by providing defined property rights in information. In some cases private mechanisms, such as market lead times, difficulty in copying or imitating particular technologies, and marketing strategies, provide natural incentives to create and exploit information. Accordingly, the strength of this dynamic argument for protection depends on circumstances of market structure and technological complexity.

The fundamental trade-off in setting IPRs is inescapable. On the one hand, static efficiency requires wide access to users at marginal social cost, which may be quite low. On the other hand, dynamic efficiency requires incentives to invest in new information for which social value exceeds development costs. These are both legitimate public goals, yet there is a clear conflict between them.

Economists often state this problem by noting that IPRs operate on the mixture of these two market distortions. Excessively weak property rights satisfy the static goal but suffer the dynamic distortion of insufficient incentives to create intellectual property. There the economy suffers slower growth, more limited culture, and lower product quality. Excessively strong IPRs favor the dynamic goal but generate the static distortion of insufficient access. The economy suffers from inadequate dissemination of new information. A common alternative expression of this trade-off is that IPRs generate monopoly positions that reduce current consumer welfare in return for providing adequate payoffs to innovation, which then raises future consumer welfare.[1]

The basic trade-off is illustrated in figure 3.1, which demonstrates a linear demand and marginal revenue for a product that has been invented and may be supplied to the market at constant marginal cost. Once the product is available, ex-post optimality requires that it sell for marginal cost at point C, generating consumer benefits in the area AP_cC. However, the solution at C, which would emerge in a competitive market in which all firms could costlessly imitate the product and sell a close substitute, generates no rents with which to cover the costs of the

---

1. This description is most apt for patents, which support exclusivity over the use of an idea. Patents are the subject of the overwhelming majority of theoretical studies by economists. It is somewhat less apt for copyrights, which generate ownership of a particular expression, and trademarks, which protect the use of a distinctive mark or symbol.

Figure 3.1 Basic access innovation trade-off in IPRs

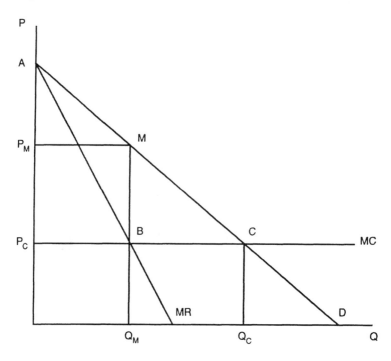

original research and development program. Therefore, there would be no such investment, the product would go undeveloped, and the entire consumer benefit area would disappear.

An alternative solution is to create a monopoly in the good through an intellectual property right, such as a patent. In this case the firm would offer the product at point M, earning monopoly rents of area $P_M P_C BM$. These rents, which represent a transfer from consumers to inventors, are the return on the original investment in product development. The economy suffers a deadweight loss of area MBC in comparison with the competitive (but unattainable) solution at point C. Compared to having no innovation, however, society achieves a net gain of the remaining consumer surplus plus monopoly profits, less associated R&D costs.

This simple theory shows the need for public intervention to stimulate invention in cases where ex-post competition would reduce market price to the competitive level and deter the ex-ante costly investment. In principle, society would provide support that is just sufficient to induce the introduction of all innovations for which optimal ex-post consumer surplus exceeds R&D costs. Because IPRs are incapable of operating so precisely, they are second-best remedies for the underlying market distortions. Protection might be too weak, resulting in forgone innovation, or too strong, generating surplus transfers to inventors and sacrificing available benefits from consumer access. Note also that a poorly struck bargain could slow economic growth to the extent that access to protected technologies is required to induce incremental innovations and artistic creation, which is how the bulk of innovation occurs.

Within this fundamental problem of dual distortions lie numerous economic issues of considerable concern. First, rights to own information impose other costs on society. For example, rent seeking for IPRs may be a serious problem because the property is being invented or discovered anew. There is no ownership until the right is created. Thus, a strong IPRs system may cause wasteful duplication of investment in R&D (that is, patent races) plus costly effort to assert ownership rights. Further, technical and judicial actions to enforce rights through excluding free riders may be costly. Finally, the costs of transferring rights to information can be high if there is uncertainty about the value of the information, about monitoring its use by those who buy or license it, or about other contracting costs. This problem leads to serious issues of antitrust policy in determining "fair" or "efficient" means of transferring intellectual property rights. These costs should be taken into account in assessing IPRs systems.

So also should external benefits that emerge from invention. The social value of information may be greater than the private market revenues it generates, because there may be market failures in creation of intellectual property. For example, the social value of an invention would exceed private revenues if there were positive consumption externalities, such as network effects from computer systems, software standards, or inoculations. Similarly, there is surplus social value whenever cost reductions spill over to other uses without market compensation. Examples here might include accounting systems and weather satellites. Note the implication that if such spillovers were easier under weak patents, an economy optimally could choose to provide limited protection. Risk aversion in undertaking high-cost R&D programs also could result in deficient private incentives to create the socially optimal amount of innovation, while such deficiencies would also sacrifice potential scale economies in research activities.

The main goal of an intellectual property system should be to create economic incentives that maximize the discounted present value of the difference between the social benefits and the social costs of information creation, including the costs of administering the system. The net effects of IPRs on social values versus private values are unclear. Much depends on demand parameters, the cost-reducing effects of process innovations, and market structures. The evidence suggests that there are large spillover gains from major inventions, while IPRs on smaller inventions generally do not create significant monopoly rents. Thus, there is likely a presumption in favor of strong IPRs in most societies on the grounds that private markets are inadequate to induce socially optimal information creation.

Setting an optimal policy for promoting invention and innovation requires accounting for numerous market characteristics in each product or artistic area. These characteristics include prospective demand and growth in demand, potential spillovers, the costs of R&D and duplicative races, potential impacts on market structure, and competitive aspects in the economy. Because many of these characteristics are highly uncertain at the time decisions on providing IPRs are made, finely tuned policies are probably unworkable. If it were possible to do so precisely, an economy could create a system of IPRs that would vary in the scope and length of protection with each potential new invention or creation. Further, there would be limits on protection due to the costs of providing and enforcing IPRs. But this task is not only impossible due to uncertainty, it is itself subject to severe government failure associated with poor choices and rent seeking.

An alternative policy regime would call for the government to retain a monopoly over technology and product creation, funding all development itself. It could then provide wide dissemination at low cost. As economists note, however, it is unlikely that governments would react efficiently to changing market preferences and technical information. Monopolized research in the former Soviet Union and China, for example, largely failed to produce technologies and products that could be moved into commercial streams.

Between these extremes countries might pursue systems that mix incentives for private information creation through IPRs with various public supports. In the United States, for example, research in the defense and aerospace industries is largely undertaken in or funded by public agencies. Large public research subventions are made to university researchers working on applied solutions that could find their way into private markets. Governments also subsidize artistic creation, libraries, and museums.

While the issue is complex, it is fair to say that provision of new goods and technologies through government procurement and nationalized research programs has not proven effective in stimulating and disseminating knowledge. Market-based approaches, in which governments set rules for protecting the fruits of invention but ensure competition in the creative stages, seem to be more flexible. IPRs are an obvious solution to this problem.

In setting rules governing IPRs, societies must strike a balance between the needs of inventors to control exploitation of their new information and the needs of users, including consumers and potential competitors working on follow-on inventions and innovations. Stated another way, the system should find an appropriate balance between creating and disseminating intellectual property. A system that creates innovations that are not put widely into use may be less beneficial than a regime that places less emphasis on creation but ensures broad dissemination of new ideas and creative works.[2] For instance, where many patents are never placed into commercial use because their holders do not see them as commercially viable, commercialization incentives are as important as incentives for creation.

In this context, the system should (1) allow market-based incentives for creation, (2) try to minimize the costs of innovative activity, and (3) provide for timely disclosure of innovation or creation and reasonable fair use with economic and social goals in mind. Moreover, it is important that IPRs interact coherently with other regulatory or economic systems, including antitrust policy, trade and FDI policies affecting the values of IPRs, and general technology development strategies. These last, which include industrial policies such as R&D subsidies, R&D joint ventures, and public grants to universities and agencies for basic R&D, are influenced by how IPRs are granted and protected.

Intellectual Property Rights in an Open Economy

The preceding captures the essence of the argument for intellectual property rights in a closed economy. The situation is more complicated in a world of many countries linked by trade and investment. The first difference is evident from figure 3.1. For a country that imports or produces an imitative product or technology at the competitive price, a decision to award protection transfers monopoly rents to foreign firms; the country thereby suffers a static loss of area $P_M P_C CM$ from the worsened terms of trade. It also reduces output by local firms that the rights holder has not authorized. If the country is too small for such a transfer to induce foreign firms to spend more on R&D of products that meet local demands, there is a straightforward loss in welfare. This simple observation underlies much of the resistance to stronger IPRs in many developing countries.

Technology-importing countries may prefer weak IPRs as a form of strategic trade policy. In addition to the discipline on monopoly pricing indicated in figure 3.1, weak patents, trade secrets, trademarks, and copyrights allow uncompensated imitation and copying of foreign products and technologies. Thus, limiting IPRs may provide inexpensive technology transfer, to the extent that imitative and adaptive capabilities are effective. International technology spillovers through uncompensated imitation have long been an important justification for refusing to grant patents (Vaitsos 1972).

Thus, countries that import goods and technologies that may be subject to IPRs coverage count several costs of protection, including higher prices for imports, potential competitive abuses in the exploitation of

---

2. Again, this is essentially a utilitarian statement. Different societies may value creation and novelty per se differently than they do social use and commonality.

IPRs, employment losses in imitative and copying industries, and restricted access to international technologies.

However, greater IPRs protection in developing countries does generate domestic benefits. One gain would be more domestic innovation, which would be better suited to local needs than foreign innovation. The prospects for such innovation depend, among other things, on local market size and domestic technological capacities. Benefits from trademarks seem particularly important, because product development reacts elastically to such protection in developing countries (Maskus 1997b). Further benefits stem from the fact that stronger IPRs expand incentives for trade and inward FDI and reduce the costs of writing and monitoring contracts for technology licenses.[3]

IPRs are national in scope, permitting considerable differences across nations in their protection regimes. International variations in IPRs have been the subject of trade conflict for a long time. For example, the US Copyright Act adopted by the first American Congress actively sought to encourage the development of the publishing industry by awarding rights to print, reprint, publish, and sell literary works only to domestic citizens and residents (Post 1998). Foreigners were not allowed to obtain copyrights and the law explicitly permitted parallel importation of works copyrighted abroad. In consequence, American publishers were able to publish and sell foreign literary creations cheaply; this attracted sharp criticism, especially from British authors.

Throughout several revisions of the law in the 19th century, discrimination against foreign authors and publishers remained central to US copyright law, as it did in many other major countries. Only with the passage of the International Copyright Act of 1891 did the US government recognize equal treatment for foreigners, and then only for countries offering reciprocal treatment to American authors. The change was made because of both pressures from foreign governments and, more importantly, growing interests on the part of US authors and publishers to receive protection abroad. Even so, the new law, which imposed discriminatory requirements on foreigners, remained explicitly protectionist.[4] Only with American accession to the Berne Convention in 1989 did all vestiges of discrimination in the publishing industry disappear.

The history of US copyright law demonstrates convincingly that countries that are substantial net importers of products and technologies that

---

3. These issues are discussed at length in chapter 4.

4. This law still imposed difficult formalities, such as requirements for copyright notice, registration, and deposit of works, with which foreign publishers found it difficult to comply. Moreover, it added the so-called "manufacturing clause," which mandated that, in order to receive copyright protection, any book or journal in the English language had to be printed from type set in the United States or Canada, and be printed and bound in the United States or Canada. The manufacturing clause, which was the subject of an adverse GATT ruling, remained a part of US law until 1986.

potentially are subject to IPRs protection consider weak protection to be a form of infant-industry support. To the extent that the losing interests from weak protection are foreign, they command little weight in the policy framework. The creation of indigenous firms that develop and produce items that require security from piracy has been the traditional spur toward stronger IPRs.

It is interesting to note one substantive potential difference between infant-industry trade protection and IPRs, however. Trade protection tends to create inefficient industries that block trade liberalization. Thus, to the degree that weak IPRs induce the development of innovative firms, they generate a future constituency for systemic reform.[5] Whether weak protection of intellectual property in fact has such an impact remains open for debate, as will be discussed later.

The copyright story also demonstrates that weak IPRs can be viewed as a means for achieving noneconomic objectives, such as the growth or maintenance of domestic cultural industries. The most prevalent of such objectives in the global economy is the preservation of public health through limiting the costs of procuring medicines simply by not patenting them. Thus, many developed nations, including Italy and Japan, did not provide patents for pharmaceutical products until the late 1970s; Canada only removed compulsory licensing of patented drugs in 1993.

Indeed, significant controversies persist over differences in IPRs among developed countries. For example, the United States remained dissatisfied with aspects of the Japanese patent system until its recent reform, claiming that it encouraged excessive filing of narrow patent claims and discouraged patenting by foreign firms. The US and the EU have moved toward patenting software with demonstrated industrial utility, but they differ considerably in their rules on acceptable decompilation of computer programs for purposes of reverse engineering. Negotiations continue over the scope of protection for geographic indications, with the US preferring less protective standards than the EU. Developed countries also differ markedly in their treatment of copyrights. In the world economy today, however, the largest differences in intellectual property protection occur along North-South lines. Information developers in the innovative countries of the North see several primary shortcomings in the regimes of many developing countries:

■ Inadequate enforcement of copyrights and trademarks allows extensive copying of entertainment and software products and unauthorized use or misrepresentation of well-known trademarks.

■ Pharmaceutical and chemical products have generally been excluded from patent protection.

---

5. I am grateful to Catherine Mann for this insight.

- The absence of patent protection for biotechnological inventions and patents or *sui generis* rights for plant varieties has been controversial.

- There is concern about the practice, albeit rare, of issuing compulsory licenses with inadequate compensation to firms that are perceived to be exercising their patent insufficiently to achieve desired consumer benefits or technology transfer.

- Also problematic is the often weak or poorly defined system of rules protecting trade secrets.

Structures and Objectives of IPRs

Despite the terminology related to figure 3.1, it is inaccurate to think of IPRs as mechanisms for creating monopolies. Intellectual property rights define the extent to which their owners may exclude others from activities that infringe or damage the property. Thus, IPRs set out and protect the boundaries of legal means of competition among firms seeking to exploit the value of creative assets. In principle, efforts to extend the rights beyond these boundaries are denied. In this context, it is more fruitful to conceive of IPRs as rules regulating the terms of static and dynamic competition, rather than mechanisms for creating legal monopolies. While IPRs do create market power, the impact on competition varies as widely across products, technologies, and countries as it does across the form of rights granted and the scope of protection. Indeed, the strength of the protection depends not only on the scope of the rights granted, but also on the ability of competitors to create non-infringing products and technologies and the ability of consumers to substitute among supply sources.

This section describes the general structure of various forms of IPRs, noting the different objectives they try to fulfill and the limitations placed on them to ensure their proper functioning.[6] While the focus is on the economics rather than the legal characteristics of IPRs, it is useful to introduce certain legal terms that come up throughout the volume. Table 3.1 lists each area of intellectual property and its main forms of protection.

Patents

A patent gives its owner the right to exclude all others from making, selling, importing, or using the product or process named in the patent without authorization for a fixed period of time. In principle, it is the

---

6. An excellent source on this material is Besen and Raskind (1991).

Table 3.1 Instruments and agreements for protecting IPRs

Types of intellectual property	Instruments of protection	Protected subject matter	Primary fields of application	International agreements
Industrial property	Patents and utility models	New, nonobvious inventions with industrial utility	Manufacturing, agriculture	Paris Convention Patent Cooperation Treaty Budapest Treaty Strasbourg Agreement TRIPs
	Industrial designs	Ornamental designs of products	Automobiles, apparel, construction tiles, others	Hague Agreement Locarno Agreement TRIPs
	Trademarks	Identifying signs and symbols	All industries	Madrid Agreement Nice Agreement Vienna Agreement
	Geographical indications	Identifying place names	Wines, spirits	Lisbon Agreement TRIPs
Artistic and literary property	Copyrights and neighboring rights	Original expressions of authorship	Publishing, electronic entertainment, software, broadcasting	Berne Convention Rome Convention Geneva Convention Brussels Convention WIPO Copyright Treaty WIPO Performances and Phonograms Treaty Universal Copyright Convention TRIPs

(table continued next page)

Table 3.1 Instruments and agreements for protecting IPRs (*continued*)

Types of intellectual property	Instruments of protection	Protected subject matter	Primary fields of application	International agreements
Sui generis protection	Integrated circuits	Original designs	Computer chip industry	Washington Treaty TRIPs
	Database protection	Databases	Information processing	EC Directive 96/9/EC
	Plant breeders' rights	New, stable, distinct varieties	Agriculture, food	UPOV TRIPs
Trade secrets	Laws against unfair competition	Business information held in secret	All industries	TRIPs

Source: Adapted from Primo Braga, Fink, and Sepulveda (2000).

most powerful instrument in the IPRs system because it provides exclusive rights to the physical representation—in the forms of goods, blueprints, formulas, and designs—of ideas with industrial applicability. Because they protect technologies and products to which follower countries wish to have access, patents are also among the most controversial forms of IPRs.[7] This is particularly true in sectors where the public interest may call for wide dissemination at moderate prices.

Legal and Economic Principles

Patents may be awarded in any area of technology to any new and useful process, product, composition of matter, or, in the United States, ornamental design of a product. However, some subject matter may be excluded from patentability in order to preserve morality, national security, or public health. In most systems patents also are not awarded for fundamental scientific discoveries flowing from the basic physical laws of nature, including mathematical algorithms. Under the nearly universal "first-to-file" rule, patents are granted to the applicants who first submit the appropriate documents. The United States is an exception, awarding patents to inventors who can document that they were the first to invent the product or technology (a "first-to-invent" rule).

To be patentable, an invention must meet three criteria: (1) it must be novel (that is, previously unknown), (2) it must contain an inventive step (that is, a step that is nonobvious to one skilled in the area of technology it represents), and (3) it must be useful or have industrial applicability. Novelty and nonobviousness are important, for they set the technical bar that patent examiners must certify has been met before protection can be awarded.

In general, an inventor may apply for one of three types of patents, though not all countries recognize all three forms:

1. *Invention patents* (or simply patents) require significant nonobviousness, meaning that they embody discrete advances in technology. They receive the longest term of protection, with the global standard under the TRIPs agreement being 20 years.

2. *Utility models* are awarded to mechanical inventions with less stringent nonobviousness standards. These inventions, which tend to be incremental improvements in existing products and technologies, embody less technological progress and receive shorter protection.

3. *Industrial designs* protect the aesthetic or ornamental aspects, such as shape, pattern, or color, of a useful commercial article. The design

---

7. Others are copyrights for software and electronic databases.

must be associated with the industrial article itself. TRIPs requires that designs be protected from unauthorized copying or imitation for a minimum period of 10 years.

Inventors make claims about the protectable novelty of their inventions but examiners may narrow the claim or reject it. Patent *breadth* refers to the precise claims that make up the protected subject matter. It is a technical matter; examiners do not try to consider economic efficiency in patent grants. Patent *scope* refers to the effective coverage awarded by the patent and associated instruments. For example, coverage may be complemented by a legal "doctrine of equivalents." This doctrine permits patent owners to litigate against competing products and technologies shown to rely on techniques that are essentially equivalent to those in the patent grant. The power of the doctrine may depend on national legislation.

In economic terms, whether a patent should cover narrow claims over a long life or broad claims for a short time depends on expected market competition and the likelihood of spillover effects (Klemperer 1990). These considerations argue for structuring patents to meet the specific conditions of each application, which is impractical. Some economists mention also the height of patent protection, which refers to the power of a particular grant to permit its recipient to limit or control development of follow-on technologies.

Four arguments may be put forward to justify the award of market power through patent grants:[8]

First, patents provide an incentive to take on the research effort and the costs of inventing new technologies and products and bringing them to market. Thus, patents are a primary solution to the problem of ensuring that inventors may appropriate the returns to R&D in the area of industrial invention and innovation. Note that the incentives must be sufficient not only to induce invention but also to encourage commercialization. A patent that is not "worked" through production or sales, even if it were commercially viable to do so, locks up an area of technology with little gain to consumers. In consequence, some countries include working requirements, within particular time periods, for patent grants to be sustained.[9] An important variant of the commercialization-inducement theory of patents is that patents may reduce the transaction costs of licensing, resulting in broader sharing of new information.

A second argument is that patents serve to expand the public stock of technical knowledge. It has long been recognized that in return for

---

8. Mazzoleni and Nelson (1998) provide a trenchant analysis.

9. Note that domestic production requirements may be effectively equivalent to a trade restraint or an investment mandate, pointing out the intricate interplay between IPRs and commercial policy.

cre-ating market exclusivity through a patent, society requires compensation. For this reason, patents bear a disclosure requirement, in which the technical aspects of patents are made known and others are free to incorporate the information into new inventions that do not violate the patent claim. Note that the narrower the claim, the easier it is to invent around the patent. Similarly, the sooner the patent application is laid open for inspection by the public, the more rapidly the technical information it contains becomes known. In this sense, patents may be dynamically procompetitive even if they are statically anticompetitive. Indeed, advocates of strong patent rights believe that they create significant competition, with long-run consumer benefits.

A third justification is that the awarding of market power through patent grants may facilitate the establishment of markets for developing and disseminating knowledge.[10] Absent exclusive rights to new information, these markets themselves might fail to develop—an observation that is consistent with the practical situation in some developing countries, as I discuss later.

A final argument is that well-recognized patent claims encourage orderly follow-on innovation, much as do prospecting claims for mineral deposits.[11] In this view, ownership of a broad patent on an invention supports fruitful development of related innovation by the owner or its licensees. Without such rights, there may be wasteful duplication of R&D targeted to applications of the controlling technology. This justification for awarding monopoly rights on a technology that permits control of subsequent exploratory research is controversial, even within leading technological nations such as the United States.

Clearly, the market power associated with patents may impose social costs even as it encourages invention and commercialization. Accordingly, societies limit the power of patent grants. Not only are patents limited in duration and breadth, they also carry disclosure requirements and, in many nations, must be worked if protection is to be sustained. These limitations vary across countries and, as will be discussed in later chapters, may be selected to affect the competitive conditions associated with the patent regime. Moreover, the potential for abusing the market power inherent in patent grants is recognized in national competition policies. Attempts to extend protection beyond the patent grant are considered anticompetitive. They may be subject to antimonopoly remedies, including orders to cease the practice, compulsory licenses to competing firms of key products or technologies, and even patent revocation. Some examples of abuses include the horizontal restraints on trade associated with patent licensing, tied sales that extend the patent to an unpatented

---

10. See David (1993).

11. The "prospect theory" of patents is associated with Kitch (1977).

product, exclusive grant-back conditions in technology contracts, and conditions preventing challenges to patent validity. These are taken up further in chapter 7.

The Effectiveness of Patents

Many observers question whether strong patent systems are needed to achieve their stated goals. An obvious question is whether patents are necessary to stimulate investment in invention and commercialization. Competitive rivalry in technology development may spur invention naturally. Further, market and technical barriers to imitation may allow inventive firms to charge a price above current production costs long enough for them to recover investment costs and compensate for risks taken. Scherer (1980) notes some conditions under which this situation might prevail, including imitation lags due to secrecy, imperfect information transfer, and the complexity of successful imitation. Being first to market a new product may also confer an advantage by establishing a company's reputation for quality.

Thus, the ability of firms to appropriate the economic returns to invention and innovation depends on several characteristics, among them the degree of market imperfection, the technical ease of imitation, the pace of information diffusion and firms' abilities to control it, and market demand parameters. In cases where innovation and development would happen naturally, patent protection is redundant and potentially costly. In practice, however, it is difficult to identify such cases, since inventors generally do file for patents. It may not be possible to determine whether the promise of a patent was the stimulus to invention or whether registration is a means of establishing claims to an invention that would have emerged anyway.

There is suggestive evidence on some of these questions. In the United States, information about new products and processes becomes available to a firm's competitors (including foreign competitors) fairly rapidly, generally within one to two years (Mansfield 1985). The information is transferred through shifts of personnel, technical meetings, communication with suppliers and customers, reverse engineering, and the study of patent applications. Thus, the ability of firms to retain technological advantages in-house without protection is limited.

However, there is a big step from learning the information to imitating the new product or process. Imitation takes time and requires investment in R&D, marketing, production facilities, and start-up costs—and, if necessary, the need to invent around the original patent. In the United States, these costs can be substantial in many industries. In a sample of firms in four industries, average imitation costs totaled some 65 percent of innovation costs and imitation time equaled about 70 percent of innovation time (Mansfield, Schwartz, and Wagner 1981). These costs depended significantly on market structure. Further, except in the pharmaceuticals industry, patents had small impacts on imitation costs and patented innovations were relatively easily imitated, generally within four years of introduction.

Mansfield (1986) sampled 100 firms in 12 US manufacturing industries on their views of whether patents are important to their decisions about investment in innovation. His results suggested that only in the pharmaceutical and chemical industries were patents considered essential; here more than 30 percent of the inventions would not have been developed without potential protection. In these sectors, fixed costs of R&D are high and imitation is fairly easy. In three industries (petroleum, machinery, and fabricated metal products), patents were seen as important in the development of 10 to 20 percent of inventions; in the other seven industries, patents were viewed as unimportant or only marginally significant in inducing R&D. These results are consistent with those reported in Levin et al. (1987).[12]

That patents may not be considered important incentives for invention in US industry does not mean that firms decline to patent. In Mansfield's sample, a high percentage of patentable inventions were patented, ranging from 50 percent in the primary metals sector to 86 percent in the petroleum and machinery industries. The remaining inventions were protected, to the extent possible, with trade secrets and private actions. Thus the benefits of patent protection were seen as worth incurring its costs.

This evidence suggests that the elasticity of invention with respect to patents is rather small, except in certain industries. However, these surveys are rather dated. Newer technologies such as biotechnology and plant genetics find patent protection important. Moreover, inventor attitudes toward the importance of patents are surely endogenous to the strength of the system. At the international level, the general weakness of the global patent system and the ease of technological spillovers may have contributed to the view of patents as unimportant (Mansfield 1988). If so, stronger protection could alter this view and potentially increase inventive activity and economic growth. Further, any dynamic linkages or spillovers between product generations would be enhanced by stronger patent regimes, causing firms to view patents as more significant over time.

A second question is whether patents are the least-cost means of stimulating invention. Patents may be a crude means of compensating inventors, resulting in inadequate returns if protection is weak or excessive returns if protection is so strong as to transfer to inventors revenues above their investment. This latter outcome often happens, at times spectacularly (Scherer 1980). It is evident that the fixed-term patent structure is ill designed to effect optimal dynamic resource allocation. Cheung (1986) suggests that it is possible in principle to design lump-sum transfers from

---

12. Taylor and Silbertson (1973) present similar evidence for the United Kingdom.

consumers to inventors that could stimulate the same investments in innovation without suffering the price distortions of patent grants.

This argument is a variant of the case for using tax-cum-subsidy schemes rather than tariffs and quotas to promote certain social objectives—and from a practical standpoint it has the same shortcomings, chiefly the difficulty of making such transfers efficiently and political resistance to cash transfers. Further, it would be practically impossible to compute the required surplus transfer ex ante, given the uncertain nature of technology development. The third alternative of government provision of R&D is, as noted earlier, also unwieldy and ineffective. Thus, for all its imperfections the patent system is probably the most efficient system for promoting inventive efforts, though this hypothesis cannot be tested.

There is little systematic evidence that patent disclosure enhances the dissemination of technical information, though Mansfield mentions the importance of this requirement in his 1986 survey. The more significant factor is that the patent system may provide the necessary incentive for firms to undertake the risky, long-term R&D that leads to major technological breakthroughs, such as copying technologies, computers, and semiconductors (Scherer 1980). Around these inventions grow whole industries that use their technologies, improve on them, or develop residual applications. The social gains to large technological advances can far exceed private returns because their associated spillover benefits have a substantial positive impact on growth, a point on which there is virtually no doubt (Bresnahan 1986). While there is little empirical evidence on the role of patents in this process, largely due to the difficulty of constructing counterfactual cases to study, practitioners suggest that patent protection plays an important role.

Copyrights

Copyrights protect the rights of creators of literary and artistic works to communicate, display, or perform those works in some medium, plus the rights to make and sell copies. Copyright laws protect the expression of an idea—its arrangement and presentation in words, musical notes, dance steps, colors, and so on—rather than the idea itself. By tradition, literary and artistic ideas are without industrial applicability, which renders them different from patentable inventions, though this distinction has been blurred by recent technological developments, as will be discussed later. Thus, the idea to render a painting of a mountain cannot be protected from others who also wish to paint it. But the particular rendition by one artist is protected from being copied, either literally or so closely as to constitute "slavish copying."

To receive a copyright, the item must be a demonstrably original work, but there is no need for novelty in the underlying idea. The particular expression must be fixed in a medium, such as a book, recording, electronic broadcast, software, or even electronic mail. It is generally not necessary to undergo registration formalities to receive a copyright because any original expression is protectable upon creation regardless of its inherent quality. Rather, it is sufficient to establish the date on which the work was created. Formal registration, however, may be of material assistance in defending the copyright.

Copyrighted works are protected from unauthorized copying for long periods, typically the lifetime of the creator plus 50 to 70 years (50 years for corporate copyrights). The longer period compensates for the lower monopoly power of copyrights compared to patents. Copyrights cannot be renewed. When they expire, the works enter the public domain for free use.

A copyright confers the rights to prevent unauthorized duplication, performance, recording, broadcast, translation, or adaptation of a work. Further, the Berne Convention requires member countries to provide "moral rights" or "authors' rights," by which the creator may prevent any prejudicial modification of her work even after she has sold its economic rights. Further, most countries provide "neighboring rights," which protect the rights of those who disseminate an author's work, such as performers, phonogram producers, and broadcasters, to prevent unauthorized duplication of their efforts. Copyright laws also typically extend rights to authors to control the development and use of derivative products, such as the affixation of literary characters on clothing.

The main exceptions to copyright protection come under the "fair-use doctrine," the terms of which vary from country to country. Under this doctrine, countries define activities that can make use of protected works in the interests of educational, scientific, and technical advance. Thus, limited uncompensated quotation of a work is allowed, subject to appropriate citation, as is the making of a limited number of copies for educational and research purposes.

More controversial is the treatment of decompilation of computer programs for purposes of developing competing applications. In the United States, for example, many software developers consider this form of reverse engineering to be free riding that injures their investment in program development.

The fundamental objectives of copyrights in literary and artistic property are like those in patents for industrial property: creative works provide social, cultural, and economic benefits that society wishes to secure. These works involve investment costs, including training, time, materials, technology acquisition, and the like. Moreover, marketing copyrighted products requires costly investment that is more readily recouped given the greater certainty provided by protection. If other members of society were allowed to free ride on works without compensating their creators, the incentives to create would be severely dampened. Static economic efficiency might be achieved, but at the cost of lower growth in cultural identity and reduced investment in "industrially useful" expressions such as software. At the same time, providing exclusive rights limits the dissemination of literary works and raises the static costs of education, research, and entertainment. The copyright system reflects a compromise between these difficulties, attempting to balance the needs of creators with society's interests in wide access to their creations.

There may be natural market mechanisms that would provide adequate remuneration to creators in the absence of copyrights. Examples include subject matter that is relatively inaccessible, the advantages of being first to market the creation, embedded devices that defeat copying of electronic products, and demand characteristics. However, most cultural creations are not naturally protected because second comers may appropriate their value through low-cost duplication and distribution, with little or no investment in mastering the underlying creative effort. Indeed, free-riding competitors would focus their efforts on those creations that had proved successful in the marketplace, relieving them of any uncertainty costs and allowing them to take advantage of the marketing efforts of creators. The returns to original developers would be significantly reduced.

The rapid and dramatic improvements in copying technologies that have emerged in recent decades underlie growing demands for stronger global protection, as well as extension of protection to subject areas such as software, internet transmissions, and broadcasts. These issues are complex and subtle. For example, the technologies required to receive a satellite broadcast have become sufficiently inexpensive that it is costly for the broadcaster to practice exclusion. Some who receive the broadcast without authorization may then benefit commercially by displaying it to paying patrons or by retransmitting it over local cable systems. Such actions reduce the value of both the copyright owned by the program's producer and the neighboring right owned by its broadcaster, resulting in lower appropriability.

The private solution, in which broadcasters scramble their signals to make them unintelligible to all but authorized receptors, may be socially inefficient. It achieves exclusion at the sacrifice of consumer benefits, but the cost to the broadcaster (or its consumers) may approximate the original loss in copyright value, leaving a net potential loss. The United States has effected a compromise solution, in which broadcasters get limited copyright protection plus remuneration from cable operators at a price set by the government, effectively giving cable operators a compulsory license to carry the broadcast. This solution may also be suboptimal, because compulsory licenses imply involuntary transactions by the broadcaster that may stifle further program development.

Related questions surface with respect to electronic transmission of databases and other proprietary information among computers. Again, exclusion, though feasible, is costly, particularly when transmission is over networks with multiple users. To encourage their development and sale, databases may be copyrighted in some nations, while laws covering trade secrets may help protect proprietary information. However, when such information is transmitted, the difficulty of excluding unauthorized users raises policy concerns like those in broadcasts. There is a substantive international component to this issue: such transmissions are often transborder and countries assert the right to regulate the amount and type of information flows crossing their borders.

Information technologies are particularly vulnerable to low-cost and massive copying, raising thorny issues about copyright and fair use, as I will discuss later. These are critical issues on the global IPRs agenda.

Trademarks and Geographic Indications

Trademarks and *service marks* protect rights to use a particular distinctive mark or name to identify a product, service, or company. Such marks are of material value in distributing goods and services. Because the pool of potential trademarks is limitless, they typically require only registration formalities, with an opportunity for others to protest the award of a trademark if it can be shown to infringe a prior mark. Trademarks typically may be renewed indefinitely.

Related rights include *geographic indications*, which certify that a consumer product (wines, spirits, and foodstuffs) was made in a particular place and that it embodies physical characteristics of that location, such as soil conditions and climate, or that it meets quality conditions implicit in the reputation of a location. Though there is variation in how these mechanisms operate and how they affect economic incentives, they all have the same basic purposes: to lower consumers' search costs, protect consumers from fraud regarding the origin of a product, and safeguard commercial reputations for quality.

Like patents and copyrights, trademarks carry legal authority to enforce the exclusive use of an asset created by human thought. In this case the asset is a symbol or other identifier that conveys information to the consumer about the product. If consumers view the mark as a reliable indicator of desirable product characteristics, they would be willing to pay a premium for the good. This premium compensates the firm for the cost of developing and advertising the trademark. If competitors were allowed to duplicate the mark or use a confusingly similar mark these costs might not be recoverable.

It is important that trademarks be distinctive, because protecting non-distinctive marks could impose confusion and litigation costs on society without lowering consumer search costs. Similarly, generic names like "car" or "microwave oven" are not eligible for protection.

In most countries other than the United States, trademarks are awarded to the first person to register them. Though this system provides legal certainty about ownership and helps avoid inadvertent duplication of trademarks, it may encourage excessive investment as firms attempt to register all potentially interesting or descriptive names and symbols in a prospective product line.[13] In other countries it is simply first commercial use that procures a trademark; registration serves to buttress claims to first use. The advantage of this system is that trademarks provide little social benefit except when they are actually used to identify a good being sold. Its main difficulties are ambiguity about where the trademark may have been used first and the geographic extent of protection, along with an inability to avoid inadvertent duplication.

Unlike patents and copyrights, trademarks do not protect the creation of additional knowledge; rather, they identify the origin of a product. Critics claim that this substantive difference renders trademarks less socially valuable, in that they sustain market power without providing dynamic incentives to create new products.

A balanced view recognizes that trademarks have positive impacts that offset the market power they might generate.[14] Because trademarks indicate the inherent quality or other distinguishing features of identified products, the consumer's costs of searching for preferred quality characteristics are lowered. This gives firms an incentive to maintain or improve quality over time in order not to erode the value of their marks. Thus, trademark protection may be expected both to raise the average quality of products on the market and to generate further product differentiation. Moreover, trademarks offer an inducement for new firms with distinctive products to enter markets, a process that can be of considerable importance for growth and market deepening in developing economies.[15] Trademark protection establishes incentives for orderly distribution, which can be important in securing economies of scale. Finally, trademarks provide an outlet for consumers who desire exclusivity in their consumption. The need to protect high-end consumer trademarks, such as Chanel and Calvin Klein, is evident, since otherwise free riders would duplicate the marks and attach them to goods of lower quality and lower cost. Indeed, such well-known trademarks are the targets of most product counterfeiting in international markets.

Potential monopoly costs and consumer damages from trademarks are limited for several reasons:

---

13. Landes and Posner (1987) suggest that this has been a problem in Japan, and stories about speculative or fraudulent registration are common in many countries. A modern variant is the practice of registering domain names on the internet that are quite similar to the names or trademarks of familiar enterprises.

14. See Landes and Posner (1987) and Besen and Raskind (1991) for discussion.

15. Maskus (1997b) discusses the importance of this process in Lebanon, while Maskus, Dougherty, and Mertha (1998) describe its operation in China.

- The market power associated with a particular trademark is likely to be small because the potential supply of competing trademarks is virtually unlimited (the exceptions occur where a highly successful brand in a sector with substantial fixed investment costs serves to augment entry barriers).

- Legal structures covering unfair competition generally prevent fraudulent passing off of goods and services and false and misleading advertising.

- Consumers are capable of assigning quality variations to goods. If the claimed quality is consistently not forthcoming, consumers will discount the trademark. Because firms have strong incentives to safeguard their reputations, misleading activity should be minimal in well-functioning markets that are complemented by adequate legal systems.

Unauthorized duplication of a mark or use of a confusingly similar name or mark constitutes trademark infringement. The primary international area of contention is the production, sale, and importation of counterfeit goods that are represented as legitimate goods. While counterfeiting may enhance consumer welfare by providing lower-cost alternatives, it also reduces welfare by increasing confusion, raising search costs, diminishing the value of trademarks, and lowering incentives to maintain product quality and develop new products. Worse, the fraudulent sale of low-quality food items and medicines could endanger human safety. Rights are usually enforced through private litigation; it is up to the courts to determine the likelihood of confusion, whether infringement was deliberate, and what damages to assess.

Trade Secrets

Trade secrets are proprietary information about production processes, including such mundane but commercially valuable items as customer lists and organizational methods. A trade secret is protected by standard liability laws against unauthorized disclosure through commercially unfair means. Because these laws define torts, not IPRs in the classic sense, they do not fit well into the standard intellectual property framework. In particular, there is no exclusive right to use the information if in leaking out fairly it enters the public domain. Trade secrets cannot be protected against learning by fair means, such as independent creation, reverse engineering, or reading public documents. Thus, while a trade secret has no statutory time limit, it can run out in the regular course of competition.

Traditionally, economists doubted that trade secrets could provide net economic benefits. If no disclosure is required but market power is created, by protecting trade secrets society must lose.

This view has changed with the growing recognition that protecting trade secrets may efficiently fill gaps created by the patent system and also provide important incentives for innovation (Reichman 1994). There are three such gaps: (1) An inventor might judge his creation to be unpatentable in legal terms but hard to imitate. (2) A firm could prefer not to disclose its process, as a patent requires, because disclosure could reduce expected profits. (3) A firm might wish to avoid the costs of patent filing.

Society could achieve economic gains from protecting trade secrets in comparison with patents: trade secrets laws could generate innovation, especially of the smaller, incremental kind that would have value for a limited time. Trade secrets could reduce incentives for R&D races because no patent might be awarded or sought. Learning trade secrets by reverse engineering would be more common than under patent protection since the follower firm may use its findings without liability. Indeed, this could be a cheaper route for competitors to learn new technologies than reading patent applications and inventing around patent grants.

There is an interesting reason, in principle, that there is no liability for lawful copying in trade secrets law. Firms are at some times likely to be creators and at other times copiers of trade secrets. All have a joint interest in being able to reverse engineer each other's products in order to learn the underlying processes. Legal protection against reverse engineering would impose costs on the system that, in expected value terms, could be higher for every firm than the expected costs of imposing limited trade secrets protection.[16]

Trade secrets law is dichotomous. There is full liability when the attempt to learn a proprietary process is illegal but no liability when the attempt is legal. This structure acts as an incentive to firms to engage in legitimate learning activities, which in turn could stimulate greater dynamic competition. The task for policymakers in each country is to define the boundaries of legal attempts to learn a rival firm's trade secrets.

Hybrid Forms of Intellectual Property Protection

Recent advances in technology have strained the classical categories of intellectual property because new forms of creative activity do not easily fit into them.[17] For example, computer software embodies elements of both literary expression, in the form of its binary code, and industrial utility, to the extent that programs are integral to production processes. In the former case, protection via copyrights is indicated, which is largely

---

16. This claim was articulated most forcefully by Reichman (1994, 1998). See also Besen and Raskind (1991) and Landes and Posner (1987).

17. Some of these issues are explored further in the next section.

the global standard. However, programs of industrial utility that meet novelty and nonobviousness requirements are patentable in many systems, including the United States, the EU, and Japan. There are also questions about the extent to which decompilation of programs should be permitted in order to facilitate competing applications and maintain software interoperability.[18]

Similar comments apply to aspects of semiconductor topography (chip design). Such designs do not seem to be literary expressions, yet it is relatively easy to copy them. At the same time, patent protection of layout designs seems excessive because the designs themselves may not meet novelty requirements. Accordingly, chip topographies have attracted their own form of *sui generis* protection that requires originality (as in copyrights) but provides only 10 years of exclusive rights in production, sales, and imports.

An additional form of protection is plant breeders' rights (PBRs), which permit developers of new plant varieties to control their marketing and use. These rights operate much like patents, being provided for fixed terms. However, rather than PBRs requiring that new plants be nonobvious and have industrial utility, plants need only be distinctive from earlier varieties and genetically stable. PBRs are controversial in developing economies with significant farming sectors but little capacity in the private sector for innovation in agriculture and horticulture.

Finally, questions persist about whether copyright protection is adequate to encourage electronic transmission of broadcasts, internet materials, and databases (Reichman and Samuelson 1997). While copyrights have emerged as the global standard in these areas, additional mechanisms may be required to discipline unauthorized copying and commercial use of materials transmitted electronically. This point is discussed further below.

Sectoral Reliance on IPRs

Just as IPRs vary considerably on functional grounds, their importance differs greatly among economic sectors. In order to understand the sources of pressure for change in global protection it is useful to discuss the dependence of critical sectors on various forms of IPRs. This discussion should not obscure the fact that all sectors make extensive use of IPRs. Patents are important in machinery, equipment, and motor vehicles, for example, and virtually all goods and services are marketed with trademarks. Copyrights protect publishers of magazines, industrial manuals,

---

18. Samuelson et al. (1994) advocate *sui generis* protection for software, but their proposal has not yet been adopted in any national legislation.

and blueprints. Moreover, various IPRs can interact in a portfolio of protection. Characters developed by the Walt Disney company may be copyrighted in films, books, and derivative products, but they are equally protected by the Disney trademarks.

The "Patents Complex": Pharmaceuticals, Biotechnology, and Plant Varieties

Patents in all fields of technology are sought by innovative firms in all industrial sectors. However, patent protection is seen as particularly critical for capturing returns to basic invention in pharmaceuticals, agricultural and industrial chemicals, and biotechnology. These industries have high R&D costs but face considerable appropriability problems. It is not difficult for competitors to determine the molecular composition of pharmaceutical compounds or the genetic makeup of biotechnological inventions, and to develop imitative products. Such inventions wear secrets "on their face," in the terminology of Reichman (1994). Accordingly, drug manufacturers and biotechnology firms in the United States and Europe are in the forefront of programs to strengthen global patent protection. The situation is similar for new plant varieties, which typically entail substantial innovation costs that may not be recoverable if exclusionary limits are not placed on the ability to duplicate and resell seeds.

At the same time, IPRs related to drugs, genetic inventions, and seed varieties are precisely the technologies that attract the greatest controversy. There is widespread concern in developing countries over the potential for monopoly pricing and limited distribution of new technologies and products in response to stronger patents. I address these concerns in a later chapter. At this point it is useful to discuss briefly the economics of each of these sectors in order to demonstrate the importance of patents. Note that these three lines of business are closely related. Research and production activities are often conducted in all of them by firms that are ordinarily classified as chemical, pharmaceutical, or agribusiness companies. Biotechnological inventions are themselves sources of new medicines, industrial processes, and food products.

Pharmaceuticals

The global pharmaceutical industry is both hierarchical and intensely competitive. At the top lie a relatively small number of large multinational enterprises, headquartered in the United States, Switzerland, Germany, the United Kingdom, and Japan, that undertake virtually all the basic pharmaceutical research done by private entities. A wave of mergers in the 1990s has increased concentration at this level of the industry.

These enterprises are truly global in scope. For example, the American pharmaceutical industry has far more foreign production and distribution facilities per parent enterprise than any other US manufacturing sector (Maskus 1998b). In large part this internationalization reflects cost savings from transporting bulk ingredients, with assembly into dosages and distribution undertaken locally. It also reflects the significant price advantages that trademark recognition affords in the industry, even in countries with weak patent laws, such as India (Lanjouw 1997).

Patented pharmaceutical products face competition from a variety of sources. Depending on patent scope, substitute products within each therapeutic group may be widely available. Upon expiry of a patent, all firms are free to market versions of the product. And because patents may not be sought or recognized in various markets, there are numerous imitations for nearly all therapeutic treatments—a situation that presumably will change considerably after TRIPs is fully implemented. The vast majority of pharmaceutical firms in the world produce generics, other substitutes under their own brand names, or imitative varieties of patented goods. Thus, beneath the top level of major pharmaceutical companies the thousands of medicine producers in the world make the industry highly competitive in most markets.

In the countries where innovative research in pharmaceuticals is undertaken, the industry is the most research intensive of all sectors. Approximately 18 percent of pharmaceutical sales is spent on R&D by American drug companies (US Congressional Budget Office 1994). The after-tax R&D cost per new chemical entity (NCE) that is placed on the market has been estimated recently at between $194 million ($359 million before tax credits) and $241 million (US Office of Technology Assessment 1993; DiMasi, Grabowski, and Lasagna 1991). The Pharmaceutical Research and Manufacturers' Association (1999a) currently estimates that it requires an average of $500 million to introduce a new marketed medicine. These costs per marketed product have risen considerably in real terms in the last decade.

An important reason for these high R&D costs is that many failed compounds are investigated for each product that is shown to be safe, effective, and patentable. Another is that it takes a long time, on average 12 to 15 years in the United States, for a product to make it from preclinical research through clinical testing and regulatory marketing approval to product launch. This imposes a heavy capital cost in forgone interest on funds tied up in R&D. Given the high research costs and the low probability of product success, it is easy to see why appropriability problems in this sector are extreme. Follower firms need only target those successful product launches with proven market demands, rather than undertake a comprehensive exploratory research program.

Distribution in the pharmaceutical sector is heavily regulated in most nations (Danzon 1997) in order to control prices to consumers (hospitals and patients) and to limit budgetary costs of public health facilities. Prices may be regulated directly based on costs, wholesale and retail

markups, inflation adjustments, and reference prices set through negotiations or by inspection of foreign prices. In some regulatory systems
specific manufacturers and physicians are subject to revenue limits in an
attempt to control prices or prescription practices. In others, firms are
regulated by limits on returns to capital invested. Patient co-payments
and managed care systems also limit pharmaceutical prices and company revenues.

The effectiveness of various systems in controlling prices and procurement costs is debatable because of the many distortions these systems
impose (Danzon 1997). Among OECD countries, pharmaceutical price
indices tend to be lower in countries with extensive price regulation,
although in these countries fewer generics and over-the-counter drugs
are available. However, real expenditures for drugs are not necessarily
restricted by extensive regulation. Innovative pharmaceutical research seems
to be encouraged in countries, such as the United States and the United
Kingdom, where firms are relatively free to set prices, while imitative
research is encouraged in nations, such as France and Italy, where price
and revenue regulations are extensive.

It is not surprising that before TRIPs many developing countries failed
to use patents to protect pharmaceutical products, viewing the absence
of patents as a form of limiting public health costs. Though a number of
developing nations have extended their patent laws to pharmaceutical
compounds in recent years, many still have not. Indeed, as noted earlier,
even in some industrial countries recognition of patents has come only
in recent decades. In part, this situation reflects the political power of
local pharmaceutical firms that have grown up behind weak patent systems that allow them to produce and sell imitative products. Such firms
will come under considerable competitive pressure as their governments
enact patent protection for pharmaceutical products as required by TRIPs.

Biotechnology

The biotechnology industry remains dynamic, with most firms being created
to develop and sell a single new genetic technological process or product. Thus, research in this field is performed largely by small firms, though
the major pharmaceutical, chemical, and agribusiness firms do undertake research, as do university scientists. Biotechnological inventions consist
of genetic research tools, pharmaceutical products, transgenic strains of
plants and animals, and biological industrial processes. It has been estimated that roughly half the "important" drugs on the market and under
development are based on biotechnological inventions (Rathmann 1993).

R&D costs are also significant in this industry. Estimates of the costs
of launching a biotechnological medicine are comparable to those for
pharmaceuticals more generally, while it is thought that costs for successful food products and genetic plant improvements are perhaps even

higher (Rathmann 1993). However, learning a biotechnological formula through reverse engineering is typically straightforward and inexpensive, again making it hard for original inventors to recoup investment costs where there is no protection.

Early forms of biotechnology products came from cloning proteins found in nature in order to produce commercially viable quantities. Because this research involves discovering genetic sequences rather than inventing them, there is considerable uncertainty about the patentability of its outcomes (Barton 1993). Moreover, though knowledge of gene sequences (such as those being mapped in the Human Genome Project) is of potentially great value, the gene sequences themselves may not have industrial utility, rendering questionable the idea of patentability. Courts also find it difficult to identify a specific point of invention (isolation versus sequencing, which might be achieved by different claimants) for purposes of enforcing rights.

For these reasons and because of ethical and environmental concerns, there is a natural tension over the patentability of products involving living organisms. The United States Supreme Court first addressed the issue in 1980, when it upheld the patent claim for an organism that would attack oil spills.[19] Although this organism was never commercialized, the recognition of organism patentability was a critical inducement to the US biotechnology industry. Within two years, more than 100 companies had been formed and today annual global sales exceed $20 billion (Rathmann 1993). Since that time, the American courts and the US Patent and Trademark Office have moved sharply in the direction of strong and broad patent protection in biotechnology. Patents have been upheld covering all potential products from the genetic engineering of a particular plant or a critical research tool, such as a genetic sequence developed for one drug but that could be required in developing numerous pharmaceutical products, all of which would be subject to the initial patent (Barton 1995).[20] Moreover, such patents encourage filing for protection of all potential genetic combinations, potentially limiting follow-on competition. Thus, critics characterize the American system as overprotective. Indeed, recent statements from the Clinton administration encouraging the developers of maps of genetic sequences to make these maps of the human genome available widely to scientists, rather than to limit access through patents, points to rising concern about the effects of protection in core technologies.

The EU generally has taken a more cautious view, though recently it has strengthened patent rights for microorganisms. Nonetheless, concerns

---

19. *Diamond vs. Chakrabarty*, 444 US 1028 (1980).

20. See US Patent 5,195,135, 7 December 1994, Agracetus cotton patent covering genetic engineering of cotton plants and lines; and US Patent 5,328,987, 12 July 1994, Maliszewski (Immunex) IgA FC receptors.

over unknown health risks and the potential environmental impacts of engineered genetic materials merging with natural materials have caused numerous European nations to restrict their use in plants and animals used for food.[21] Such concerns appear to be spreading to the United States, where numerous farmers have chosen to forgo further sowing of genetically modified plants.

Many developing nations do not permit patenting of biotechnological inventions. This situation does not seem to reflect protection for local biotechnology firms, because few developing economies have successfully established a presence in the industry. Rather, it indicates concern over potential impacts of patents on the costs of biologically activated pharmaceuticals, food products, and agricultural inputs, plus complex questions about regulating the exploitation of domestic genetic resources. Under TRIPs, the obligation of countries to provide biotechnology patents remains ambiguous, although the definition of excludable subject matter clearly is broader than that practiced in the United States (Maskus 1998a; Watal 2000b).

Plant Varieties

The development of new plant varieties that may be higher yielding or more disease resistant than prevailing varieties is accomplished by both biotechnological research and genetic mixing. In the industrialized countries such research is performed in private chemical and agribusiness firms, university research laboratories, and public research institutes, including extension services. In developing economies such work is largely undertaken by public universities and research institutes, which make seeds available to farmers at low cost. Publicly funded international research institutes also provide new strains to agricultural ministries for dissemination to farmers. The best-known example is the International Rice Research Institute, which is commonly credited with perfecting higher-yielding and more robust rice strains that were widely planted in some developing countries.

As these comments suggest, agricultural research has long been considered something of a public good, because food supplies depend on widespread dissemination of new seeds. Limited intellectual property protection for new varieties reflected a policy tilt toward dissemination, requiring public research procurement. However, this view has changed fundamentally in recent years, with more countries recognizing the advantages of shifting research into private facilities, supported by exclusive rights to research results. Indeed, under considerable pressure to reduce budgets or become self-financing, a number of public research

---

21. Pollin (1998) provides an entertaining and cogent summary of these concerns.

institutes in developing countries have shifted sharply toward a more commercial orientation in order to remain competitive with a growing number of private breeders (UNCTAD 1996). Limited evidence suggests that such institutes support IPRs in plant strains because they also wish to protect their own research results.

As with drugs and biotechnology, appropriability problems are significant in seed varieties. Plant varieties are protected by systems of plant breeders' rights, which combine patent-like protection with limitations on the scope of rights. Thus, inventors are given exclusive rights to produce, sell, and import seed varieties. One key exception is the farmer's privilege, which allows farmers, after initial purchase of protected seeds, to retain for their own use sufficient quantities of seeds to plant the following year's crops. Another is the breeder's exemption, which allows competing breeders to use varieties freely in developing new strains. Such exceptions to the exclusive use of seed varieties are not allowed under the US system of patent protection, so the choice between patents and this form of *sui generis* protection is important in determining the competitive nature of PBRs in each country.

TRIPs obliges nations to provide either patents for new plant varieties or less restrictive protection of the kind just discussed. The privatization of rights to the outcomes of agricultural research is among the most controversial areas of IPRs. Concerns arise on behalf of farmers in poor countries who might not be able to afford new agricultural inputs priced under IPRs protection, inducing them to use older technologies that would be less competitive. It is also argued that extensive recognition of PBRs could eventually reduce genetic diversity, with unforeseen consequences for plant diseases and public health.

The "Copyrights Complex": Recorded Entertainment, Software, and Internet Transmissions

Copyrights protect original artistic and literary expression in numerous media, including print publishing, audio and video recording, live performances fixed in some medium, derivative products and services, broadcasts, software, video games, electronic databases, integrated networks, and electronic transmissions over the internet. Classical copyright doctrine envisioned only the first of these activities. Thus, it is not surprising that strains on the copyright system have emerged as its purview has extended to newer technologies and products. I illustrate these issues through a brief discussion of three critical areas that are at the forefront of the international policy debate in copyrights. Although recorded entertainment, software, and electronic commerce are commonly considered distinctive economic sectors, they are interrelated through their extensive reliance on information technologies.

Recorded Entertainment

Among the more dynamic industries in the United States is film and music production. Global sales of such products have expanded dramatically in recent years, as has American employment in film and music production. The industry depends critically on advanced technology to achieve special effects and sound quality. It also invests considerable amounts in talent. Thus, there are substantial investment costs at the creative end. Moreover, marketing is costly as firms attempt to establish quality reputations for differentiated acts and products. Thus, industry profits are protected both by copyrights and trademarks.

Unauthorized copying of recorded films and music lies at the center of international disputes over IPRs. Incentives for pirating (copying and selling such goods without authorization) are easy to understand. It is cheap to acquire machinery for duplicating videotapes, digital video disks, and compact disks, and this machinery can produce many copies with minimal diminution in quality. Copies are sold, with minimal distribution costs, at prices near marginal costs because pirating industries are generally fluid and competitive.

Piracy is the classic example of free riding in the copyright area. Pirating firms absorb no research costs and free ride on the creativity of performers and producers, allowing the firms to sell duplicates of original movies and records at a fraction of the price that would be supported by copyrights. The International Intellectual Property Association (IIPA) annually estimates the revenue losses American firms suffer from limited copyright enforcement around the world. It claims that in 1995 such losses amounted to $2.3 billion in motion pictures and $1.3 billion in records and music. Estimated "piracy rates" ranged from 20 percent in Western Europe to 99 percent in Africa in films and from 5 percent in Western Europe to 70 percent in Eastern Europe in music.[22]

The United States has expended considerable diplomatic energy convincing developing countries to enact and enforce copyright laws that would reduce piracy. Numerous countries have done so, both because of this external pressure and because emerging creative interests in those countries favor stronger copyrights. Moreover, TRIPs requires antipiracy efforts through adequate enforcement. Accordingly, copyright protection in recorded entertainment should soon improve markedly, which is a signal victory for US entertainment firms. However, effective enforcement of copyrights in developing economies will be delayed because of administrative costs and economic interests in pirating that will be difficult to overcome.

---

22. These estimates are likely exaggerated because they assume that current sales levels would not fall if prices rose as a result of eliminating piracy. See IIPA (1998a).

Computer Software

At the international level, software developers face problems similar to those in recorded entertainment, again because the high margins between protected software prices and costs of unauthorized duplication create large markets for pirated programs. The IIPA estimates that piracy losses to US software firms in 1995 amounted to $7.2 billion in business applications software (including platforms) and $3.1 billion in computer games. Piracy rates tend to be higher in business software than in any other form of recorded media. Illegitimate copies of programs such as Microsoft's Windows 98 and Office 97 are sold over the counter (with copies sometimes made while the customer waits) and loaded onto hardware systems. This activity constitutes literal copying of software code, meaning that copyright protection should be sufficient to reduce the problem. Hence, the global standard in software, as written into the TRIPs agreement, is for countries to recognize computer programs as copyrightable expression. Again, this is a significant improvement from the standpoint of software developers, though adequate enforcement is years away.

While American software firms are pleased that there is a global commitment to protect their products with copyrights, it is a minimum standard. In the United States protection is considerably stronger, thanks to a combination of copyrights and patents, along with maintenance of trade secrets (Samuelson et al. 1994). The need for additional protection arises from the fact that literal application of traditional copyright precepts to computer programs may be too weak to provide incentives for innovation. Classical doctrine would make illegal only "slavish copying" of computer code, rendering it easy for competitors to produce rival programs by simply rewriting code in imitative ways. Thus, through judicial interpretation copyrights have been extended considerably to protect programs. For example, the Third Circuit Court upheld the claim that the "structure, sequence, and organization" of programs are copyrightable, extending protection to interfaces and structural features of programs.[23] In another case the "look and feel" of programs through its computer interfaces was protected from being mimicked by competitors.[24] Critics think such extensions do not fit comfortably with copyright doctrine; they equate protectable expression with functional aspects of programs. Because copyright provides very long protection (copyrights last for author's life plus 50 years) to functional areas without corresponding novelty requirements, it may be overprotective.

---

23. *Whelan Associates, Inc. vs. Jaslow Dental Laboratories, Inc.* 797 F. 2d 1222 (3d Circuit, 1986).

24. *Lotus Development Corporation vs. Paperback Software International*, 740 F. Supp. 37 (D. Mass. 1990).

Similarly, American policy precludes reverse engineering of programs by allowing software firms to license their products subject to a no-decompilation clause. This structure is unusual in the copyrights area, where other forms of expression, such as books and published music, may be studied by definition. Computer programs prevented from decompilation bear no automatic disclosure. This policy is restrictive, for decompilation is an important source of follow-on innovation and permits interoperability of programs in an open environment. For this reason, the EU follows a compromise solution by allowing decompilation to the extent needed to obtain information to create an interoperable program.

Computer programs and algorithms are patentable in the United States and Japan subject to novelty and utility demonstrations. Such patents recognize the functional aspects of software, such as programs that effectuate an industrial process. Software patents are criticized on two grounds. First, some critics complain that algorithms as discovered "truths of nature" are not patentable under classic doctrine. Second, patents provide strong rights to exclude others from using the idea underlying a particular functional program design, potentially according considerable market power to software firms that could be exercised in user industries and through computer networks.

This description points out that technology can render classical IPRs concepts difficult to sustain. The essence of the problem is that computer programs are "industrial literature" that embodies elements of both functional utility and literary expression. Some experts call for a hybrid form of protection that would combine shorter patent terms for functional aspects and copyrights for the textual expression (Reichman 1994). This view has not affected policy to date; the United States continues to provide full copyright and patent protection on various programs. It is not clear what the competitive implications of this system are but many observers, particularly within the software industry, consider it to be excessively protectionist.

Internet Transmissions

Electronic transmissions over the Internet pose complex questions for copyright (World Trade Organization 1998; Shapiro and Varian 1999). TRIPs applies standard copyright principles to such transmissions. Therefore, the copyright owner holds duplication and distribution rights. However, enforcing these rights is difficult in digital products, which may be easily downloaded with no deterioration in quality. Indeed, users may compile their own music disks or videos without paying royalties to any of the original rights holders. Technology for such activity continues to improve, leading to calls for technical means to deter unauthorized downloading and distribution.

The Copyright and the Performances and Phonograms treaties (concluded at the World Intellectual Property Organization in December 1996) allow countries to bar the use of technical means to circumvent electronic measures to control copying. They also facilitate collective management of copyrighted materials on the internet by permitting identifying markers, the unauthorized removal of which is illegal. The treaties further clarify the rights of performers and music producers to authorize electronic trans-mission of their works.

The United States and the EU have adopted these treaties and amended their copyright laws in light of the concerns of content providers that their materials were not well protected. For example, under the Digital Millennium Copyright Act, enacted in the US in 1998, it is illegal to circumvent antipiracy measures built into commercial software and to manufacture or distribute devices that defeat encryption codes, unless this is done to conduct encryption research or to assess program interoperability. Limited exceptions for the anticircumvention rules are provided to nonprofit libraries and educational institutions. Internet service providers are excused from infringement liability for transmitting materials submitted by content providers, but are expected to remove clearly infringing material from users' Web sites. Fair-use exceptions are provided to faculty members and students who wish to download a single copy of protected material for research or study, but the exceptions are subject to rigorous conditions. The law also requires Webcasters to pay licensing fees to record companies. Finally, it clarifies that it is illegal to distribute, in any form, electronically downloaded or uploaded materials without the authorization of the copyright holder.

Such laws in effect not only extend copyright protection to internet transmissions but also extend copyright scope to regulations intended to defeat electronic piracy. Stronger copyrights should expand the supply of electronic materials and contribute to the growth of electronic commerce. There should be significant additional gains associated with network externalities, which may markedly reduce transaction costs in international trade and introduce new electronic products and services to wide areas of the globe.[25]

However, some users, such as university libraries and researchers, worry about the effects of this additional protection on their access to, and ability to duplicate, research materials. Again, the issue is essentially the same as it is generally with IPRs: stronger rights increase returns to creative activity but raise the costs of enjoying that activity. Finding a balance between these two objectives is never easy.

The tension is illustrated well by the ongoing controversy over legislative attempts to extend copyright protection to databases. The European Union has done so through its Directive on the Legal Protection of

---

25. See Mann and Knight (1999) and Organization for Economic Cooperation and Development (1999) for discussions of the market-expansion impacts of electronic commerce.

Databases.[26] The United States has legislation pending in the form of the Collections of Information Antipiracy Act.[27] Both strive to protect the investments of firms and researchers in the creative assembly of data compilations from copying for commercial use by second comers—a laudable goal in principle. However, they go too far—their conditions could throw significant and costly barriers in the path of scientific researchers and educational institutions (Reichman and Samuelson 1997; Reichman and Franklin 1999).

For example, as written, their provisions would extend copyright protection to data compilations that require nothing more than arranging publicly available data into a particular order, thereby protecting materials that, under standard interpretation, should not be copyrightable. Researchers seeking to use scientific data so protected would be obligated to seek approval through a licensing arrangement, which could extensively raise research costs, particularly if the scientists needed to combine several databases from disparate sources. More chillingly, the owners of scientific databases could choose not to license them, tending to reduce the pace of technical change and scientific progress.

Licensing would be technically and legally feasible, given the ability of providers to attach binding licensing contracts (e.g., shrink-wrap licenses and standard-form contracts) to electronic data downloads. A researcher who obtained a license could be prevented from sharing the data with other researchers, because exhaustion of rights at first sale does not extend to licensing contracts. The 15-year protection could be indefinitely extended if the database were improved. In principle, this provision would award to databases—a creation of limited inventive activity—protection that exceeds even the patent grant.

In response to significant protest from the research communities, libraries, and universities, a number of amendments to the US legislation have been proposed. The objective is to extend standard concepts of fair use to database protection. Thus, researchers would be permitted to make and use single copies of data to the extent that their use and discoveries did not harm the commercial interests of the developer—a standard that is vague as currently written. Libraries would be allowed to make (at least) single copies for archival purposes and universities would have limited liability if the law were infringed by faculty and students.

The strongly protective EU directive and proposed US legislation essentially reflect the accelerating view of data as a commodity. In part, this reflects the growing private use of data for marketing products and services. There is merit in providing copyright protection to expensively accumulated customer lists, for example. However, it also further blurs

---

26. Directive 96/9/EC, March 1996.

27. H.R. 354, 106th Congress; H.R. 2652, 105th Congress.

the distinction between public research and its private uses. On current trends an increasing amount of research data will become private property, either because they were generated with funding by private grants or because the researcher, working from public grants and data, sees commercial value in exploiting them.

The "Trademark Complex": Status Goods and Quality Inputs

Trademark infringement is common in many developing countries. Rising incomes in the rapidly growing economies of Asia and Latin America account for a shift in demand toward status goods like high-quality apparel, cosmetics, jewelry, and accessories. The substantial gap between the market prices of legitimate products and the costs of producing knockoff goods creates a thriving market for counterfeit merchandise sold without authorization under marks that are identical or confusingly similar to registered trademarks. It is the classic free-rider problem. Creation of recognizable trademarks and reputations for quality requires significant investment in design, marketing, and quality control. Once this investment is made it is difficult to prevent expropriation or dilution of the trademark by second comers.

The problem plagues both well-known international brands and local enterprises that invest successfully in trademark development. Indeed, while stories of illegitimate use of foreign marks are well known, the unauthorized exploitation of local brand names may be even more prevalent, both because they may be more familiar to consumers and because their owners may be less capable of enforcing their rights. Inadequate enforcement of trademark regulations and unfair competition laws are a drag on business development and economic growth.

Trademark infringement is far more common than is often recognized. Beyond the obvious attempts to pass off counterfeit goods under names like Gucci, Chanel, and Rolex, marks and brand names are falsified in, among other sectors, prepared foods and beverages, medicines, transport equipment, industrial machinery, electronic equipment, personal computers, and software. Thus, unauthorized versions of Compaq computers and Microsoft programs have a market at least as much because of their reputations for quality as for their functional characteristics. Well-known manufacturers of industrial machinery, such as transformers, heating equipment, and construction cranes, also experience problems with local competitors selling like products with a false representation of trademark, licensing rights, or technology.

Because trademark infringement is ubiquitous and cross-sectoral, many firms harmed by it have widely varying interests in their operations in developing countries and are not easily organized into an effective lobbying campaign. In contrast, the concentrated patent (pharmaceuticals) and copyright (software and recorded entertainment) interests exert more influence on global policies through their national trade authorities (Ryan 1998). Nonetheless, multinational firms are pursuing their rights more aggressively in key markets, such as China, while pushing for regulatory reform and additional enforcement. Moreover, TRIPs calls for countries to recognize well-known trademarks, to remove onerous registration and use requirements, and to improve administrative and judicial enforcement.

Geographical Indications

When food products, wines, and spirits bear a reputation for quality that is essentially attributable to their geographical origin, there is a special category of protection. Otherwise, competitors may pass off their products even if made in other locations, thus diminishing the value of investments in improving the original locations and marketing products. TRIPs envisions two levels of protection. First, there is a requirement for countries to provide legal means to prevent false or misleading claims of geographical origin, applicable to any products. Second, there is special protection for wines and spirits that precludes the use of geographical terms with products that do not originate in the indicated area, even if accompanied by expressions such as "imitation" or "kind." The agreement further calls for negotiation of an international system of registration for wines and spirits in order to implement the higher level of protection.

Protecting geographical indications has long concerned French vintners and Scottish whiskey distillers. The recent explosion in global demand for distinctive wines, spirits, and food products lends further urgency, with high-quality winemakers in the United States, Australia, Chile, and elsewhere recognizing the potential value of such protection. At present the issue is largely contested among food and wine producers in developed countries and such key developing countries as Chile, Argentina, and South Africa. Many firms undertake global advertising campaigns based on production *location*. However, increasing numbers of firms in developing economies are exploiting the value of distinctive place *names*.

Trade Secrets

There is no identifiable "complex" of industries that rely on trade secrets for competitive advantage. The term "trade secrets" covers any form of industrial or commercial know-how that (a) supports efficient production and (b) is maintained within the enterprise and its licensees as proprietary information. Such secrets could be chemical formulas underlying production of foods, medicines, and industrial chemicals, methods for heat transfer, construction techniques, bookkeeping or management systems, customer lists, and so on. Trade secrets are transferred internationally through FDI and technology licensing contracts.

Laws governing trade secrets define as illegal any attempts to learn and disclose proprietary information or to use it without authorization to develop competing production. Such laws vary widely across countries and even across states within the United States. The main source of contention, however, is inadequate laws and weak enforcement in developing economies. For example, it is alleged that public agencies, in reviewing proposed FDI or technology licensing agreements, leak confidential information to domestic competitors. It may be difficult to prosecute competitors that pay employees to divulge proprietary know-how. And there may be few restraints on the ability of managers and technical employees to leave a company and start a competing firm based on their acquired knowledge of trade secrets.

While TRIPs accords considerable discretion in the protection of undisclosed commercial information, it requires that countries develop systems for safeguarding such information from unfair competition, consonant with specified minimum definitions of illegal conduct. Further, undisclosed test data submitted for regulatory approval of agricultural chemicals and pharmaceutical products must be protected against unfair commercial use and any disclosure that is not necessary to protect the public. Legal and administrative enforcement of trade secrets must be improved as well.

The Evolving US System: Protectionism Unchained?

The remainder of this book focuses primarily on the implications of weak IPRs systems in developing nations. However, this policy overview would be incomplete without noting that in important respects the American regime has become overly protectionist by almost any utilitarian standard. For example, the United States recognizes virtually no exceptions to patentable subject matter. Claimants need only to document that the invention is nonobvious, bears an inventive step, and has industrial utility, without reference to the area of technology. These standards raise only minimal bars under American practice. These weak requirements could be offset in principle by certifying only narrow patent claims. Yet US patent examiners often award patents with broad coverage to inventions with limited inventiveness. This problem was mentioned earlier in the biotechnology area, where patents are granted on both genetic combinations and research tools. Patents on the functional aspects of computer programs are also common.

Most recently, American patent examiners extended protection to basic business methods on the Internet. The most visible examples are the patent awarded to Amazon.com, Inc.'s "one-click" ordering process and

Priceline.com, Inc.'s patent on its process for permitting shoppers to propose transaction prices.[28] These patents cover broad methods of facilitating electronic distribution, yet cannot reasonably be considered novel. The idea that consumers could propose a price at which they would be willing to purchase a product dates back thousands of years; there can be little public benefit to protecting exclusive rights to it. The "one-click" patent rewards an idea that has similar antecedents in regular commerce and is excessively broad in any case. Pending litigation between Amazon.com, Inc. and BarnesandNoble.com could sort out these issues. In recognition of these problems, some observers call for shorter duration, say 5 rather than 20 years, for business-methods patents on the Internet.

The United States also has increased dramatically the scope of copyright protection. Problems surrounding copyrights on electronic transmissions and databases were discussed earlier. Regarding copyrights generally, in October 1998 Congress passed Senate Bill 505, the "Sonny Bono Copyright Term Extension Act," which extended the term of protection by an additional 20 years. It is possible to argue that the additional protection could induce greater creative activity in the future. However, this act also covers works already in existence, serving only to increase their economic value while delaying their entry into the public domain. There can be no justification for this inclusion in the economic conception of copyrights; it was passed only to transfer more profits to past creators.

Each of these issues is the subject of intense debate in the United States. Thus, it is inaccurate to suggest that the highly protective regime encounters no opposition or that the community of intellectual property experts speaks with one voice. Nevertheless, the legislative and judicial "balance" struck in the United States in recent years heavily favors intellectual property developers. Perhaps this wave of excessive protection ultimately will reverse itself. At a minimum, it seems unwise to advocate the exportation of such protection to developing nations.

Globalization and the Technology Content of Trade

The preceding discussion set out the essential trade-offs and complexities in IPRs protection, including sectoral interests and international variations in protection. Differential standards among countries are consequential because intellectual property accounts for a substantial and growing share of international trade and investment. Inventors and creators market their products and technologies globally, a fact that collides

---

28. See "U.S. Will Give Web Patents More Scrutiny," *Wall Street Journal*, 29 March 2000. Part of the problem seems to be that patent examiners have insufficient resources to conduct adequate searches for prior art and are therefore incapable of detecting what is actually novel within the broad claims.

with weak and variable protection. Indeed, in recent years perhaps no other area of international commercial policy has come under greater pressure to expand the global reach of standards that have traditionally been set in developed countries. This section discusses the extent of international exchange of intellectual property.

The Use of Intellectual Property Rights

It is difficult to accurately measure the outputs of intellectual creation. Such outputs range from major inventions to minor product innovations, all of which may be patented though they have vastly different economic and social values. They include slogans, logos, and brand names that may be trademarked but not necessarily put into use. Research activities may generate trade secrets, which by definition are not published. Finally, copyright registrations do not cover the vast amounts of creative materials for which registration is not sought; nor do they reflect the underlying value of particular literary and artistic expressions. Thus, the contributions of intellectual work to economic activity, growth, and wealth creation are not easily measured.

Nonetheless, such contributions are important and growing in many countries, as judged by standard counts of intellectual property applications. For example, table 3.2 lists the number of patent applications in several countries or regions for the years 1990 and 1996. The 12 countries first comprising the European Union (through the accession of Spain and Portugal) saw no increase in applications (row N) through their own patent offices, which handle perhaps 104,000 per year in total. The main reason for this is the diversion of applications to the European Patent Office (EPO), either directly or through the Patent Cooperation Treaty (PCT). The treaty allows centralized EPO patent applications to be designated as valid in all EPO member nations.[29] For example, the PCT permits an applicant to seek patent protection in multiple designated countries by filing one international patent application, thereby economizing on application fees.

It is evident that the EPO provides considerable economies to both resident and nonresident applicants. In 1996 there were 86,614 EPO applications, a rise of 88 percent over 1990. When extended to national coverage within the EU, these applications supported over 800,000 filings, suggesting that each EPO filing requested extension to nine countries on average. Nonresidents are particularly likely to use the EPO to achieve coverage throughout the region.

In the United States, annual patent applications rose by 27 percent in the early 1990s, from 176,100 to 223,419. The mix between domestic and

---

29. The EU12 countries comprise most of the members of the EPO.

Table 3.2   Patent applications in selected countries

Country	1990 Resident	1990 Nonresident	1990 Total	1996 Resident	1996 Nonresident	1996 Total
EU12	94,614	443,284	537,898	112,115	805,362	917,477
N	69,900	34,007	103,907	81,500	22,492	103,992
Percent PCT/						
EPO	26	92	81	27	97	89
EPO	23,505	22,549	46,054	38,546	48,068	86,614
USA	91,410	84,690	176,100	111,883	111,536	223,419
PCT	1	13	7	4	21	13
Japan	333,373	43,419	376,792	340,861	60,390	401,251
PCT	0	36	4	1	65	10
Canada	2,782	35,135	37,917	3,316	45,938	49,254
PCT	8	31	29	22	75	71
Australia	6,948	19,559	26,507	9,196	34,125	43,321
PCT	11	47	37	12	84	69
Mexico	750	4,539	5,289	389	30,305	30,694
PCT	n.a.	n.a.	n.a.	1	87	86
Brazil	2,430	10,004	12,434	2,655	29,451	32,106
PCT	0	59	47	1	89	81
China	4,780	4,872	9,652	11,698	41,016	52,714
PCT	0	0	0	1	74	57
South Korea	9,083	22,304	31,387	68,446	45,548	113,994
PCT	0	37	26	0	69	27
MIT	299	8,100	8,399	408	12,424	12,832
PCT	n.a.	n.a.	n.a.	n.a.	n.a.	n.a.
India	1,147	2,673	3,820	1,660	6,632	8,292
PCT	n.a.	n.a.	n.a.	n.a.	n.a.	n.a.

EU12 = the first 12 members of the European Union.
N = national patent office.
EPO = European Patent Office.
PCT = Patent Cooperation Treaty.
MIT = combined figures for Malaysia, Indonesia, and Thailand.
Note: Figures for PCT are percentages of applications.

Source: World Intellectual Property Organization, *Industrial Statistics Yearbook*, various years.

foreign applicants remained roughly consistent, indicating a mature and open system. Nonresident applicants rapidly increased their filings through the PCT.

The rising numbers of patent applications in the EU and the United States in the 1990s are significant because they seem to reverse the widely discussed "patenting slowdown" in those countries in the 1970s and 1980s

(Evenson 1984; Segerstrom 1998). American resident patent applications in the United States fell from approximately 72,000 in 1970 to a low of around 59,000 in 1983, returning to 1970 levels only in 1988; the trends in Europe were similar. These facts occasioned concerns about the declining productivity of R&D programs, because over the same period real R&D spending and the number of scientists and engineers employed in R&D rose sharply. It thus appears that after some lag these increasing investments are now resulting in growing patent applications.

Japan has long had a system that encourages large numbers of applications filed to cover narrow claims (Ordover 1991). Moreover, specific features of the Japanese patent system, including utility models and pregrant disclosure, favor frequent filings by domestic residents for small claims over infrequent filings by foreign residents over somewhat larger claims (Maskus and McDaniel 1999). These characteristics are reflected in the patent data: 85 percent of all applications in 1996 were filed by residents. This is a far higher percentage than anywhere else. However, the growth of foreign applications was larger than that of domestic applications, reflecting an expanding interest in protection in Japan. Overall applications rose by about 6 percent.

Canada and Australia represent developed economies in which nonresident applications are far larger than resident applications, though both types are rising rapidly. In both countries use of the PCT by foreign applicants rose dramatically over the period. Total applications rose by 29 percent in Canada and by 59 percent in Australia.

The first four developing nations listed in table 3.2—Mexico, Brazil, China, and Korea—exhibited explosive growth in patent applications in the 1990s:

- Filings rose by a factor of five in Mexico and by 158 percent in Brazil. However, this was due entirely to nonresident applications, particularly through the PCT.

- In contrast, South Korea's near trebling of total applications featured a massive increase in domestic applications.

- China registered substantial increases in both resident and nonresident applications.

Thus, both domestic residents and foreign firms are increasingly registering for protection in South Korea and China, reflecting the importance of those markets, the ability of domestic enterprises to develop patentable technologies and products, and improving technology protection. The PCT is an attractive route to registration in both nations.

The Southeast Asian economies of Malaysia, Indonesia, and Thailand also saw total applications rise dramatically, dominated by increased foreign filings. Thus, in the 1990s these markets, characterized by high growth

Table 3.3 Trademark applications in selected countries

Country	1990			1996		
	Resident	Nonresident	Total	Resident	Nonresident	Total
EU12	219,854	116,630	336,484	235,524	130,294	365,818
MP		38	13		51	18
USA	106,693	20,653	127,346	183,925	28,585	212,510
Japan	151,935	19,791	171,726	163,518	24,642	188,160
Canada	13,948	11,733	25,681	17,895	15,446	33,341
Australia	12,826	9,189	22,015	21,777	15,569	37,346
Mexico	15,863	9,579	25,442	19,562	12,774	32,336
Brazil	57,769	6,111	63,880	56,481	12,910	69,391
China	50,853	6,419	57,272	122,057	28,017	150,074
MP		32	4		19	4
MIT	25,897	14,459	40,356	33,368	28,527	61,895
South Korea	33,564	13,262	46,826	60,852	14,846	75,698
India	18,713	1,968	20,681	35,799	6,924	42,723

EU12 = the first 12 members of the European Union.
MP = Madrid Protocol.
MIT = combined figures for Malaysia, Indonesia, and Thailand.
Note: Figures for MP are percentages of applications.

Source: World Intellectual Property Organization, Industrial Statistics Yearbook, various years.

rates, successive rounds of economic liberalization, and some attempts to strengthen IPR regimes, became more attractive locations in which to protect intellectual property.

Table 3.3 lists the number of applications for trademarks and service marks in the same years. In all countries the number of resident exceeds the number of nonresident applications, but especially in Brazil, China, South Korea, and India. This attests to the fact that emerging economies tend to experience significant entry of new domestic enterprises that find it advantageous to protect brand names for purposes of investing in product recognition. Except for Brazil, there was dramatic growth in annual trademark registrations over the period, with the number in China rising by 163 percent. The United States, Canada, Australia, and Mexico also registered significant expansion in trademark use. Within the EU there was a nearly 10 percent rise in trademark filings, with nonresidents making growing use of the registration procedures available under the Madrid Protocol (MP). Foreign enterprises also extensively employ the MP in China.

The figures in table 3.4 are for applications to register new plant varieties in various countries in 1992 and 1996. In the EU, resident applications

Table 3.4   Applications for registrations of plant varieties in selected countries

Country	1992			1996		
	Resident	Nonresident	Total	Resident	Nonresident	Total
EU12	2,812	2,211	5,023	2,016	669	2,685
CPVO	n.a.	n.a.	n.a.	1,209	169	1,378
USA	463	178	641	677	374	1,051
Japan	620	97	717	736	203	939
Canada	14	149	163	99	162	261
Australia	65	123	188	137	154	291
Argentina	80	23	103	69	76	145
Chile	11	27	38	16	13	29
South Korea	0	1	1	3	36	39

EU12 = the first 12 members of the European Union.
CPVO = Community Plant Variety Office.
n.a. = not available.

Source: World Intellectual Property Organization, *Industrial Statistics Yearbook*, various years.

through national intellectual property offices, combined with applications through the Community Plant Variety Office (CPVO), rose from 2,812 to 3,225 over this period. Nonresident applications were heavily supplanted by applications through the CPVO. The United States saw a substantial increase in applications from both residents and nonresidents, while in Japan nonresidents chose to increase their protection for plant varieties rapidly. Both Canada and Australia experienced rapidly rising registrations from domestic firms.

Argentina and Chile are listed as representative developing economies. It is only in South America that protective systems for plant varieties were commonly implemented in developing nations in this decade, though Brazil (among others) had not established such a system by 1996. Argentina saw a substantial rise in applications, dominated by nonresident filings, though applications in Chile fell off somewhat over the period. Since South Korea established an application system for plant varieties in 1992, it has registered a marked rise in nonresident applications. Thus, although this form of protection is relatively new in developing nations, interest in it seems to be rising rapidly.

There are no centralized data for copyright registrations in different countries; even if there were, because in general copyrights need not be registered to be valid, such data would reflect only a small part of the materials being created. One indirect way of representing the importance of copyrights is to consider that publication and other production of

Table 3.5 Indicators of demand for copyright products in selected countries

	Book titles		TV receivers per 1,000 population		PCs per 1,000 population	Internet hosts per 10,000 population
	1991	1996	1990	1995	1996	1996
EU12	315,736	354,303	453ᵉ	532ᵉ	176ᵉ	92.4ᵉ
USA	48,146	68,175	799	805	362	442.1
Japan	35,496	56,221	611	684	128	75.8
Canada	22,208ᵃ	19,900	612	714	193	228.1
Australia	n.a.	10,835	486	554	311	382.4
Mexico	n.a.	6,180	148	270	29	3.7
Brazil	27,557ᵇ	21,574ᶜ	208	223	18	4.2
China	92,972ᵃ	110,283	267	319	3	0.2
South Korea	29,432	35,864ᵈ	210	337	132	28.8
MIT	13,198	18,003	91ᵉ	132ᵉ	17ᵉ	2.1ᵉ
India	14,438	11,903	32	61	2	0.1

EU12 = the first 12 members of the European Union.
MIT = combined figures for Malaysia, Indonesia, and Thailand.
n.a. = not available.
a. 1993.
b. 1992.
c. 1994.
d. 1995.
e. Weighted by GDP levels.

Sources: United Nations Educational, Scientific, and Cultural Organization, *Statistical Yearbook*, various years; World Bank, *World Development Report*, various years; and World Bank, *World Development Indicators 1998*.

creative activities reflect demand for copyright protection. Thus, table 3.5 presents information on book titles produced, television receivers and personal computers per 1,000 members of the population, and internet hosts per 10,000 people in selected nations.

Because annual figures on book production are subject to considerable cyclical pressures, they must be treated with caution. Nonetheless, between 1991 and 1996 most countries reported notable increases in the output of titles, the exceptions being Canada, Brazil, and India. EU members collectively published over 350,000 titles in 1996, with nearly a third of this sum accounted for by the United Kingdom, which is the world's largest publisher of books by title. The number of books published in the United States rose by 42 percent over the five years. China, South Korea, and the Southeast Asian economies also became significant centers of publishing in the 1990s.

Televisions receive copyrighted programming and display copyrighted videos. The developed economies saw relatively small increases in the penetration of TV receivers into households (see table 3.5), reflecting near saturation of that medium by the early 1990s. However, substantial increases were registered in Mexico, China, South Korea, the Southeast Asian economies, and India. Clearly, as incomes rise the demand for televised services and entertainment expands, suggesting a rising need for copyright protection.

Finally, the penetration of personal computers and internet services into households and businesses provides a measure of demand for computer software. While the figures in table 3.5 are for a single year and therefore do not indicate growth rates, it is evident that software usage is growing rapidly in many countries (Mowery 1996). Developing nations lag far behind in personal computers and internet connections, suggesting substantial room for growth as these economies expand.[30] In turn, copyright protection will prove vital for growth in the use of legitimate software and for the international spread of internet commerce.

International Trade in IPR-Sensitive Goods

As I have noted elsewhere (Maskus 1993), goods that rely extensively on IPRs protection tend to be among the fastest-growing items in international trade and also are distinctive in terms of international comparative advantage. This is not surprising in light of underlying product characteristics, including advanced technological content, rapidly evolving dynamics in technology, and marked quality differentiation.

Strong support for these statements is provided in table 3.6, which shows trade growth and a simple measure of revealed comparative advantage (RCA) for a selection of product categories in 1990 and 1996. The first set of columns lists both nominal gross trade (exports plus imports) in billions of US dollars for total merchandise and percentage growth in nominal trade. Clearly, this growth rate depends not only on volume increases but also on inflation and exchange rate variations. However, my interest here is in demonstrating the relatively rapid expansion of sectoral trade. Thus, a comparison of trade growth by sector with aggregate trade growth should be largely free of inflation and exchange rate effects. Finally, for each product group I list an RCA index, which is the ratio of group exports to group imports, divided by the ratio of total merchandise exports to total merchandise imports. Thus, RCA measures the extent to which the sectoral trade pattern differs from each country's overall trade pattern. An index well in excess of unity suggests an under-

---

30. The data on personal computers surely underestimate the number of PCs in place in developing economies, because there is often a thriving underground business in the PC and software sectors (Maskus 1997b).

Table 3.6 Trade in IPR-sensitive goods for selected countries

Country	Year	Total merchandise			Pharmaceuticals			Polymerization products		
		Total	Percent of change	RCA	Total	Percent of change	RCA	Total	Percent of change	RCA
		($b)*			($m)			($m)		
EU12	1990	2,784		1.00	41,694		1.30	58,536		1.10
	1996	3,718	34	1.00	78,970	89	1.21	66,656	14	1.14
USA	1990	911		1.00	6,717		2.16	7,952		2.83
	1996	1,447	59	1.00	14,480	116	1.35	13,806	74	2.42
Japan	1990	523		1.00	3,714		0.25	3,461		2.79
	1996	760	45	1.00	6,391	72	0.36	5,719	65	3.52
Canada	1990	251		1.00	1,117		0.29	2,443		0.89
	1996	377	50	1.00	2,708	142	0.29	5,111	109	0.91
Australia	1990	82		1.00	927		0.33	478		0.27
	1996	126	54	1.00	2,254	143	0.53	864	81	0.33
Mexico	1990	58		1.00	359		0.38	779		0.59
	1996	117	99	1.00	1,346	274	0.72	2,308	196	0.27
Brazil	1990	54		1.00	445		0.15	545		1.68
	1996	105	94	1.00	1,226	176	0.22	1,253	130	0.69
China	1990	115		1.00	1,060		1.32	1,292		0.16
	1996	290	151	1.00	1,867	76	3.97	7,079	448	0.05
South Korea	1990	135		1.00	396		0.44	1,295		0.99
	1996	281	108	1.00	1,044	164	0.42	4,038	212	3.80
MIT	1990	162		1.00	598		0.17	2,106		0.12
	1996	377	132	1.00	1,334	123	0.25	3,838	82	0.45
India	1990	42		1.00	711		2.30	553		0.04
	1996	70	69	1.00	826	16	0.86	863	56	0.16

Country	Year	Special industry machines			Metalworking machines			Data processing equipment		
		Total	Percent of change	RCA	Total	Percent of change	RCA	Total	Percent of change	RCA
		($m)*			($m)			($m)		
EU12	1990	36,669		1.58	29,941		1.25	63,598		0.66
	1996	39,601	8	2.05	26,571	-11	1.47	103,362	63	0.77
USA	1990	8,474		1.55	6,426		0.96	31,439		1.31
	1996	17,236	103	1.95	12,061	88	1.00	65,155	107	0.83
Japan	1990	5,731		3.40	6,054		4.58	15,122		3.38
	1996	13,167	130	4.16	10,578	75	6.84	28,254	87	1.09
Canada	1990	1,870		0.45	1,218		0.36	4,190		0.29
	1996	2,980	59	0.58	1,940	59	0.42	7,687	83	0.24
Australia	1990	693		0.27	323		0.19	1,696		0.10
	1996	1,314	90	0.50	584	81	0.28	3,093	82	0.12
Mexico	1990	662		0.08	466		0.09	807		0.88
	1996	1,589	140	0.24	1,191	156	0.17	4,025	399	2.10
Brazil	1990	297		0.13	370		0.14	242		0.20
	1996	1,232	314	0.14	986	167	0.27	1,143	372	0.25
China	1990	4,865		0.26	1,053		0.28	462		0.23
	1996	8,608	77	0.05	4,048	284	0.10	4,655	907	3.52
South Korea	1990	2,067		0.15	1,431		0.14	2,992		2.07
	1996	6,725	225	0.28	3,724	160	0.23	7,233	142	2.15
MIT	1990	2,446		0.04	1,267		0.05	888		0.84
	1996	6,600	170	0.07	3,114	146	0.08	9,143	930	4.34
India	1990	313		0.37	334		0.28	119		1.30
	1996	1,152	268	0.05	496	49	0.15	272	128	1.06

(table continued next page)

Table 3.6 Trade in IPR-sensitive goods for selected countries (continued)

Country	Year	Electromedical machines Total ($m)*	Percent of change	RCA	Electronic microcircuits Total ($m)	Percent of change	RCA	Measuring, control instruments Total ($m)	Percent of change	RCA
EU12	1990	6,764		1.44	20,166		0.76	37,428		1.04
	1996	9,799	45	1.49	53,162	164	0.81	42,208	13	1.12
USA	1990	3,671		1.49	22,142		1.41	13,235		2.82
	1996	5,961	62	2.32	64,900	193	1.27	22,570	71	2.44
Japan	1990	1,837		3.25	10,286		2.41	6,112		1.36
	1996	2,737	49	1.58	34,010	231	1.61	11,606	90	1.59
Canada	1990	327		0.14	3,166		0.53	2,501		0.37
	1996	375	15	0.25	8,413	166	0.43	3,945	58	0.38
Australia	1990	147		0.09	187		0.02	813		0.22
	1996	290	97	0.25	799	326	0.02	1,281	58	0.29
Mexico	1990	76		0.05	99		0.12	508		0.20
	1996	212	179	0.60	2,903	2,822	0.27	2,051	303	0.52
Brazil	1990	111		0.01	348		0.08	422		0.12
	1996	208	87	0.06	781	125	0.06	809	92	0.12
China	1990	210		0.08	23		0.52	850		0.16
	1996	380	81	0.14	3,145	13,498	0.19	2,267	167	0.20
South Korea	1990	159		0.15	6,831		1.99	1,796		0.18
	1996	432	171	0.25	22,368	227	2.87	4,149	131	0.09
MIT	1990	84		0.06	5,075		2.58	1,015		0.11
	1996	213	153	0.05	20,759	309	1.48	2,451	141	0.19
India	1990	74		0.10	115		0.03	388		0.09
	1996	196	166	0.13	219	90	0.02	755	94	0.10

Country	Year	Alcoholic beverages			Perfume, cosmetics			Printed matter, sound recordings		
		Total	Percent of change	RCA	Total	Percent of change	RCA	Total	Percent of change	RCA
		($m)*			($m)			($m)		
EU12	1990	25,889		1.73	11,894		1.56	36,550		1.05
	1996	33,457	29	1.67	20,794	75	1.68	45,396	24	1.20
USA	1990	4,410		0.19	1,727		1.43	10,582		2.55
	1996	6,280	42	0.28	3,775	119	2.00	16,777	59	2.40
Japan	1990	1,773		0.03	540		0.42	3,881		1.98
	1996	1,878	6	0.06	1,213	125	0.34	6,041	56	1.11
Canada	1990	1,093		0.99	365		0.38	2,941		0.20
	1996	1,262	15	0.82	1,051	188	0.45	4,390	49	0.29
Australia	1990	401		0.85	199		0.25	1,121		0.16
	1996	755	88	2.08	407	105	0.49	1,539	37	0.26
Mexico	1990	355		2.68	80		0.08	556		0.70
	1996	706	99	4.43	360	350	0.46	1,937	248	0.63
Brazil	1990	93		0.64	25		0.76	130		0.14
	1996	322	246	0.55	143	461	0.68	385	196	0.09
China	1990	62		5.43	158		14.72	457		0.65
	1996	125	99	5.75	152	-3	8.01	1,455	218	0.82
South Korea	1990	58		0.35	65		0.41	1,225		4.04
	1996	307	431	0.41	413	532	0.20	2,159	76	1.74
MIT	1990	248		0.20	220		0.88	402		0.16
	1996	417	68	0.50	446	103	0.66	2,139	432	0.65
India	1990	12		1.59	127		9.93	131		0.50
	1996	19	60	2.57	46	-63	8.43	492	277	0.69

EU12 = the first 12 members of the European Union.
MIT = combined figures for Malaysia, Indonesia and Thailand.
*All figures are in US dollars.

Source: United Nations, *International Trade Statistics Yearbook*, various issues.

lying comparative advantage; an index below unity suggests a comparative disadvantage.[31]

The product groups chosen cover sectors that figure prominently in international debates over IPRs: patents in pharmaceuticals, chemicals, machinery, and instruments; chip topography protection in microcircuits; trademarks in alcoholic beverages and perfume and cosmetics; and copyrights in printed matter and sound recordings. Clearly these sectors do not exhaust all categories in which IPRs loom large. Moreover, they are broad aggregates covering a large mix of products of varying ages and technological contents, so they do not necessarily correspond closely to product-specific demands for IPRs. Nonetheless, they seem to tell a consistent story.

As might be expected, in the 1990s aggregate merchandise trade rose most rapidly for the developing economies in the sample, especially South Korea, China, and Southeast Asia (MIT). Among the developed economies, US trade rose most rapidly in nominal terms, though overall the EU12 nations saw a 34 percent rise. (The aggregation of European economies clearly masks considerable national variation in trade performance, a fact that carries over into, and clouds, the sectoral analysis.)

There is much to digest in table 3.6 and I simply highlight interesting cases. The pharmaceuticals and medicines group saw relatively rapid trade growth in all countries except China, MIT, and India. The United States maintained a substantial, though declining, RCA in pharmaceuticals as its gross trade more than doubled. Japan demonstrated a comparative disadvantage in the sector, in considerable contrast to the other high-technology industries in the table. China's RCA indices were well above unity, mainly reflecting a near absence of imports in drugs and medicines but a substantial export trade. These ratios are likely to moderate as China improves its patent protection for imported drugs and liberalizes import restrictions. India saw a marked deterioration in its RCA for pharmaceuticals in the 1990s. India's export strength in this sector has been based on competitive imitation and production of products that were not patentable in India and its export markets (Watal 1996; Marino 1998). Recently India, after rapid growth in imports of medicines, is again a net importer.

Nearly all countries experienced relatively fast trade growth in special industry machinery, machine tools, electromedical machinery, measuring and controlling instruments, and computers.[32] Save for the last category,

---

31. RCA indices should be treated with caution, as they depend also on sectoral trade protection, subsidies, and other factors. However, ratios quite different from unity are surely meaningful, as are comparisons over time within a country. Moreover, because these indices are computed solely on trade flows they do not reflect production advantages associated with FDI for local markets.

32. The EU12 is a frequent exception, reflecting cross-currents in trade data that emerge through the aggregation of disparate countries.

these high-technology machinery sectors are not only areas of revealed comparative advantage for the United States, the EU, and Japan but also areas in which patents are common. Thus, these countries clearly are net exporters of the technology embodied in such machinery, which helps explain their keen interest in stronger global patent rights. At the same time, these machinery categories revealed significant comparative disadvantages in nearly all other countries, especially developing countries. Mexico and South Korea are noteworthy in registering marked increases in their RCA indices in high-technology machinery, providing a crude explanation for their rising interest in implementing stronger patents during this period. Canada and Australia remain net importers of these machinery categories.[33]

Perfume and cosmetics represent highly differentiated consumer goods that are sold under familiar trademarks and that are subject to considerable infringement. Trade growth has been especially rapid in this group, except in China and India, whose unusually low import levels account for their high RCA indices. Mexico, Brazil, and South Korea are rapidly expanding markets for such goods. Again, these are decided net export commodities for the EU and the United States, consistent with their strong push to crack down on trademark piracy. Trade growth has been less rapid in alcoholic beverages, an area of strong comparative advantage for the EU, Australia, and Mexico. As noted earlier, the EU has been the strongest advocate of a global system of registration and protection for geographical indications in wines and spirits.

Finally, trade growth in printed matter and sound recordings has been especially great in the developing economies. The United States, Japan, and the EU (especially the United Kingdom) retain net export positions in publishing at this aggregate level.[34] Canada and Australia are significant net importers of published materials, a fact that helps explain Canada's support for its cultural industries and Australia's recent decisions to permit parallel importation of books and music compact disks. In any event, these figures suggest that effective copyright protection in developing countries is of rising interest to publishers in the developed world.

Licensing and Foreign Direct Investment

Table 3.7 provides perspective on trade trends in services that are sensitive to IPRs protection. Indicators include net trade in computer and information services (IT) and royalties and license fees (RLF). The latter

---

33. Again, these categories are aggregates of detailed machinery subgroups. At more disaggregated levels Canada and Australia would undoubtedly register RCA indices above one in many subgroups.

34. Unfortunately, software is not broken out separately in the international trade data.

Table 3.7 Trade in IPR–sensitive services and royalties and license fees

Country	Service	1990 ($billions)			1996 ($billions)		
		Receipts	Payments	Balance	Receipts	Payments	Balance
EU12	IT	0.6	1.4	−0.8	6.6	6.7	−0.1
	RLF	8.8	13.6	−4.8	13.9	20.4	−6.5
USA	IT	n.a.	n.a.	n.a.	n.a.	n.a.	n.a.
	RLF	16.6	3.1	13.5	27.3	6.7	20.6
Japan	IT	n.a.	n.a.	n.a.	1.1	2.2	−1.1
	RLF	2.9[b]	6.1[b]	−3.2[b]	6.1	9.0	−2.9
Canada[a,d]	IT	n.a.	n.a.	n.a.	n.a.	n.a.	n.a.
	RLF	854	855	−1	1266	993	273
Australia[a]	IT	n.a.	n.a.	n.a.	151	179	−28
	RLF	162	827	−665	229	992	−763
Mexico[a]	IT	n.a.	n.a.	n.a.	n.a.	n.a.	n.a.
	RLF	73	380	−307	111	328	−217
Brazil[a]	IT	n.a.	n.a.	n.a.	39	229	−190
	RLF	12	70	−58	29	482	−453
South Korea[a]	IT	3	50	−47	5	69	−64
	RLF	37	136	−99	168	2214	−2046
MIT[a]	IT	n.a.	n.a.	n.a.	n.a.	n.a.	n.a.
	RLF	0	170	−170	23	653	−630
India[a]	IT	n.a.	n.a.	n.a.	n.a.	n.a.	n.a.
	RLF	1	72	−71	1[c]	82[c]	−81[c]

EU12 = the first 12 members of the European Union.
MIT = combined figures for Malaysia, Indonesia, and Thailand.
IT = computer and information services.
RLF = royalties and license fees.
n.a. = not available.
a. Millions of dollars.
b. 1991.
c. 1995.
d. Data for technology balance of payments. Data for 1996 are deflated by US wholesale price index (1990 = 100).

Sources: International Monetary Fund, Balance of Payments Statistics Yearbook 1997 and International Financial Statistics, various issues; and Organization for Economic Cooperation and Development, Basic Science and Technology Statistics 1997.

variable is what the OECD refers to as the "technology balance of payments." It comprises "money paid or received for the use of patents, licenses, trademarks, designs, inventions, know-how, and closely related technical services" (OECD 1998). Because not all countries report each of these flows, there are some gaps in the coverage. All data are reported in US dollars at prevailing exchange rates. Accordingly, the 1996 figures are deflated by the US wholesale price index to achieve a crude measure of changes in trade volumes.

There are several reasons why published data on RLF may not capture adequately the amount of technology being traded. Licensing fees are determined through complex contracting procedures, which attempt to price the implicit value of information. Information is unlike standard commodities in that its ultimate economic value may be unknown at the time a contract is struck. Further, the fees paid may be influenced by tax laws, accounting rules, and management decisions regarding the extent and form of income repatriation. Finally, joint ventures, business alliances, and cross-licensing agreements may encompass different volumes of licensing than would be suggested by straightforward licensing fees. Thus, these figures should be treated with caution.

Data on credits and debits for the EU countries are sums of gross flows and therefore do not net out intra-EU trade. However, in principle two-way flows within the EU should cancel in computing trade balances, which therefore do indicate extra-EU net trade. With this caveat, note that gross receipts from and payments for computer and information services amounted to around $6.6 billion in 1996, a substantial rise from 1990 levels. Both receipts from and payments for royalties and license fees rose by over 50 percent within the EU over the period, indicating a substantial increase in international licensing of technologies and trademarks. The EU12 nations remain net payers of RLF, reflecting the existence of substantial net importers of intellectual property (including France, Germany, Ireland, and Spain) in that region.

The United States also experienced significant increases in receipts from and payments for RLF, with payments more than doubling. However, the near-doubling of RLF receipts earnings from abroad generated a large rise in net receipts for intellectual property. Indeed, the United States remains by far the largest global net supplier of technology, trade secrets, and IPRs for which royalties are paid. Japan as a net importer of both computer services and intellectual property has also seen a marked rise in transactions requiring license fees.

That rapid growth is associated with rising technology imports seems clear from looking at the remarkable increases in the volume of RLF payments by Brazil, the Southeast Asian economies, and especially South Korea from 1990 to 1996. South Korea's outward payments rose fifteen-fold in this six-year period, resulting in net outward payments for RLF of over $2 billion by 1996. In contrast, India's gross RLF payments grew only marginally; Mexico's payments actually fell, probably as a result of the macro-economic crisis in the middle of the decade.

A final way to trade intellectual property is to transfer information to subsidiaries through foreign direct investment. Table 3.8 presents basic indicators on trends in the stocks of inward and outward FDI between

Table 3.8 Inward and outward stocks of foreign direct investment

Country	1990				1996			
	Inward ($b)	GDP (percent)	Outward ($b)	GDP (percent)	Inward ($b)	GDP (percent)	Outward ($b)	GDP (percent)
EU12	691	10.9	724	12.0	1,026	13.0	1,309	16.8
USA	395	6.9	435	7.6	630	8.3	793	10.4
Japan	10	0.3	201	6.8	30	0.7	259	5.6
Canada	113	19.7	85	14.8	129	22.0	125	21.3
Australia	74	25.2	31	10.3	117	29.7	46	11.7
Mexico	33	13.2	0.6	0.2	75	22.3	2.2	0.7
Brazil	37	8.5	2.4	0.5	110	14.2	7.2	0.9
China	19	4.8	2.5	0.6	172	24.7	18	2.6
South Korea	5.7	2.3	2.3	0.9	15	2.6	14	2.8
MIT	61	32.2	2.7	4.6	130	31.0	18	11.0

$b = billions of dollars.
EU12 = the first 12 members of the European Union.
MIT = combined figures for Malaysia, Indonesia, and Thailand.
Note: For both EU12 and MIT percentages of GDP are weighted by national investment stocks.

Source: United Nations Conference on Trade and Development, *World Investment Report 1998: Trends and Determinants.*

1990 and 1996. That FDI has risen in recent years more rapidly than output in most areas of the world is clear from the figures on investment stocks as a percentage of GDP. With few exceptions these ratios rose sharply during the early 1990s. The European Union, the United States, and Japan remained large net suppliers of FDI, while Canada and Australia had larger inward investment. The inward rise was especially large in Mexico, Brazil, and China, while South Korea has become a significant investor in its own right. To the extent that such investments embody intellectual property, these figures suggest that FDI has also become an important source for trading and exploiting IPRs internationally. These are issues to which I devote considerable attention in the following chapters.

Pressures for Change in the Global IPRs System

The figures just reviewed suggest two broad conclusions: (1) the 1990s have been a period of rapidly expanding international economic activity, particularly with regard to implicit or explicit trade in technology and goods protected by intellectual property rights, and (2) resort to IPRs through patent applications and trademark registrations is strengthening rapidly, particularly in major developing economies.

That the international demand for IPRs is rising stems largely from the fact that in a globalizing economy the creation of knowledge and its adaptation to product designs and production techniques are increasingly essential for commercial success. In this environment firms wish to exploit their technical advantages on an international scale and also to limit expropriation costs from potential rivals. These tasks are made easier by the adoption of stronger and more uniform IPRs in different countries. Thus, globalization of technology trade is itself the key factor in explaining systemic change in intellectual property rights.

Two other factors are also critical. One is that the costs of copying and imitating products from important sectors of technology are falling, making infringement easier and more prevalent. This is evident with electronic media, such as software, computer games, compact disks, and videos, which may be reproduced cheaply and in bulk with little or no quality degradation. Similar problems plague unauthorized duplication of broadcasts and Internet products and services, a fact that has materially retarded the international provision of electronic information. In pharmaceuticals, the costs of original product research and marketing continue to grow rapidly, but imitation costs remain low. Many biotechnological products, in particular, are subject to considerable investment costs but may be copied at a small fraction of the original expense. It is also straightforward to duplicate industrial designs, such as tile patterns or machine configuration. In all of these cases, copying costs are falling relative to original development costs, in large part because of efficiencies from using computer technologies to imitate.

A final strain on the classical IPRs system, as discussed earlier, is that many of these newer technologies do not fit comfortably within standard conceptions of industrial property and artistic property. Computer microcircuits, software programs, biotechnological inventions, and electronic transmissions all strain the limits of classical patent or copyright laws. Thus, even within developed countries intellectual property law remains in considerable flux.

These elements explain the substantial rise in demand from intellectual property owners for stronger and more harmonized global standards of protection. They underlie the massive efforts mounted by authorities in the United States and the European Union to reform the global IPRs system. These efforts have been ubiquitous, encompassing numerous bilateral negotiations with particular developing nations under threat of trade sanctions, comprehensive regional trade agreements that cover IPRs, the multilateral TRIPs agreement, ongoing efforts to unify legal practices within the EU, and international negotiations under the auspices of WIPO over intricate aspects of copyright for electronic transmissions.

Summary

Intellectual property rights are complex phenomena that cannot readily be captured by the phrase itself. They exist in a variety of forms—patents, copyrights, trademarks, trade secrets, and mixed forms of protection—that each operate distinctively. They are aimed at achieving somewhat different goals, which vary by subject matter and economic sector. Ultimately, however, IPRs attempt to strike a balance between (1) providing adequate incentives to develop new technologies, products, and artistic creation, and (2) ensuring effective distribution of those inventions into the economy. As policy tools, IPRs are second-best solutions to the difficult and delicate mix of failures that arise in markets for developing and selling information. Nonetheless, because they are market-based incentives they are generally much more efficient than direct public support for invention.

While all industries make use of a portfolio of IPRs, certain sectors have a need for particular types of intellectual property protection, and these sectors dominate the global policy debate. Patents are especially critical in the pharmaceutical and biotechnology industries, while plant breeders' rights add a complementary form of protection. Each of these areas raises contentious issues about the economic and social implications of protecting exclusive rights to new knowledge. Even within the United States, the bastion of strong protection for intellectual property, debate persists about the wisdom of awarding broad patents to biotechnological tools, genetic sequencing, and life forms. This approach is unlikely to be widely adopted in developing countries for the intermediate future.

Copyright-dependent sectors include software, recorded entertainment, electronic broadcasts, databases, and internet commerce. Because computer software falls uncomfortably between copyright and patent principles, it is subject to varying treatment in different countries. Copyright procedures seem adequate in principle for the protection of internet transactions but may require supplementation with technical solutions to endemic problems of appropriability. The protection of databases remains controversial because it could reward activity that is of limited creativity and yet pose potentially significant difficulties for scientific and educational uses of information.

The use of trademarks is widespread in all forms of business. It generally poses little threat to competition while providing important incentives for product development and quality improvements, thereby benefiting consumers and reducing their search costs. Trade secrets permit firms to protect proprietary information that they do not wish to patent. Often such information consists of small and incremental, subpatentable inventions. Trade secrets protection can promote the development of such inventions and also encourage their diffusion into competition via reverse engineering.

Given these potential impacts of IPRs and the growing need, stemming from globalization of technology, to exploit new information in international markets, the registration of intellectual property is expanding rapidly. Patent and trademark statistics point to rising recourse to protection in virtually all countries. Figures on trade, FDI, and licensing receipts suggest further that the relative IPR-intensity of international economic activity is growing.

Nonetheless, these increases are not shared equally across nations. Patent applications from firms in developed economies continue to dominate global registrations. Developing countries continue to be overwhelmingly net importers of technology and new products. Thus, an inherent tension exists between countries at different levels of economic development in their perceived interests in the global and national systems of protection. This theme is developed at length in chapter 4.

4

The Global Effects of Intellectual Property Rights: Measuring What Cannot Be Seen

Despite the obvious practical importance of the question, economists did not attempt until the 1990s to assess empirically the effects of international variations in the strength of IPRs. Without such evidence, the field lay open to strong claims on both sides of the debate—a situation that remains largely true today. Thus, for example, advocates of global harmonization of strongly protective standards made powerful assertions about the trade-distorting effects of weak and variable IPRs in order to buttress the case for their inclusion in the Uruguay Round negotiations. Their opponents argued that strengthening global IPRs would cause monopolization of trade and technology transfer, leading to widespread competitive abuses. These arguments clearly were based on strong assumptions with limited systematic evidence available to support any of them. The situation was even more stark than the earlier acute shortage of information on how patent systems affect innovation and welfare, which had prompted Priest (1986, 19) to lament, "The ratio of empirical demonstration to assumption in this literature must be very close to zero."

In the last decade, a number of economists have made strenuous efforts to help close this information gap. Some analysts developed numerical indices to characterize the strength of patent rights across nations. These in turn were used to study the impact of patent regimes on international trade, FDI, and technology licensing. This chapter reviews the evidence compiled in such studies; it concludes that, in the main, the strength of IPRs is a significant and positive determinant of international commercial activity. Stronger global IPRs could enhance the dynamic efficiency with which resources are allocated internationally, which should help mitigate any adverse distributional consequences.

This literature remains young. There is much room for further work. Moreover, how IPRs affect international business specifically is not well understood by economists. Some of the evidence suggests that they may operate in subtle and indirect ways, prompting analysts to think in broad terms about how to structure IPRs within wider policy frameworks.

Measuring Intellectual Property Rights across Borders

The most fundamental task is to measure the existence and strength of IPRs on a consistent international basis. This is especially difficult; any numerical measures that claim to capture IPRs accurately are subject to sharp criticism. After all, IPRs fall into the category of general rules supporting (or hindering) the legal operation of business, along with competition policies, environmental regulations, and labor standards. Indeed, they may be compared to the characteristics underlying economic structure, such as factor endowments, infrastructure, and the judicial system. Unlike tariffs and taxes, IPRs are not readily measurable; nor do they have obvious price-based equivalents like those used to assess the restrictiveness of quotas. Complicating the picture is that, as fundamental rules governing behavior, IPRs surely interact in complex ways with other policies in reaching their full effectiveness. Thus, identical laws may have quite distinct effects in countries that differ in their market structures and preferences.

Such difficulties render impossible a full accounting of the magnitude and strength of IPRs, especially on a comparative basis; the best analysts can do is to make qualitative rankings of IPRs as measures of inputs into economic and social production. Alternatively, market outcomes, which should be correlated with the underlying laws, may be used as output measures of the stringency or effectiveness of IPRs.

Input Measures

The most sensible approach to quantifying IPRs is to conceive of them as legal entities that serve as fundamental inputs into production. Note that they are public inputs, much like public infrastructural investments, which are available to all users meeting certain legislated requirements. Thus, input measures focus on the laws in place in each country and perhaps on their enforcement as well. This context suggests three distinctive approaches.

First, the most straightforward way to assess a nation's legislation is to list its memberships in international conventions promoting IPRs. Except for the TRIPs agreement, which is a core component of the WTO,

Table 4.1 Membership trends in key intellectual property conventions (number of countries)

Convention	1985	1990	1995	1999
Paris Convention	93	99	136	155
Berne Convention	76	86	116	140
Budapest Treaty	16	23	35	46
Patent Cooperation Treaty	44	49	85	103
UPOV	17	19	29	44

UPOV = Union for the Protection of New Varieties of Plants.

Sources: World Intellectual Property Organization (1999) and UPOV (1999).

and various regional agreements on intellectual property, these conventions are maintained largely under the auspices of the World Intellectual Property Organization (WIPO). There are 23 such pacts, including the recent Copyright Treaty and Performances and Phonograms Treaty, that either establish minimum standards for members or facilitate international cooperation in registering intellectual property. The structure of these conventions has been well described elsewhere (e.g., WIPO 1988; Primo Braga 1996). Many in effect before TRIPs were criticized for advancing weak standards; none was endowed with powers of dispute settlement. These shortcomings were a significant motivation for advocates of stronger standards to incorporate intellectual property into the WTO.

Despite these problems, a country's decision to join any WIPO conventions may be taken as a signal that its laws recognize at least minimal standards, such as national treatment and minimum periods of protection. Moreover, a country that accedes to a treaty setting out cooperative registration procedures envisions enjoying not only the cost savings such arrangements might entail but also an increase in applications for protection in its own jurisdiction. Thus, membership in basic WIPO conventions has been used by a number of analysts (e.g., Ferrantino 1993) as an input measure of the strength of IPRs.

In this context, it is instructive to look at figures for membership trends in five key conventions (see table 4.1).

The Paris Convention covers industrial property of all kinds: patents, industrial designs, trademarks, geographical indications, and trade secrets. It requires national treatment as a main principle, provides for priority of application in the case of patents, marks, and designs, and sets out rules for the administration of these IPRs. After a small rise in the late 1980s, accessions to the convention mushroomed throughout the 1990s. All new members since 1985 have been developing countries and countries in transition, implying a considerable extension of the convention's requirements into new areas.[1] While several key developing economies, including Venezuela, Singapore, India, and Chile, chose to join in the 1990s, most of the newer members are small and poor or new republics in transition. No doubt much of the increase in membership stems from the need of WTO parties to implement TRIPs, which incorporates by reference the substantive legal provisions of the Paris Convention while not requiring membership per se. In any case, at the present time global membership is comprehensive.

Similar comments pertain to the Berne Convention, which protects literary and artistic works. This convention also rests on national treatment and requires the extension of protection to nationals of all members. It enumerates in general terms the rights covered by copyright laws and exceptions to those rights, and also establishes minimum periods of protection. Membership in the Berne Convention expanded rapidly in the 1990s, indicating growing and globally comprehensive acceptance of traditional copyright protection. Again, virtually all of the new members are small developing economies and economies in transition, though China joined in 1992 and Indonesia in 1997.[2] Like the Paris Convention, substantive provisions of the Berne Convention are incorporated into TRIPs by reference.

The Budapest Treaty is an example of an international cooperative structure in patent mechanisms, in this case those for biotechnological patents. In particular, it allows the deposit of a microorganism into a recognized depositary authority to support patent applications in member nations without the need to make similar deposits with each member. The treaty, concluded in 1977, initially attracted members from only a limited number of developed economies. As biotechnological inventions have multiplied, the cost and security advantages of single deposits have attracted a rising number of developing economies, including China (1995), South Korea (1988), and South Africa (1997).

The Patent Cooperation Treaty (PCT) is also collaborative. It permits an applicant to seek patent protection for an invention in each of many countries by filing one international patent application, designating those nations in which the inventor wishes the application to have effect. A major patent office makes a single international search for prior art, which is preliminary and nonbinding on any member. Because of the considerable cost savings for the applicant and national examination authorities, membership in the PCT rose dramatically in the 1990s, to 103 countries.

Finally, the International Union for the Protection of New Varieties of Plants (UPOV), sets out minimum standards for protecting the fruits of

---

1. The number actually undercounts true accessions, because several, such as Brazil and Indonesia, joined the Paris Convention earlier but only quite recently adopted the amendments accepted by the 1967 Stockholm conference.

2. The United States joined the Berne Convention only in 1989.

invention in new plants.[3] Rapid technological progress in developing new seeds and hybrids has expanded global interest in such protection; membership in UPOV rose rapidly in the 1990s, again with the greater expansion coming in the latter half of the decade.

The nearly universal international membership in the Paris and Berne Conventions and the WTO requirement of adherence to TRIPS are perhaps the clearest indication that intellectual property protection is pushing forward broadly across the world. Ironically, the fact that few countries remain outside these conventions makes it difficult to use their membership decisions to proxy international differences in the strength of intellectual property protection.

Of course, dummy variables based on membership can be at best only a crude indicator of the strength of a nation's IPRs. The Paris Convention standards for patents, for example, are weak in comparison with those in developed economies and allow wide discretion in limiting patentability, issuing compulsory licenses, and setting opposition procedures. The convention simply requires countries to protect against unfair business competition without setting out procedures for doing so. The Berne Convention does not explicitly cover software; nor does it address the particular problems of other information technologies. Enforcement of standards is implicit in the conventions but effective enforcement varies from country to country, often to the point of absence. Accordingly, some analysts have attempted to capture the strength of IPRs and their enforcement more comprehensively through detailed consideration of each nation's laws. The authors in Gadbaw and Richards (1988) pioneered this effort by analyzing laws and observing enforcement efforts in seven major developing countries as of the mid-1980s. With rich description of policy variations in different functional areas of IPRs the study demonstrated that standards were decidedly weaker in developing than in industrial countries. However, the authors did not construct any comparative indices of strength in IPRs, and the limited country and period coverage precluded much systematic analysis based on their descriptions.

It is possible to use the annual National Trade Estimate Reports of the United States Trade Representative (USTR) to track changes over time in IPRs of major nations as perceived by US business interests. Table 4.2 is a rough overview of the situation as it evolved from 1986 to 1998. The descriptors chosen—weak, moderate, good, and strong—reflect the nature, frequency, and severity of the complaints issued by USTR, though such words cannot precisely describe a country's IPR laws or their enforcement. Thus, for example, while I list significant changes only in patent and copyright laws during this period, there were also changes in trade secrets regulations, plant variety protection, trademarks, and the like.

---

3. UPOV is a separate entity and is not administered by WIPO. The acronym UPOV derives from its French title.

Table 4.2 Qualitative trends in intellectual property protection, selected countries

Country	1986	1998	Year of major law changes
Argentina			
Laws	Weak	Moderate	Patent 1996; CR 1994
E/A	Weak	Weak	
Brazil			
Laws	Weak	Good	Patent 1997; CR 1996
E/A	Weak	Weak	
China			
Laws	Absent	Good	Patent 1993; CR 1992
E/A	Absent	Weak	
Egypt			
Laws	Weak	Moderate	CR 1994
E/A	Weak	Weak	
India			
Laws	Weak	Weak	Patent 1999; CR 1995
E/A	Weak	Moderate	
Indonesia			
Laws	Absent	Moderate	Patent 1991, 97; CR 1997
E/A	Absent	Weak	
Japan			
Laws	Good	Strong	Patent 1995; CR 1992
E/A	Weak	Good	
South Korea			
Laws	Weak	Strong	Patent 1987, 95; CR 1987, 96
E/A	Weak	Good	
Mexico			
Laws	Weak	Strong	Patent 1991; CR 1991, 93, 96
E/A	Weak	Moderate	
The Philippines			
Laws	Weak	Good	Patent 1997; CR 1997
E/A	Weak	Moderate	
Spain			
Laws	Moderate	Strong	Patent 1986, 92; CR 1987, 93
E/A	Weak	Strong	
Taiwan			
Laws	Weak	Strong	Patent 1993, 95; CR 1985, 95
E/A	Weak	Weak	
Thailand			
Laws	Weak	Good	Patent 1992, 98; CR 1995
E/A	Weak	Weak	
Turkey			
Laws	Weak	Good	Patent 1995, 99; CR 1995
E/A	Weak	Moderate	

E/A = enforcement and administration.
CR = copyright.

Source: Author's inferences from descriptions in USTR, various years.

Moreover, while a word like "moderate" is meant to convey the overall tenor of IPRs protection, it may mask considerable variation in the individual laws covering functional areas of intellectual property.

Keep in mind, finally, that the descriptions summarize the views of USTR, which accord heavy weight to treatment that is parallel to, or even stronger than, the protective standards found in the United States. A law that is "moderate" by American standards may not be unreasonable by the standards of a particular country.

The descriptions in table 4.2 leave the strong impression that the 1990s indeed saw considerable strengthening of the legal structures and enforcement mechanisms for IPRs in many countries. Moreover, the dates given represent only years in which major legislative changes were made; many of these laws continue to evolve through technical adjustments and implementation.

The countries included in the table illustrate a number of avenues toward adopting stronger IPRs. For example, Spain, which had moderate protection for industrial property in 1986, experienced high levels of piracy due to lax enforcement. However, one condition of its entry into the European Union was the adoption of laws harmonized with the (still-evolving) EU standards. Thus, in 1986 Spain revised its patent law to include pharmaceutical products (though protection was phased in only by 1992). Spain adopted the EU software directive in 1993, providing copyrights and the prospect of patents for computer programs.

Turkey resisted changing its laws for some time, but in anticipation of a free trade agreement with the EU recently enacted legislation considerably tightening industrial property rights and copyrights. Similarly, Mexico adopted laws based on highest global standards as early as 1991 and has tightened them further in the context of NAFTA. Indeed, one of the more significant aspects of current regional trade agreements between rich countries and poor countries is that the latter are expected to significantly reform their IPRs regimes.

South Korea and Taiwan are examples of countries that adopted considerably stronger IPRs in the late 1980s and early 1990s, in large part because domestic commercial interests emerged to push that agenda, though American diplomatic and trade pressures contributed.[4] Japan's prior patent procedures—which provided for pregrant opposition, were subject to lengthy delays, and encouraged "patent flooding"—were long an irritant to US multinational enterprises (MNEs). Extensive bilateral discussions led to an agreement in 1994 under which Japan shifted the emphasis of its patent system toward promoting innovation and reduced examination terms.

Argentina, Brazil, the Philippines, and Thailand engineered notable strengthening in their laws only recently. Argentina's 1996 patent law

---

4. Ryan (1998, chapter 4), provides a trenchant discussion.

revision, since enhanced, retained significant limitations on patentability and patent scope. Brazil has adopted stronger laws in anticipation of meeting its TRIPs requirements. Both countries extended copyright protection to software, though allowing liberal decompilation. The Philippines, despite considerable American pressure throughout the decade, adopted major legislative changes only in 1997, also responding to TRIPs obligations. Thailand's policy evolution was similar. All four of these nations continue to experience significant piracy in copyright and trademark goods. For its part, Egypt updated its copyright law in 1994 and undertook a number of publicized raids on unauthorized distributors of software and electronic entertainment products. However, piracy remains a significant problem and Egypt has yet to update its patent law.

China eagerly embraced IPRs reform in this decade. Beginning from a situation of near absence, China erected laws covering patents (including pharmaceutical patents), trademarks, integrated circuits, plant varieties, unfair competition, and copyrights (LaCroix and Konan 1998; Maskus, Dougherty, and Mertha 1998). China joined nearly all the major international IPR conventions and is also now a member of international procedural treaties on the classification of patents and trademarks and the deposit of microorganisms. The country must make further minor revisions to conform to TRIPs but those revisions are under consideration. China has also made considerable progress in establishing education and training programs in IPRs and in upgrading its administrative and legal enforcement systems. Nonetheless the economy continues to experience massive product counterfeiting, suggesting that enforcement has a long way to go.

Indian law conforms with TRIPs in copyrights and trademarks but is weak in patents. The 1999 revisions to the Indian patent law, passed over considerable and lengthy opposition, meet current transition requirements but remain short of ultimate TRIPs standards. Indonesia's reforms have progressed to the point where legal systems provide moderate coverage of IPRs, though administration of the system remains in its infancy and there are endemic enforcement problems. Looking at the table as a whole, it is no surprise that as the decade ended, the lowest-income economies—India, Indonesia, and Egypt—retained the weakest protection.

Such qualitative descriptions are informative but of limited use for comparisons of large numbers of countries or for statistical analysis. Several researchers have thus undertaken a close analysis of the components of legal structures in order to develop numerical indices of IPRs strength.

The first cross-country index was developed by Rapp and Rozek (RR) (1990). They consulted the legal texts of each country's patent laws and made a rough assessment of their conformity with the minimum standards proposed as guidelines by the US Chamber of Commerce (1987). Their approach considered only the presence or absence of particular features of patent laws, such as working requirements, compulsory licenses, and product patents for pharmaceuticals. It did not consider enforcement ef-

Table 4.3 Indices of the strength of IPRs laws

	RR 1984	GP 1985	GP 1990	GP 1995
Full sample				
N	116	108	109	116
Average	2.90	2.44	2.45*	2.73*
Median	3	2.52	2.52	2.71
CV	0.49	0.39	0.40	0.32
Increases	n.a.	n.a.	9	34
Decreases	n.a.	n.a.	4	3
High-income				
N	27	26	28	30
Average	4.14	3.37	3.43*	3.70*
Median	4	3.32	3.32	3.86
CV	0.26	0.19	0.23	0.17
Increases	n.a.	n.a.	5	15
Decreases	n.a.	n.a.	1	1
Mid-income				
N	33	27	27	34
Average	2.62	2.24	2.29*	2.54*
Median	2	2.26	2.01	2.61
CV	0.41	0.29	0.30	0.23
Increases	n.a.	n.a.	2	13
Decreases	n.a.	n.a.	2	1
Low-income				
N	56	55	54	52
Average	2.46	2.11	2.12*	2.33*
Median	2	2.41	2.41	2.57
CV	0.56	0.44	0.44	0.33
Increases	n.a.	n.a.	2	6
Decreases	n.a.	n.a.	1	1

RR = Rapp and Rozek.
GP = Ginarte and Park.
N = Number of countries.
CV = Coefficient of variation.
n.a. = non-applicable.
*Average scores are computed for an unchanged set of nations between adjoining years.

Sources: Adapted from Rapp and Rozek (1990), Ginarte and Park (1997), and data provided by Park.

fort or effectiveness. Their scale ranged from zero, signifying the absence of a patent law, to five, indicating full conformity with minimum standards. The index was therefore subjective, with each unit increase attempting to capture differences in a large range of complex legal issues.

The first column of table 4.3 provides summary statistics on the RR index for 116 countries in 1984. High-income economies are those with real per capita GDP levels above US $7,000, using 1985 data, taken from the Penn World Tables, for purchasing-power-parity adjusted incomes. Middle-income economies have real per capita GDP levels between $2,500 and $7,000; low-income economies have incomes below $2,500.

It is immediately evident that the strength of patent rights rises with per capita income, though the increase in the average from the low-income to the middle-income economies is not large relative to the rise from middle-income to high-income countries. This point is explored further in the next section. Moreover, as income levels rise, variation in patent rights falls, as evidenced by the lower coefficients of variation (CV) for richer countries.

The RR approach was extended significantly by Ginarte and Park (1997). They examined the patent laws of a comprehensive number of countries quinquennially from 1960 to 1990, considering five components of the laws: duration of protection, extent of coverage, membership in international patent agreements, provisions for loss of protection, and enforcement measures.[5] Each component was further broken down into important characteristics determining its effective strength. For example, patent coverage refers to the patentability of pharmaceutical products and chemical products and to the existence of utility models. Enforcement measures included the availability of preliminary injunctions, contributory infringement actions, and reversals of the burden of proof in process patent cases. (The authors made no attempt to assess how well the laws in fact were enforced.) Each of these subcomponents was assigned a value of one if present and zero if absent, with the component score being the sum of these values as a percentage of the maximum value. Thus, the minimum possible national score was 0.0 and the maximum was 5.0. Although each subcomponent was binary, the aggregate score was more continuous than the unit-increment approach in the RR index. Thus, the Ginarte and Park index (GP index) is more nuanced to reflect variations in patent laws. Moreover, its computation for different years permits analysis of the index over time.

The GP index is summarized in the final three columns of table 4.3. I present figures for 1985, 1990, and 1995 because of the interest here in recent changes in IPRs. The index averaged 2.44 for all countries in 1985, indicating that roughly half the various subcomponents in patent rights were available in the average nation. Again, the high-income economies had indices that were both considerably higher and less variable than those of the middle-income and low-income economies. Further, the increase in average protection from poor countries to middle-income countries was much less than that from the next progression in incomes.

The late 1980s saw little effective increase in the strength of patent laws, according to the GP index. For example, both the mean and median scores increased almost imperceptibly between 1985 and 1990 across the full sample.[6] While nine countries increased their protection, four weakened

---

5. These data have now been updated to 1995 and were kindly provided by Walter Park.

6. In the table, the average scores refer to an unchanged set of countries between 1985 and 1990 and between 1990 and 1995 to avoid confusion arising from entry or exit of nations into the database.

their patent laws. Within the high-income economies, the average index rose from 3.37 in 1985 to 3.43 in 1990, suggesting an average increase of 1.5 percent in the index among wealthy countries. Nonetheless, one country (Belgium) in this group registered a reduction in its patent score. Among the middle-income countries, the average index rose from 2.24 to 2.29, or 2.2 percent. Two countries (Mexico and South Korea) strengthened their laws and two (Malaysia and Greece) weakened them. Among the low-income economies there was little improvement in patent laws, with the average index rising only from 2.11 to 2.12, or 0.5 percent. The indices of two nations (Guatemala and Benin) went up while that of one (India) went down.

The GP index for 1995 indicates that there was considerably more strengthening of patent laws in the 1990s than earlier. Of the 109 countries in the sample for both 1990 and 1995, fully 34 engineered more protective patent regulations; 15 of these were high-income countries and 13 middle-income countries. Six of the low-income economies saw rising indices. Across the groups, the average percentage increases in the mean indices were 7.9 percent (high-income), 10.9 percent (middle-income), and 9.9 percent (low-income). From this evidence it appears that in the 1990s many poor and medium-income nations were induced to strengthen their IPRs, whether for internal economic reasons, because of external pressure, or both. Middle-income countries raising their standards were Argentina, Brazil, Chile, South Korea, Malaysia, Mexico, Thailand, and Venezuela, among others.[7]

A final approach to measuring IPRs regimes as inputs into production is to survey MNE managers, who likely are aware of effective differences in systems across countries. These surveys typically ask for the respondents' views on the adequacy of local intellectual property protection. Accordingly, they pay considerably less attention to the structure of laws and considerably more attention to how effectively the laws may be used to protect technological information. Thus, respondents rank their views of patents, trademarks, trade secrets, and copyrights in the aggregate, including not only how the laws operate but also how well they may be enforced. While such surveys are crude in that they ignore technical aspects of the law, they are informative in terms of perceived effectiveness. Unlike indices based on laws, however, the responses likely are endogenous to a host of issues that may not be closely related to IPRs, such as market structure and growth prospects in each country. They also depend on the sensitivity of the firms sampled to IPRs protection, which could vary over time. Thus, they must be treated with caution.

---

7. I should call attention also to the index developed by Sherwood (1997), who developed a subjective assessment of several components of IPRs, including patents, trademarks, trade secrets, protection of new life forms, copyrights, treaty adherence, and enforcement and administration, in 18 developing countries as of the mid-1990s. Another index was constructed for 33 countries by Kondo (1995).

Table 4.4   Survey indices of perceived strength of IPRs

Country	1990	1995	Percent change
Industrial countries (selected)			
USA	69.2	80.80	16.8
Japan	70.2	66.3	−5.6
Canada	58.4	72.3	23.8
Germany	70.6	78.9	11.8
France	67.2	72.9	8.5
Spain	40.4	58.1	43.8
United Kingdom	59.7	74.4	24.7
Average of 21	*59.0*	*70.5*	*19.4*
Developing countries			
Brazil	36.3	35.3	−2.9
Hong Kong	52.1	63.1	21.1
India	44.3	40.6	−8.4
Indonesia	35.4	45.3	27.9
South Korea	57.1	54.2	−5.1
Malaysia	52.1	62.0	19.0
Mexico	42.0	56.1	33.6
Singapore	71.9	78.8	9.6
Taiwan	53.9	63.8	18.4
Turkey	35.8	25.3	−29.3
Venezuela	32.5	32.1	−1.2
Average of 11	*46.7*	*50.6*	*8.4*
Other developing countries			
Argentina		47.1	
Chile		61.8	
China		33.6	
Egypt		60.0	
The Philippines		37.3	
Russia		15.8	
Thailand		52.1	

Source: World Economic Forum, *World Competitiveness Report* (various issues).

The most familiar survey measure is published by the World Economic Forum in its annual *World Competitiveness Report*. Respondents are asked to provide a subjective answer to the question of whether IPRs in each country are adequate to meet their needs for security and exploitation of proprietary technical information. The answers are compiled into a numerical index ranging from zero to 100, with higher numbers indicating stronger faith in the system of IPRs.

Table 4.4 lists indices for selected countries for the years 1990 and 1995.[8] The most striking aspect of these figures is that MNE managers consider that developed economies have done more to strengthen intellectual property protection than developing economies. Canada's decision to phase out compulsory licenses in pharmaceuticals, for example, seems largely responsible for the 24 percent rise in its index, while Spain's

---

8. Intellectual property entered the survey in 1989.

adherence to EU standards explains the 44 percent rise in its measure. For 21 industrial countries, the average perceived rise in IPRs protection was 19 percent.

In contrast, for 11 developing countries the average perceived rise was 8.4 percent. Policy in Mexico, Indonesia, Hong Kong, and Taiwan was seen as becoming markedly more protective of foreign intellectual property in this period. However, perceived conditions of protection in Turkey deteriorated significantly in the early 1990s, while Brazil and Korea registered small declines. Thus, it appears that, from the standpoint of MNEs, the ability to protect IPRs improved considerably in the early 1990s in the industrial countries, but considerably less on average in developing economies.

The third section of the table shows the indices for certain developing countries in 1995. By this measure, Chile and Egypt provide relatively strong protection, while Russia, China, and the Philippines do not. Russia's laws are adequate but their enforcement is nil (USTR 1999). China is in a similar position, though perceptions of its protection may be improving: China's index rose by 13 percent between 1994 and 1995.

In summary, together the various measures discussed permit us to draw some conclusions with reasonable confidence:

1. Standards for protecting intellectual property have increased globally, with much of that strengthening coming in the 1990s. Legal reforms in a number of countries, such as Mexico, Taiwan, Thailand, and China, have been especially marked. In many countries such reforms emerged only in the late 1990s, with their adoption mandated by the TRIPs agreement.

2. Enforcement efforts in developing countries tend to lag significantly behind legislative changes.

3. High-income economies continue to strengthen their IPRs. Indeed, it is difficult to determine whether standards in developed and developing economies are converging or diverging, even as minimum standards rise virtually everywhere. This seems especially evident from the survey responses summarized in table 4.4, where on average perceived IPRs protection in the industrial countries rose faster than in developing countries.

While these inferences are reasonable, given various shortcomings the measures discussed here must be treated with caution. Moreover, there are troubling discrepancies among the measures. For example, the qualitative passages in USTR (1999) are laudatory of the modern structure of Mexico's IPRs laws, but the Mexican GP index for 1995 (2.52) remains no higher than the average for middle-income developing countries. Nonetheless, the index rose by 55 percent, which is consistent with the large

Table 4.5   Estimated rates of software piracy and lost revenues

	1994		1998	
	Piracy Rate (percent)	Revenues ($mil.)	Piracy Rate (percent)	Revenues ($mil.)
North America	32	3,931	26	3,196
USA	31	3,590	25	2,875
Western Europe	52	2,783	36	2,760
Germany	48	671	28	479
Spain	77	191	57	235
Eastern Europe	85	1,101	76	640
Russia	95	516	92	273
Latin America	78	981	62	978
Brazil	77	294	61	395
Guatemala	94	9	85	9
Mexico	78	192	59	133
Asia/Pacific	68	3,145	49	2,955
China	97	364	95	1,193
Japan	66	1,400	31	597
South Korea	75	511	64	198
Thailand	87	68	82	49
Middle East/Africa	80	406	63	380
Egypt	84	8	85	11
World Total	49	12,347	38	10,977

Source: BSA/SIIA (1999).

increase between 1990 and 1995 in the perceived strength of Mexican IPRs put forward by survey respondents in *World Competitiveness Report*. Thus, despite the differences in approach, there is broad agreement across these measures.

Output Measures

Some analysts attempt to assess IPRs by considering outcomes that may correlate with the underlying effectiveness of intellectual property regimes. The most common approach is to estimate the extent to which rights are violated in different countries. For example, the Business Software Alliance and the Software and Information Industry Association (BSA/SIIA; 1999) publish estimates garnered from their member firms about the degree of copyright infringement in key nations. Similarly, the International Intellectual Property Association (IIPA; 1999) compiles estimates of piracy rates and revenue losses in motion pictures, recorded music, and software for those countries it recommends to receive designations from USTR under the "Special 301" provisions.

Table 4.5 lists estimated piracy rates and revenue losses for US software firms in various regions and countries in 1994 and 1998. The methodology for estimating revenue losses is simplistic: Firms are asked to report the level of pirated software sales, through any medium, they believe to exist. These sales are considered to displace US revenues, regardless of how markets would react to price and structural changes if copyrights were stronger. In this sense, the estimated revenue losses are excessive, though it is impossible to know by how much. Moreover, the estimated revenue losses are sensitive to business conditions. For example, piracy losses in South Korea are reported to have fallen precipitously by 1998, but this is related foremost to slackening demand there.

Subject to such caveats, the reported figures can be instructive. American software firms claimed that globally they lost over $12 billion in sales in 1994 and nearly $11 billion in 1998. The United States is not impervious to piracy. In 1998, 25 percent of software copies put into use here were obtained without copyright authorization; the associated revenue losses were the largest of any country. The period from 1994 to 1998 saw declining piracy rates in most countries, with the overall rate falling from 49 percent to 38 percent. Rates remain high in Russia, China, and Egypt, where unauthorized duplication is endemic. Clearly, piracy rates vary negatively with economic development: higher-income economies, which tend also to be the major software producers, have strong interests in vigorous protection and awareness campaigns.

Similar measures in trademarks and patents are more difficult to come by. Because patent coverage and scope vary widely from nation to nation, it is rarely clear whether particular business actions should be adjudged infringements, which they might be under US law but not in another national jurisdiction. To get an idea of the complexities involved in pharmaceutical patenting, for example, consider the submission of the Pharmaceutical Research and Manufacturers' Association (PhRMA 1999a) to USTR regarding "Special 301" designations. India and Argentina were listed as priority foreign countries largely due to deficiencies in patent coverage. PhRMA tentatively estimated its member firms' annual sales losses to be some $500 million in India and $600 million in Argentina. South Korea was also listed in this category, mainly because of trade barriers and administrative deficiencies in the patent regime, with an estimated sales loss of $500 million. South Africa was placed on this list because its new Medicines Act significantly weakens effective protection of patented pharmaceutical products through aggressive pricing regulations and compulsory licenses. Complaints about other nations included failure to provide retroactive patents (Canada, no estimated damages), discriminatory marketing rights and price controls (China, damages of $1.4 billion), and inadequate treatment of foreign test data along with price regulation (Japan, damages of over $2.5 billion). The report claims that the policies it targets are current or likely violations of TRIPs obligations, an interpretation that must await dispute settlement procedures.

As suggested, estimated rates of copyright, trademark, and patent infringement might be indirect measures of the strength of IPRs if the analyst believes they correlate strongly with weakness in the laws and enforcement. This is true, other things being equal—but unfortunately other things may not be equal. Copyright infringement depends not only on laxity of enforcement, for example, but also on local business conditions, pricing strategies of rights owners, and cultural preferences. In this context, law-based measures are likely more suitable for analytical use.

While these various measures leave much to be desired as indicators of the true strength of IPRs, they are the best available. One reason for using them is to investigate whether their measures of IPRs may be fruitful for analytical work. Two general questions emerge, one relating to IPRs as endogenous policy variables, and the other to IPRs as determinants of economic activity. Thus, economists have analyzed both the cross-country determinants of the strength of patent rights and the impacts of international variations in patent rights on trade, investment, and technology transfer. Because the latter impacts are critical in thinking about the likely effects of stronger global IPRs, they dominate much of the attention in this chapter.

Determinants of Intellectual Property Rights

It is obvious from the figures already given that IPRs tend to strengthen as economic development and incomes rise. That optimal protection of intellectual property is an increasing function of income and technological capacity is easy to explain. As incomes rise, the demand for higher-quality, differentiated products also rises, leading to growing preferences for protection of trademarks and copyrights or, in political economy terms, an increase in the supply of IPRs. As an economy's technological sophistication increases, inventors and creators require stronger protection for their works; thus, demand for IPRs rises. Of course, causation may go both ways, with stronger property rights also contributing to growth in incomes. The latter point remains subject to debate, being not yet well understood in empirical terms. I elaborate these points in chapter 5 on IPRs and economic development.

That IPRs are positively correlated with real GNP per capita was first demonstrated by Maskus and Penubarti (1995), using the RR index,[9] though they corrected it for two econometric problems. First, because the index is subjective, there is significant potential for measurement error. For example, a number of poor nations, such as Ghana and Nigeria, have strong laws on paper because they were British colonies and modeled their

---

9. Rapp and Rozek (1990) chose to use their index as an explanatory variable in an analysis of income levels; they were not concerned with the opposite causation.

regimes on the United Kingdom Patents Act. However, enforcement difficulties significantly reduce the effective strength of patents in those
countries. (This problem may not be of much consequence because few
foreign firms are likely to apply for patents in such small markets.)[10]
Second, an adjustment problem arises because levels of economic development and trade flows may influence the structure of patent laws and
their enforcement.

Maskus and Penubarti used instrumental variables to try to purge the
raw RR patent index of these problems. The instruments included prior
indicators of the level of economic development (GDP per capita, primary exports as a share of total exports, infant mortality rate, and secondary enrollment ratios for 1965, 19 years prior to 1984, the year of the
patent index). They also used dummy variables for former British and
French colonies and alternative measures of intellectual property protection, which were highly correlated with patent strength yet presumably
were not correlated with trade-regression error terms. Using the instruments to predict patent strength resulted in a corrected index with continuous values from 0.9 to 5.3 (as opposed to the incremental raw index
with integral values from 0 to 5). It is worth noting that their approach
found that GDP per capita and the secondary enrollment ratio (a proxy
for prior human capital development) were strongly positive determinants of this index, as were the dummy variables for colonial identity.
While this index was adjusted, it still does not necessarily represent the
optimal structure of patent rights.

Figure 4.1 plots the relationship between the corrected patent index, on
the vertical axis, and the natural log of real GNP per capita ("income"), on
the horizontal axis. Recall that these data are for 1984. A simple regression of the index on current income resulted in this relationship:

$$PATENT^* = -0.51 + 0.49\log(INCOME) \quad R^2 = 0.37.$$

Both coefficients were highly significant statistically. Thus, as real income rises, there is a corresponding increase in patent strength across
countries. The calculation suggests that as income rises by $1,000 (a 29
percent increase evaluated at the sample mean), the patent index would
become higher by 0.14 units (a 4.5 percent increase). Income alone is
capable of explaining 37 percent of the variation in corrected international patent rights.

Figure 4.1 actually suggests that patent rights decline as incomes rise
from low levels, then accelerate sharply toward the highest income levels.
Thus, there seems to be a quadratic relationship between IPRs and GNP
per capita, estimation of which resulted in this equation:

$$PATENT^* = 10.5 - 2.63\log(INCOME) + 0.21[\log(INCOME)]^2 \quad R^2 = 0.50.$$

---

10. I am grateful to Jayashree Watal for pointing this out.

Figure 4.1 Relationship between patent rights and per capita GNP

corrected RR patent index

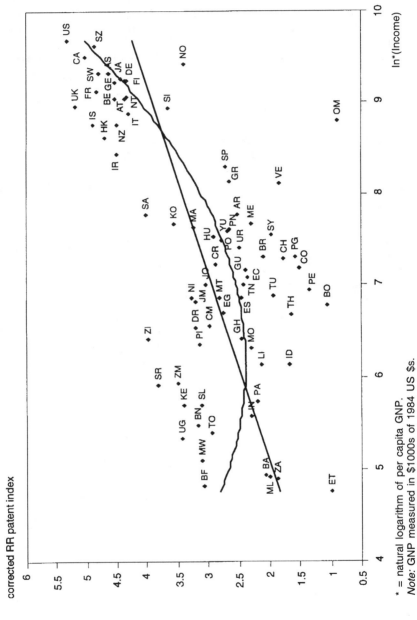

* = natural logarithm of per capita GNP.

Note: GNP measured in $1000s of 1984 US $s.

Sources: Maskus and Penubarti (1995) and author's calculations.

Adding the squared term lets income explain 50 percent of the variation in IPRs across countries. This specification strongly suggests that countries tend to weaken their patent laws as incomes begin to rise and then strengthen them after a certain point. This U-shaped curve is reminiscent of the "environmental Kuznets curve," which indicated that countries reduce their environmental standards up to some level of per capita income and then raise them continuously after that point (Grossman and Krueger 1993). The plot is shown in figure 4.1. It is interesting that the curve reaches its minimum at log(INCOME) = 6.26, which translates into a per capita GNP of only $523 in 1984. This income level exceeded those of only the 17 poorest nations in the data sample. Somewhat surprisingly, then, accounting for lagged determinants of patent strength, it seems that only for quite poor nations is protection weakened as incomes rise before it rises again. At the same time, it would require a per capita income of $2,750 [log(INCOME) = 7.92] for protection levels to return to the level for a per capita income of $100. In 1984 $2,750 was higher than the per capita income of Argentina, Turkey, Yugoslavia, Brazil, South Korea, Malaysia, and Mexico, as well as other middle-income industrializing economies.

It is interesting to update and extend this analysis. Ginarte and Park (1997) provide an econometric analysis of the determinants of their patent index using a panel of 48 countries for the years 1965, 1975, 1985, and 1990. They relate these patent indices to lagged values of several determinants, among them real GDP per capita, research and development (R&D) expenditures as a proportion of GDP, secondary school enrollment ratios, the Sachs-Warner (1995) dummy variable for an economy's openness to trade, the Barro-Lee (1994) index of political rights, and the Johnson-Sheehy (1995) index of market freedom.

Results from Ginarte and Park's ordinary least squares (OLS) regressions are presented in the first two columns of table 4.6. All variables are in logs except for dummy variables; standard errors of coefficients are listed in parentheses. Ginarte and Park initially ran the log of their index on the log of real per capita GDP, finding a positive and highly significant coefficient over their full sample. However, upon adding other determinants of patent rights, determinants that also influence income levels, they found that while the coefficient on GDP per capita becomes insignificant, there are strong positive impacts from the lagged R&D ratio, trade openness, and the index of market freedom. Human capital, as proxied by the lagged secondary school enrollment ratio, is positive but only marginally significant. Thus, their results seem to suggest that the determination of patent rights is driven in part by the demand for protection because countries with higher R&D intensities and human capital inputs have higher indices.

Their results also suggest that trade openness and market freedom (an index designed to measure how well governments abstain from market interference) expand patent rights. The effect on trade openness is

Table 4.6 Determinants of Ginarte-Park Patent Rights Index

Variable	GP (1)	GP (2)	Maskus (1)	Maskus (2)
Intercept	−1.06* (0.20)	0.68* (0.33)	13.61* (2.09)	10.76* (2.47)
GDP per capita	0.23* (0.03)	-0.03 (0.04)	−3.38* (0.53)	−2.58* (0.64)
(GDP per capita)^2			0.22* (0.03)	0.17* (0.04)
R&D/GDP		0.08* (0.02)		
School		0.06 (0.04)		-0.01 (0.08)
Political freedom		0.07 (0.06)		
Openness		0.10* (0.05)		0.06 (0.08)
Market freedom		0.52* (0.09)		
GDP				−0.01 (−0.67)
S&E/LF				0.08* (0.03)
UKCOL				0.23* (0.07)
FCOL				0.33* (0.13)
Number of observations	192	192	144	144
Adjusted R^2	0.31	0.51	0.33	0.37

(1) and (2) = different specification of regression equations.
S&E/LF = proportion of scientists and engineers in the labor force.
UKCOL = dummy variable for former colonies of the UK.
FCOL = dummy variable for former colonies of France.
* = Indicates significance at 5 percent or lower.
Notes: Standard errors are in parentheses.
Variables are in logs except dummies. Equations estimated by OLS.

intriguing, though difficult to interpret. It could be that citizens are willing to provide more protection in open economies because IPRs help preserve greater consumer choice. It could also be that more open economies find that trade interacts positively with innovative effort, raising the demand for intellectual property protection. (I will return to this in later sections.) Finally, it may be that more open economies could be more susceptible to American pressure for reform.

It is informative to extend the Ginarte-Park analysis in two ways. First, I apply the GP index to specifications similar to the Maskus-Penubarti study. Second, in order to focus on a more recent time period, I perform regressions using a panel of 72 countries in the years 1985 and 1990 rather than the 48 countries in the Ginarte-Park study. Looking at the later years makes it possible to collect data for the R&D variable for additional countries. These figures were taken from the annual UNESCO *Statistical Yearbooks,* supplemented by data on the number of scientists and engineers employed as a percentage of the labor force. Following Ginarte and Park, independent variables were lagged five years to reduce problems with adjustment.

The first specification, listed in the third column of table 4.6, mirrors the quadratic estimation discussed above on the RR index, but it is performed on the raw GP data. It again supports the inverted-U story. Clearly such a specification is simplistic. Thus, I add further explanatory variables that account for other influences on patent rights. One of these is size of the economy as measured by real GDP. It could be hypothesized that countries do not begin to provide strong IPRs until they reach a certain size, because there are fixed costs in organizing and administering a patent system.

In the regression in the final column, market size has no detectable impact on patent rights. This finding is potentially important in policy terms. It suggests that GDP itself is not a determinant of IPRs reform, as opposed to per capita income and economic development. Because US trade authorities are concerned with the strength of IPRs protection in large but poor economies, such as India and China, they have mounted considerable pressure for change. This finding suggests that, despite such pressure, effective patent rights may remain limited until incomes grow well beyond current levels. In other words, the higher standards required by TRIPs may well command limited enforcement attention in many nations.

The school enrollment ratio is not significant, perhaps because published secondary enrollment figures mask huge differences in actual human capital formation. However, the proportion of scientists and engineers in the labor force has a strongly positive impact on the GP index, again suggesting that as economies devote more resources to inventive activity, the demand for intellectual property protection grows. Finally, the dummies for countries that are former colonies of Britain and France are strongly significant.[11]

The notable feature here is that, even controlling for other influences, the inverted-U relationship between patent strength and lagged real per

---

11. In principle, it would be beneficial to include country fixed effects to control even more tightly for unmeasured, idiosyncratic national factors influencing patent rights. However, such an approach would be difficult with only two years of data.

Table 4.7   1985 income levels and 1990 predicted patent indices

Country	Income	GP Predicted*	GP Actual
India	763	2.21	1.48
Ghana	922	2.09	2.90
Nigeria	1,199	1.98	3.05
Indonesia	1,253	1.97	0.33
Egypt	1,574	1.91	1.99
The Philippines	1,871	1.90	2.67
Thailand	2,149	1.90	1.85
Turkey	2,851	1.94	1.80
South Korea	3,122	1.97	3.94
Malaysia	3,778	2.04	2.37
Brazil	4,249	2.10	1.85
Mexico	5,708	2.30	1.63
Spain	7,496	2.57	3.62
Japan	10,289	3.02	3.94
Italy	10,442	3.04	4.05
USA	15,101	3.84	4.52

* = value of GP Index predicted by the final regression equation in table 4.6.
Note: For all countries, the patent index is computed assuming they were not British or French colonies. Income is measured in US dollars.

Source: Author's calculations.

capita income remains intact. Indeed, the coefficients are similar to those reported for the corrected RR index, except that the coefficient on squared GDP per capita is somewhat lower. This difference actually shifts the parabola to the right in the range of low and middle incomes. As a result, the income at which patent protection becomes weakest is approximately $2,000 per capita in 1985 international dollars. Moreover, the expected patent index is the same for economies with per capita GDP of $500 and $7,750, implying a significant range of income variation before protection becomes stronger.

To illustrate these findings, in table 4.7 I list several countries, their income levels in 1985, and their anticipated and actual GP patent rights indices in 1990. In order to preserve the quadratic ranking across income levels, I compute the predicted indices from the final regression equation in table 4.6 but assume that each country was not a British colony. Colonial status does matter: the actual indices for Ghana and Nigeria considerably exceed their predicted levels. India has been more aggressive in weakening patent rights in food products and pharmaceuticals despite its former status as a colony.

Observe that the predicted GP indices fall as incomes rise through Thailand, then at higher income levels begin to rise. In most middle-income economies, actual protection in 1985 lags behind that anticipated, as illustrated by Turkey, Brazil, and Mexico. The significant later strengthening of IPRs in the 1990s in Brazil and Mexico surely stemmed in part from indigenous interests in tighter protection. In contrast, Malaysia and South Korea adopted laws by 1990 that seemed stronger than warranted by their 1985 incomes. Spain's accession to the EU also succeeded in raising its patent rights above the predicted level.

The high-income economies uniformly have actual protection levels stronger than the model predicts. It seems likely, therefore, that the simple specification set out here misses important influences on IPRs that rise cumulatively with income. Unfortunately, the dynamics cannot readily be captured with available data.

This analysis has aimed at explaining the determinants of patent laws —input measures, in our terminology. To conclude this section one study should be mentioned that considers an output measure, software piracy rates, as an endogenous variable. Marron and Steel (2000) regressed software piracy rates, averaged over 1994-96, on per capita GDP and a variety of other determinants. They found that piracy rates are negatively related to income levels, a general measure of the strength of contracts, and an index designed to measure the power of individualism in the culture relative to collectivism. An individualistic culture, they claimed, would likely have a stronger need for property rights to avoid collective coercion or misappropriation. Their results are at best questionable, in part because output measures may not provide accurate indications of underlying IPRs. Nonetheless, the study is noteworthy for introducing culture into the determination of property rights.

The Effects of IPRs on International Economic Activity

One essential reason for developing such measures is to use them in analyzing whether the strength of IPRs has detectable effects on economic activity. My main concern is to look at international economic transactions—international trade in goods, foreign direct investment, and licensing contracts——because they are the subject of considerable debate, and hope, about the effects of stronger global property rights. Clearly, however, IPRs have wider effects—on innovation, market structure, pricing, and economic development, issues I turn to in the next chapter.

Recent empirical analysis tells us much about the international effects of variations in IPRs. I am reasonably confident in the conclusions reached here, while cognizant that much more work could be done to refine the information, given the numerous shortcomings of the available measures of IPRs. Counting the number of legal provisions in a country's regime is informative but cannot readily capture the prevailing business climate within which IPRs operate. Moreover, by their nature, IPRs are territorial and aggregated. Laws covering patents, trademarks, confidential information, and copyrights apply equally to all sectors and all competitors. Thus, a national aggregate index of the strength of patents, for example, cannot convey the differential impacts they might have across industries and between foreign and domestic enterprises. For such reasons, I advise caution in considering the following.

Are IPRs Trade-Related?

Intellectual property rights originally entered the Uruguay Round negotiations on the grounds that weak and variable standards distort international trade flows and interfere with global economic efficiency. If that were true, IPRs could be labeled "trade-related" and included in the WTO. However, because it is impossible simply to discipline the associated trade distortion, an agreement to modify IPRs regimes themselves was required. These notions gave the ultimate TRIPs agreement both its name and its extensive structure.

That limited protection could distort trade is clear. For example, weakly enforced copyrights generate incentives for domestic firms to copy foreign software and entertainment products, thereby displacing imports with home production. Weak border enforcement could expand trade by indirectly subsidizing exports of imitative products from an infringing country. Weak standards could be associated either with lower or higher trade, depending on demand and on the abilities of other countries to prevent infringing trade.

Suppose a firm in a developing country is awarded a trademark that is registered abroad by another enterprise and widely recognized. The first firm could use its trademark to (1) preclude imports of products from the foreign trademark owner or (2) raise the owner's trade costs, thereby limiting trade opportunities. Similarly, working requirements that mandate local production can reduce trade; on the other hand, requirements recognizing imports as working could induce more imports than the patent owner would choose in their absence.

Highly protective IPRs could also deter legitimate trade or, alternatively, facilitate collusive behavior that would limit competition through trade. Such measures may also be applied in a discriminatory and strategic fashion, as was the case with Section 337 in US trade law (Mutti and Yeung 1997).

Note also the possibility that foreign exporters could alter their behavior in reaction to IPRs policies in importing countries: a firm might decide to exploit a market through exports where it would normally choose to license its technology for local production. The decision could be based on limited trade secrets protection in the import market, where licensing could risk unauthorized loss of proprietary information.

The linkages between trade and IPRs may have important dynamic aspects. In principle, patents directly affect growth through incentives to innovate and to transfer technology. One primary channel through which firms earn returns to invention is international trade with different markets. Variable patent systems would present an array of policy parameters that exporters must take into account in setting trade decisions. Therefore, patent regimes could be an important factor in the relationship between trade and growth (Segerstrom, Anant, and Dinopolous 1990; Taylor 1994; Frankel and Romer 1999).

This wide menu of possibilities demonstrates that trade could be affected by IPRs. It also raises the problem that the meaning of "trade distortion" is inherently ambiguous in the intellectual property context. It is as true in the international arena as domestically that IPRs are second-best solutions to dual static and dynamic market failures. The optimal pattern of production and trade is generally unknown, which makes the normative problem quite different from an analysis of tariffs and quotas. In particular, which standards introduce distortions and which standards correct them varies by circumstance. Empirical analysis to date has therefore posed only the narrower positive question of whether the global distribution of trade depends on an importing nation's system of IPRs.

Identifying how IPRs affect international trade is empirically difficult for many reasons:

- The strength of patents and trademarks will be embedded in the prices at which goods are traded; these price effects cannot be separated from other components of pricing behavior.

- Firms owning a new product or process decide to export to a particular market as they are deciding whether to service markets through FDI or licensing.

- The essence of IPRs is to create market power in the distribution of new goods and technologies, implying that the choice of market structure matters for the analysis.

To illustrate these problems and to facilitate a review of this evidence, I create a simple verbal model of a price-discriminating firm considering the distribution of a patentable or trademarked good to various countries.[12] Consider how patent laws affect trade: weak patent systems do not necessarily deprive innovative firms of all market power because local imitation is costly and takes time, though such costs vary considerably by sector. Further, strong patents do not generally create a full monopoly on

---

12. This discussion draws on Maskus and Penubarti (1997), who provide further analysis.

a new product, because legitimate substitute products are likely to be on the market. In theoretical terms, therefore, a static model with a dominant foreign firm facing a local competitive fringe makes sense. Assume also that markets are segmented by trade costs or restrictions on parallel trade, allowing the firm to discriminate in price decisions.

In this context, it is easily shown that strengthening the patent regime has an ambiguous impact on the dominant firm's decision to export to a country. The most straightforward reason for the ambiguity is that there is a trade-off between the enhanced market power generated by stronger patents and the larger effective market size created by reduced abilities of local firms to imitate the product. The *market-power effect* reduces the elasticity of demand facing the foreign firm, permitting the firm to cut its exports to the market with stronger patents. However, the *market-expansion effect* would shift the demand curve outward and induce larger sales through export. Moreover, in larger importing markets with significant imitation capabilities, the firm would experience a *cost-reduction effect*, as the stronger patent law reduces the need to engage in costly deterrent activities (Taylor 1993).[13]

This ambiguity exists in all markets. However, as Maskus and Penubarti (1995) hypothesize, the market-expansion effect is likely to dominate in larger countries with highly competitive local imitative firms, while the market-power effect would be stronger in smaller economies with limited ability to imitate. The effects would be expected to vary by sector as well. It is worth noting that this fundamental ambiguity arises in imperfectly competitive market structures, whether they are static or dynamic.

Other factors are important in determining market responses:

First, the reactions of foreign firms to changes in IPRs cannot be considered in isolation from trade policy. It is possible, for example, that the profit-maximizing reaction of an exporter could be either to increase or decrease its volume of trade with a country that strengthens its patent law, depending on the height of the tariff. Similarly, if there is a binding quota on the product, change in the patent law cannot attract more trade. If parallel imports are allowed, the dominant firm faces a different set of competitive trade-offs in setting market prices. Finally, there are complicated interactions between patents on final goods and trade barriers on intermediate inputs.

Second, as noted earlier, the firm may face a choice of entry modes, including exports, FDI, and licensing, that would be influenced by variations in patent laws. As discussed further in the next subsection, patent reform could result in substitution effects among entry modes, in addition to the fundamental ambiguity in the market-power and market-expansion effects.

---

13. Private enforcement is common in both developed and the major developing economies (Maskus, Dougherty, and Mertha 1998).

To summarize, theoretical models do not clearly predict the impacts of variable patent rights on trade volumes. Much depends on local market demand, the efficiency of imitative production, and the structure of trade barriers. Also important are the reactions of imperfectly competitive firms. Thus, a clear picture can emerge only from empirical studies.

In a pair of studies, Maskus and Penubarti (1995, 1997) estimated reduced-form equations for 1984 bilateral trade in manufacturing sectors based on the Helpman-Krugman (1985) trade model. The data set incorporated 22 exporting countries, mainly OECD members and therefore home to most of the world's MNEs, and 71 importing nations at all levels of economic development. Explanatory variables included a scaling factor, importer per capita GNP, trade restrictions in the importer, and the adjusted-corrected RR index of patent rights in the importing nations. The patent index was interacted with dummy variables for small and large developing countries in order to capture the effects of market size and technological capacity.

The results are striking. Within the group of large developing economies, which includes nearly all countries in which there have been significant complaints about weak IPRs, the strength of national patent laws exerted a significantly positive effect on bilateral manufacturing imports in many product categories. Thus, in these countries the market-expansion effect of stronger patents tends to be dominant; weak patents in large developing economies are indeed barriers to manufacturing exports from the OECD countries. The impacts were similar, though statistically weaker, in the group of small developing countries, suggesting that net market-expansion effects largely operate in these nations as well. Perhaps as anticipated, the pharmaceuticals sector demonstrated positive impacts of patents on trade flows. This industry is particularly sensitive to patent rights for protecting innovation rents.

It is evident that the strength of patent rights is highly correlated with the effectiveness of IPRs generally. Stronger patents (as a proxy for trademarks) in the study were particularly effective in increasing imports of relatively low-technology goods, such as clothing and other consumer items. This finding suggests that the ease of knocking off such products under weak trademarks limits the incentives of foreign firms to sell them locally.

Effectively, stronger trademarks lower the costs of exporting because a firm has less need to discipline local imitators through lower prices and private enforcement. This is true also of pharmaceutical formulations, though they are more likely to be produced under local license than imported. The study found further that trade in goods that are difficult to imitate, such as certain kinds of machinery, or for which trademarks are not as significant, such as basic metal manufactures, was less sensitive to international variations in IPRs. This result presumably reflects the limited threat of losing market share to local infringing firms.[14]

These findings may be statistically significant, but the more important question is their economic significance. Thus, the implied increases in international trade flows from simulated changes in patent rights are provided in table 4.8. To make these calculations, an elasticity of imports with respect to the patent index (using mean sample values and assuming fixed expenditure levels in each country) was computed for each sector and for each country group, including small developing countries, large developing countries, and high-income countries.

These elasticities were then applied to informed guesses about the new patent effectiveness that would come about from implementation of TRIPs.[15] In particular, I assume that TRIPs will result in a rise in the average corrected RR index in small developing countries from 2.68 to 3.25, or 22 percent. I entertain two possibilities for large developing countries. First, I incorporate a rise in the average index from 2.86 to 3.25, or 14 percent, to suggest harmonization across all developing countries. Second, I consider an increase in the index from 2.86 to 3.50, or 22 percent, to reflect the possibility that large countries will implement absolutely higher levels in the strength of their patent laws. Finally, I suppose that TRIPs will result in a modest increase in the average patent index in high-income nations from 4.48 to 4.60, or 0.3 percent.

Note that while these scenarios involve significant hikes in the patent indices of developing countries, they do not envision full harmonization of those indices with laws in the developed countries. As discussed elsewhere in this book, though TRIPs requires minimum standards, it comes well short of effective harmonization. Finally, the computed trade impacts should be considered to be long-run, taking place only after TRIPs standards are phased in and markets adjust to the new policy regimes.

Consider first some implications for sectoral trade. Some of the implied elasticities are negative, as for tobacco products and petroleum and coal products in all country groups. These goods likely are not responsive to patents; in fact, the underlying elasticities are not significantly different from zero. However, among the high-income countries there is a negative impact of tighter patents in professional goods, suggesting that a slight increase in patent rights would generate lower trade volumes (the market-power impact would dominate). This holds as well for pharmaceutical products. While the positive impacts on pharmaceuticals

---

14. Such inferences raise many questions that could be considered in further work. For example, it would be interesting to employ a different specification to look at how IPRs affect net trade by sector, distinguishing between effects on goods imported for final consumption and effects on goods traded through production sharing. Further, it would be interesting to see if weak IPRs could have export-enhancing impacts.

15. Details of these calculations are available on request.

Table 4.8 Simulated increases in total imports by sector into developing countries resulting from strengthened patent laws (millions of 1984 dollars)

Sector	Small DCs	Large DCS (1)	Large DCS (2)	HICs
Food products	111	1,070	1,762	386
Beverages	82	416	686	398
Tobacco products	−4	−42	−69	−102
Textiles	111	731	1,204	205
Apparel	106	711	1,171	435
Leather and products	19	145	239	53
Footwear	26	162	266	75
Wood products	12	201	331	7
Furniture and fixtures	41	240	395	147
Paper and products	106	560	922	247
Printing and publishing	35	206	340	156
Industrial chemicals	132	−18	−30	−364
Other chemical products	33	345	568	164
Pharmaceuticals	3	9	14	−51
Petroleum refining	162	862	1,420	720
Petroleum and coal products	−0.7	−25	−42	−58
Rubber products	36	194	319	120
Plastic products	31	183	301	113
Pottery and china products	13	59	97	33
Glass and products	27	165	271	108
Nonmetal products, nec	36	188	310	112
Iron and steel	180	1,005	1,656	1,027
Nonferrous metals	132	890	1,466	818
Metal products	92	485	798	193
Industrial machinery	356	1,623	2,673	730
Electrical machinery	175	869	1,432	0
Transport equipment	556	2,837	4,673	2,036
Professional goods	24	206	340	−111
Other manufactures	70	460	758	263
Total (dollar value)	2,699	14,727	24,257	7,913
Total (percentage of imports)	6.2	5.4	8.9	0.6
Total (percentage of GNP)	1.4	1.1	1.7	0.1

DC = Developing country.
HIC = High-income country.
nec = not elsewhere classified.
Notes: This table assumes that national expenditure levels remain unchanged after patent law changes. Assumptions on patent law changes include

■ A 22 percent increase in average effective strength for small countries (from 2.68 to 3.25 on a five-point scale)
■ Either a 14 percent or a 22 percent increase in strength for large countries (from 2.86 to 3.25 and 3.50, respectively in cases (1) and (2))
■ An 0.3 percent increase in strength for industrial countries (from 4.48 to 4.60).

Sources: Calculated from Maskus and Penubarti (1995) and International Monetary Fund, *International Financial Statistics Yearbook 1987.*

trade with the developing countries are statistically significant, the implied volume increases are small: only $3 million for small countries and between $9 million and $14 million for large countries. There is also a negative impact in industrial chemicals in the large developing countries and the high-income countries.

Taking all manufacturing goods together, across the small developing economies perhaps $2.7 billion in additional annual imports would be created in the long run. While this amount seems modest, it comes to 6.2 percent of total 1984 merchandise imports of this group of countries and 1.4 percent of their combined GNP. Similarly, manufacturing imports into the large developing countries could expand by between $14.7 billion (5.4 percent of 1984 imports) and $24.2 billion (8.9 percent) per year—again indicating that stronger patent rights would engender important increases in import demand. In sectoral terms, these impacts would be concentrated on transport equipment, machinery, and food products. Finally, the small policy change simulated in the high-income countries would procure an additional $7.9 billion (perhaps 0.6 percent) in merchandise imports.

Because these results are based on 1984 activity, they may be outdated. The data review in chapter 3 showed that trade in IPR-sensitive goods has risen rapidly since 1984. Thus, it is interesting to see if this additional trade bears a more economically significant relationship to international patent rights. An important study posing this question is by Smith (1999), who updated the Maskus-Penubarti studies by analyzing sectoral 1992 manufacturing exports of US states to 96 countries. These data were compiled from the two-digit Standard International Trade Classification (SITC). She used a gravity-equation framework, accounting for per capita incomes, populations, geographic distance, trade restrictions, and the RR index of patent rights. Note that one advantage of using US state-level exports as the dependent variable is that their distribution across exporters does not depend on the trade policy of the United States, which treats each state equally.

Smith's particular focus was the identification of market-power and market-expansion effects in groups of countries identified by their ability to imitate products. Consider a classification of four country groups:

■ The industrial countries tend to have strong technological capabilities and might therefore represent a competitive threat through imitation. However, they also have strong patent rights that considerably dampen this effect. Thus, Smith hypothesizes that within this group there would be an ambiguous balance between market-power and market-expansion effects.

■ A similar conclusion applies to poor economies that have both weak patent rights and weak imitative capacities.

- In contrast, industrializing economies with weak patents but effective imitation threats, such as China, Turkey, and Venezuela, should find a dominant market-expansion effect. That is, other things being equal, within this group those countries with stronger patents should absorb higher import volumes.

- Finally, nations with strong patent rights but weak imitative abilities should absorb a net market-power effect, or lower trade volumes, as the strength of IPRs expands.

Smith's econometric results were remarkably supportive of these hypotheses. Taking each country group in turn, she discovered first that US exports to countries with high R&D ratios and strong patent laws depended positively and significantly on variations in IPRs. That is, the market-expansion effect dominates among the industrial countries, attesting to the effectiveness of their IPRs in deterring imitation. This was especially true of patent-sensitive industries, such as chemicals and instruments. In contrast, US export volumes depended negatively and significantly on patent strength in the group of countries with weak property rights and limited imitation threat. In that group, the market-power effect dominated.

As expected, the market-expansion impact was particularly pronounced in trade with middle-income economies that had weak patent rights and strong imitation. This result confirms that of Maskus and Penubarti (1997), who found that industrializing economies could attract more trade by limiting local imitation through stronger IPRs.

Finally, also as expected, the market-power effect dominated among the group of nations with weak imitation and strong patent regimes.

Smith calculated the implied elasticities of US exports to patent rights in each group for the aggregated patent-sensitive industries. These elasticities were large, reflecting in part the small average trade volumes of states to each foreign trading partner. She applied these estimates to the counterfactual experiment of assuming that TRIPs would succeed in harmonizing global standards at the level represented by 4.0 on the RR index. The results suggested that US exports to countries with weak imitation and relatively strong patents would fall slightly, by 1.4 percent ($1.7 billion in 1992 values). However, exports to those countries with weak patents and weak imitation would fall by 16.5 percent ($103 billion), as a result of additional market power. In contrast, exports to the middle-income economies with weak patent rights and strong imitation would rise by 12.5 percent ($43 billion). Trade with the industrial countries would not be affected under this scenario because their patent rights would not be changed.[16] Overall, Smith's static estimates suggest that US export

16. These calculations demonstrate an obvious weakness of partial-equilibrium simulations. Clearly, any changes of this magnitude in the distribution of global trade volumes

volumes would be quite responsive to strengthening of patent rights but would fall on net as a result of TRIPs. This finding is in contrast to the calculations reported above that global trade volumes would rise in most sectors and to each country group.

Smith's findings must be approached with caution. One particular problem is that her designation of imitative abilities came from considering solely each country's ratio of R&D expenditures to GDP. In the developing economies R&D data are highly suspect and not comparable to those in developed countries. This choice led to a number of anomalous designations: Brazil and Argentina, for example, are presumed to pose lesser imitation threats than Bolivia and Tonga. A more refined designation might push larger countries into the threat group, suggesting a larger positive trade response. Note also that Smith computed only the trade response for the United States; analysis for other manufacturing exporters might find net positive impacts. And, of course, many other static and dynamic factors could influence the responses of trade volumes to the TRIPs accord.

In summary, there seems to be convincing evidence from these studies of two claims:

1. Weak patent rights are significant barriers to manufacturing trade, particularly in IPR-sensitive goods. However, this phenomenon occurs mainly within industrializing economies that pose credible imitation threats. It is no surprise that these countries have been the main focus of complaints about weak IPRs. As these countries strengthen their IPR regimes they should attract rising import volumes of high-technology goods, which may have a beneficial growth effect, as discussed in the next chapter.

2. Because poor countries without much current ability to imitate new products do not pose a competitive threat, their weak patent rights are of limited concern to technology developers.[17] Indeed, their adoption of stronger IPRs could expose them to negative market-power effects on their terms of trade, although these studies cannot support computation of how much prices would change. Indeed, the same inference could be applied to high-income economies with a comparative disadvantage in developing new products and technologies. Taken alone, this factor would imply that TRIPs could be harmful to both

would have important interindustry and international trade effects that would spill over across borders and affect the trade volumes of all countries. To date, however, no one has assembled a computable general-equilibrium model for assessing global trade impacts.

17. Clearly, this conclusion should not be applied to copyrighted goods, which are easily copied in all countries, including those without much human capital.

country groups. Of course, in an overall assessment of harmonization, many other factors must be balanced against this scenario.

IPRs and Foreign Direct Investment

Multinational enterprises (MNEs) make multifaceted decisions about how they can serve foreign markets. They may decide to undertake FDI, which requires selecting where to invest, in what kind of facilities, whether to buy existing operations or construct new plants, which production techniques to use, and how large an equity position to take with potential local partners. They may prefer a joint venture with a defined share of input costs, technology provision, and profits or losses. Finally, they may opt to license a technology, product, or service, leading to complicated bargaining over license fees and royalty payments.

These decisions are jointly determined. For any firm, the outcome depends on a host of complex factors regarding local markets and regulations. In this section I discuss the most significant of these factors for attracting FDI and review the econometric evidence.[18] IPRs clearly play an important role in these processes, though their importance varies by industry and market structure.

MNES may undertake horizontal FDI, in which the subsidiary produces products and services similar to those produced at home, or vertical FDI, in which the subsidiary produces inputs or undertakes assembly from components. In the latter case, international production is fragmented across borders, taking advantage of location considerations and input costs (especially wage differences) at various stages of production. Incentives for horizontal and for vertical FDI are different. Horizontal FDI tends to characterize the investment decisions of MNEs operating across borders within the industrialized nations, while vertical FDI is more prevalent among MNEs that invest in developing (low-wage) economies. Horizontal subsidiaries tend to produce for local or regional markets only, without exporting much to the host country. In contrast, the output of vertical subsidiaries is more likely to be exported within the MNE, both to the host country and to countries with similar demand characteristics.

Foreign direct investment embodies two distinctive assets: (1) capital and (2) technology or some intangible advantage. While the capital for financing FDI may come from the host country or from global financial markets, it may also be raised on the local capital markets of the recipient nation. Indeed, this is by far the most common approach for financing horizontal investments among industrialized nations. Thus, FDI may or may not be associated with a net external addition to the local capital

---

18. This section draws on Maskus (1998b).

stock. External financing more commonly characterizes FDI in emerging countries.

In this light, FDI should be viewed less as a source of finance (global FDI flows are in any case small in relation to flows of portfolio capital) and more as a source of investment in capital and technology or related assets. These variables are capable of improving productivity and wages in a recipient economy.

With these comments in mind, consider how a firm decides to engage in FDI. For a firm to become an MNE, it must have a sufficient cost advantage or technical product superiority over firms in the host country to overcome the disadvantages it faces in international management, including language and cultural barriers, jurisdiction-specific tax treatments, distance from headquarters, and monitoring local operations. Thus, MNEs must enjoy some efficiency advantages; economic theories of FDI begin with a description of such advantages.

A convenient framework for thinking about this question is the ownership-location-internalization (OLI) paradigm developed by Dunning (1981). In this approach, MNEs are characterized by an *ownership advantage*, which could be a tangible asset, such as a proprietary claim in facilities producing key natural resources. Far more commonly, however, the advantage is an intangible asset, such as a trademark, a reputation for quality, or a product or production process to which other firms do not have access and which is protected by a patent or maintained as a trade secret. Such advantages provide market power and cost efficiencies that are sufficient incentives to undertake multinational organization and operation.

That ownership advantages are strongly associated with technology development, information management, and marketing strategies is borne out by key characteristics of MNEs. Such firms tend to be important in industries with high R&D intensities, large employment of professional and technical workers, significant reliance on new and technically sophisticated products, and considerable amounts of product differentiation and advertising.[19]

Thus, FDI is more likely to be important in industries in which intangible, knowledge-based assets (KBAs) specific to each firm are significant for two key reasons. First, informational advantages can be transferred easily across borders at low cost. Second, knowledge is similar to a public good in that a particular technology or trade secret can be used in several production facilities without reducing its availability for others (as is the case with labor and capital). Such knowledge is embodied in blueprints, software, chemical formulas, and managerial or engineering manuals, which may be used numerous times at low marginal cost.

---

19. Considerable evidence supporting these points may be found in Brainard (1993), Caves (1996), Grubaugh (1987), Markusen (1995), and Morck and Yeung (1992).

The important implication of this characteristic of knowledge is that MNEs enjoy scale economies from multiplant production, sometimes called economies of scope. A multinational firm can produce its technical knowledge in one location and use it in several plants in different countries, spreading the investment cost of technology development and marketing across numerous facilities (Markusen 1984). In contrast, two independent firms, each of which must make this investment, operate at a cost disadvantage. Thus, we should observe significant multinational activity in industries in which transferable knowledge and product quality are a key focus of strategy. Indeed, this is consistent with the available evidence. Possibilities for exploiting multiplant economies are now considered perhaps the most important determinant of a firm's decision to undertake FDI.

This argument is particularly relevant for horizontal FDI, in which firms base strategies for penetrating markets on the economic value of their KBAs, such as superior production processes, reputations for quality, performance, and service, and even lifestyle images. MNEs find it crucial to be able to support their investments with complementary operations, including service contracts. Economic value is increasingly related to performance of systems, including products, services, information, maintenance, technical upgrades, and close relations between producers and clients. As amplified below, this means that, in today's world, FDI is less attracted by protectionist tariff walls and more attracted by economies with open access to global markets. It also suggests that strong IPRs are taking on increasing importance as a determinant of inward FDI.

To summarize, MNEs are essentially exporters of KBAs, including technology, engineering, management, marketing, and financial services. The importance of human capital skills in generating these KBAs is evident. MNEs also license the rights to use devices that protect the value of their KBAs, including patents, trademarks, trade secrets, and copyrights. Indeed, it is common to refer to IPRs themselves as the relevant KBAs. Local subsidiaries pay for these services with royalties, license fees, shared outputs, and profit repatriations.

Even given some ownership advantage, MNEs still must decide on investment destinations. These decisions depend on the *location advantages* of particular countries. Such advantages make it profitable for the firm to produce abroad rather than stay at home and export the good. Obvious examples of location advantages are market size and growth, local demand patterns, transport costs and distance from markets, low wage costs in relation to labor productivity, abundant natural resources, and trade protection that could encourage "tariff-jumping" investment. Also important are an adequate and modern infrastructure and transparent government regulatory procedures.

Recently, location characteristics that enhance the value of KBAs have taken on greater importance. Among these are an adequate supply of highly skilled labor in order to facilitate use of technology and management techniques, close proximity to customers and unimpeded ability to build supplier-customer networks, and a vibrant business-services sector that can handle localized needs for marketing and finance. Further, the strength of each country's IPRs is a location factor of growing importance, as discussed further below.

Location advantages matter for both vertical and horizontal FDI, but they are especially important for vertical FDI, in which firms build production networks, with engineering, design, and marketing operations in the headquarters country, and resource extraction, assembly, and data processing in host countries. Indeed, the most significant recent trend in vertical FDI has been such vertically integrated networks, a process also referred to as "production fragmentation," "delocalization," or "outsourcing" (Hanson 1996). This process underlies the rapid expansion of intrafirm trade in goods and services between developed and developing economies. Investment of this kind is most attractive in low-wage, high-growth economies with markets large enough to support scale economies in assembly. While outsourcing is of concern to low-skilled workers in high-wage economies, in generating overall efficiency gains in both the source and host countries it is a critical component of modern competitive strategies.

In this context, it is interesting to observe that the volume and character of inward FDI change dramatically as countries develop (Zhang 1996). The least-developed countries attract virtually no FDI (except in extractive sectors) due to extremely low productivity, education, and skills. Further, such countries tend to have underdeveloped infrastructures, are relatively closed to trade, and maintain poorly designed, intrusive, and nontransparent government regulations that encourage corruption.

When such countries can marshal effective investments in infrastructure, capital, and education and skill, their per capita income levels rise over time. As this happens, MNEs find these economies attractive locations for vertical FDI in labor-intensive assembly operations. Intrafirm trade grows. This process expands until real wages rise sufficiently that the economies lose their competitive advantages in assembly production (the FDI itself plays a positive role in raising wages). As vertical FDI falls off, however, horizontal FDI tends to move in, because such countries achieve income levels that make them attractive markets for high-quality differentiated consumer and capital goods and even for local R&D programs. Indeed, these countries may well become sources of FDI.

Interestingly, as horizontal FDI grows it tends to displace both interfirm and intrafirm trade (Markusen 1995). Thus, so-called "North-South" investment tends to be vertical, while "North-North" investment is horizontal.[20] Rapidly developing economies like South Korea, Singapore, and

---

20. The horizontal-vertical distinction is blurred in a number of sectors, such as pharmaceuticals and chemicals. In those industries, chemicals may be produced in headquarters

Mexico may move through this investment cycle in a single generation. Thus, there is an important dynamic element to growth and investment.

Key location characteristics for horizontal MNEs include market size, income levels and growth, transport costs, and the availability of complementary business services and regulation. As noted earlier, the more horizontal the investment, the more important IPRs are. In this sense, it is not surprising that countries moving up the FDI cycle find a growing economic interest in adopting stronger IPRs, an interest congruent with their own expanding abilities to produce new products and technologies.

Finally, ownership and location advantages together may not fully explain FDI because they do not account for the advantages of internal organization over selling goods and licensing technologies on the open market. MNEs also have *internalization advantages,* which relate to gains from exploiting their KBAs within their own international operations (Rugman 1986). It is this aspect of the process that explains the decision to acquire a subsidiary rather than to license an asset to an independent foreign firm.

There are numerous reasons why the costs of international transactions may be lower if performed within a single firm rather than at arm's length. Most of these relate to the difficulties of writing and enforcing contracts between independent firms when licensing is costly and information is imperfect. For example, because the KBA that is the potential subject of a licensing contract is valuable but perhaps easily copied, the original firm may not wish to reveal its technology to an unrelated licensee during contract negotiations for fear that the latter could simply decline the contract and copy the technology. The licensee, on the other hand, would be unwilling to sign a contract and agree to royalty terms unless it knows the particulars and value of the technology. In such cases, it may be impossible to draft a satisfactory contract, forcing the original firm to acquire a subsidiary to which it transfers the KBA (Teece 1986).

This informational imperfection in the market for technology implies, other things being equal, that firms would be more likely to engage in FDI in countries with weaker IPRs and contract enforcement. An implication is that as IPRs in a particular nation become stronger, firms will tend to choose more technology licensing and joint ventures and less FDI. This is the one identifiable theoretical case in which the strength of IPRs would be negatively associated with FDI flows. It applies most readily to firms that have proprietary technologies that have been expensive to develop but are easily copied, such as pharmaceuticals, agricultural chemicals, and computerized processes. A similar phenomenon is that MNEs may find it easier to retain technical and managerial employees who might otherwise defect from a licensee after learning the technology and form their own competing firms.

---

locations, then shipped in bulk to processing plants for final formulations. These formulations are sold largely on domestic markets rather than shipped back to the parent country.

An additional contracting problem is that a potential independent licensee may attempt to convince the MNE that the market is smaller than it really is or will grow to be, thereby limiting its royalties and fees. If there is wide uncertainty on this point, the MNE may prefer to avoid having to share any potential profits by engaging in FDI and controlling local management and sales. This situation also helps explain why some firms set up complementary foreign distribution and servicing facilities (Zeile 1993).

MNEs usually experience higher costs of transferring technology through arm's-length transactions because aspects of the technology that are tied up in the firm's human capital, management, know-how, and corporate culture are not easily transmitted (Teece 1977, 1986). This factor becomes more important the more complicated the technology or management process is, helping to explain the prevalence of MNEs in high-technology industries. Transfer costs also depend on the recipient country's ability to absorb the technology efficiently, suggesting that more technology for complicated products and processes would be licensed as the human capital base of the economy rises. Also important are the transparency and certainty of the legal and regulatory systems.

Where the firm's KBA is a reputation for high quality, an additional incentive for FDI arises. Once a contract is signed, local licensees may not have sufficient incentive to maintain the quality of the product or service, tarnishing the licensing firm's reputation and profitability. Similarly, licensees may shirk their marketing or distribution efforts, degrade product quality, or contract with competing firms to whose products they devote more attention. These problems are most significant in economies where monitoring is costly and difficult, the supply of technologies and products to licensees is highly competitive, and contracts are not well enforced. While many contracts are designed to deter such behavior, firms may find it easier to exercise control through FDI.

This analysis suggests strongly that internalization issues favor the development of MNEs in industries where KBAs are important. Thus, MNEs tend to be associated with intensive R&D programs, advertising efforts, and frequent introduction of complex products. In such sectors, technology transfers are likely to be internal, especially when there are contracting, monitoring, and enforcement difficulties. Thus, internalization issues characterize horizontal MNEs.

There are also internalization advantages for vertically integrated MNEs. Largely, these relate to difficulties in setting contract prices when a single buyer (the MNE) proposes to purchase inputs or services, such as a natural resource or assembly operation, from a single seller. Where markets may be oligopolistic on both sides of the transaction, firms are likely to find it advantageous to integrate the activities and establish profit-maximizing internal pricing.

This review of the determinants of FDI leaves much room for IPRs to affect investment flows and the operations of MNEs. The means by which IPRs influence FDI are subtle and complex. Seen in the proper policy context, IPRs are an important component of the general regulatory system, including taxes, investment regulations, production incentives, trade policies, and competition rules. As such, what matters overall for FDI is joint implementation of a procompetitive business environment, as I discuss further in a later chapter. In this section, I focus strictly on mechanisms by which the strength of IPRs could affect FDI decisions, as seen by economists, in light of theories of why investment takes place.

Exports are likely to be the primary mode of supply when transport costs and tariffs are low in comparison to the costs of FDI and licensing. FDI is likely to supplant direct exports of a good where trade and transport costs are high,[21] the fixed costs of building foreign plants are low, local productivity is high relative to wage costs, the size of the host market is large, and the R&D or marketing intensity of the product is substantial. The last factor is critical for horizontal FDI in differentiated goods and advanced technologies in that it is the knowledge basis, or intellectual component, of the firm's advantage that induces it to become an MNE.

FDI exists because firms with an ownership advantage prefer to exploit it through internal organization of multinational activity, with the location of activity depending on local market characteristics. IPRs are thus likely to take on different levels of importance in different sectors with respect to encouraging FDI. Investment in lower-technology goods and services, such as textiles and apparel, electronic assembly, distribution, and hotels, depends relatively little on the strength of IPRs and relatively much on input costs and market opportunities. Investors with a product or technology that is costly to imitate may also pay little attention to local IPRs, though the fact that imitation has become markedly easier over time in many sectors points to the rising importance of IPRs. Firms with easily copyable products and technologies, such as pharmaceuticals, chemicals, food additives, and software, are more concerned with the ability of the local IPRs system to deter imitation. Firms considering investing in a local R&D facility would pay particular attention to local patent and trade secrets protection.

This perspective is consistent with results reported by Mansfield (1994), who surveyed 100 major US firms with international operations in 1991. Intellectual property executives in firms representing six industries were asked (1) their opinions of the importance of IPRs in their FDI and licensing decisions and (2) their assessments of the adequacy of IPRs in

21. This is a relative comparison only. I do not mean that raising trade barriers would attract FDI, but rather that high tariffs in relation to fixed costs are associated with FDI. In general, however, significant trade liberalization tends to attract FDI for reasons discussed elsewhere.

Table 4.9 Percentage of firms claiming that strength or weakness of IPRs has a strong effect on whether direct investments will be made, by type of facility, 1991

	Sales and distribution	Basic production and assembly	Components manufacture	Complete products manufacture	R&D facilities	Average
Chemicals	19	46	71	87	100	65
Transport equipment	17	17	33	33	80	36
Electrical equipment	15	40	57	74	80	53
Food products	29	29	25	43	60	37
Metals	20	40	50	50	80	48
Machinery	23	23	50	65	77	48
Average	20	32	48	59	80	48

Source: Mansfield (1994).

16 countries. Table 4.9 reproduces his results by type of investment facility.[22]

In no industry was there much concern about IPRs protecting the operation of sales and distribution outlets. In the chemical industry, which includes pharmaceuticals, 46 percent of firms were concerned about protection for basic production and assembly facilities, 71 percent for components manufacture, 87 percent for complete products manufacture, and 100 percent for R&D facilities. This tendency to be more concerned with IPRs the higher the stage of production carried over to all sectors. Overall, the chemical industry was the most affected in its decisions to invest, though in all sectors there was a strong concern about local IPRs in siting R&D operations. In a companion paper, Mansfield (1995) demonstrated that these findings held also for Japanese and German firms considering foreign investments.[23]

Table 4.10 presents additional results for selected countries with weak IPRs in 1991. India elicited the greatest concern about patents; fully 80 percent of the chemical firm respondents indicated they could not engage in joint ventures or transfer new technologies to subsidiaries or unrelated firms due to weak protection. Interestingly, in chemicals there was little difference between joint ventures and subsidiaries in this regard. Both evidently provided foreign firms with approximately the same level of security about their technologies (though there was more concern about joint ventures in Mexico and Indonesia). However, across all countries licensing to unrelated firms was seen as riskier because of weak IPRs. This situation was also true of machinery firms. In the other sectors, however, weakness in IPRs made little difference in the willingness to transfer technology through various modes.

That licensing is seen as insecure relative to investment in the high-technology sectors in countries with weak IPRs confirms a subtle aspect of intellectual property protection. Recall that firms are more likely to undertake FDI than licensing when they have a complex technology and highly differentiated products and when costs of transferring technology through licensing are high (Teece 1986; Davidson and McFetridge 1984; Horstmann and Markusen 1987). Under these circumstances, it is efficient to internalize the costs of technology transfer through FDI in a wholly owned or majority-owned subsidiary. As IPRs improve, other things being equal, licensing costs should fall because it becomes easier to discipline licensees against revelation or appropriation of proprietary technology and against

---

22. These results should be viewed cautiously; surveys do not control for numerous other potential influences on investment and licensing decisions.

23. This suggests that the measures of the weakness of intellectual property protection marshaled from USTR reports and discussed above may not be unduly biased by their US perspective. I am grateful to Jack Mutti for pointing this out.

Table 4.10   Percentage of firms claiming that intellectual property protection is too weak to permit types of investment, 1991

Country	Chemicals	Transport equipment	Electrical equipment	Food products	Metals	Machinery	Average
Panel A: Joint ventures with local partners							
Argentina	40	0	29	12	0	27	18
Brazil	47	40	31	12	0	65	32
India	80	40	39	38	20	48	44
Indonesia	50	40	29	25	0	25	28
Mexico	47	20	30	25	0	17	22
South Korea	33	20	21	12	25	26	23
Thailand	43	80	32	12	0	20	31
Average[a]	49	34	30	19	6	33	
Panel B: Transfer of newest or most effective technology to wholly owned subsidiaries							
Argentina	44	20	21	12	0	14	18
Brazil	50	40	24	12	0	39	28
India	81	40	38	38	20	41	43
Indonesia	40	20	31	25	0	23	23
Mexico	31	20	21	25	0	22	20
South Korea	31	20	28	12	40	22	26
Thailand	60	80	31	12	0	18	20
Average[a]	48	34	28	19	9	26	
Panel C: Licensing of newest or most effective technology to unrelated firms							
Argentina	62	0	26	12	0	29	22
Brazil	69	40	29	25	0	73	39
India	81	40	38	38	20	50	44
Indonesia	73	20	33	25	0	37	31
Mexico	56	20	28	25	0	36	28
South Korea	38	20	34	12	40	29	29
Thailand	73	80	36	12	0	25	38
Average[a]	65	31	32	21	9	40	

a. Average over the seven countries listed.

Source: Mansfield (1994).

misuse of a trademark. Thus, at a given level of complexity of innovations, we would expect to see licensing displace FDI as IPRs are strengthened.

It is useful to summarize the predictions about IPRs, FDI, and technology transfer:

■ Investment and technology transfer are relatively insensitive to international differences in IPRs in sectors with old products and standardized, labor-intensive technologies. Here, FDI is influenced by factor costs, market sizes, trade costs, and other location advantages.

■ Other things being equal, FDI representing complex but easily copied technologies is likely to increase as IPRs are strengthened, because patents, copyrights, and trademarks increase the value of KBAs, which may be efficiently exploited through internalized organization.

■ To the extent that stronger IPRs reduce licensing costs, FDI could be displaced over time by efficient licensing.

■ Whatever the mode, the likelihood that the most advanced technologies will be transferred rises as IPRs are strengthened.

One implication of this analysis is that rapidly developing countries, as they move up the "technology ladder" to an ability to absorb and even create more sophisticated innovations, should find a natural interest in improving their IPRs. This is perhaps the strongest argument to make in favor of stronger protection in nations such as Korea, Brazil, Mexico, Malaysia, China, and India. In the early stages of their industrial growth, such countries have an interest in being able freely to imitate imported technologies, which calls for limited protection. As they evolve, however, they should become increasingly interested in tightening IPRs, both in order to attract the most modern technologies and to encourage their own innovation. Indeed, this prediction is borne out by the pattern of patent protection across countries, as evidenced by the U-shaped relationship between patent rights and income levels (see figure 4.1).

A final comment about the emerging system of global IPRs should be mentioned because it is little appreciated in the policy arena. To the extent that *different* levels of IPRs acts as a location determinant of FDI and technology transfer, the trend toward harmonization of IPRs within the TRIPs agreement will offset such advantages. That is, it will increase the attractiveness of countries that are strengthening their IPRs but reduce the *relative* attractiveness of those that already have strong IPRs. In conjunction with rising *absolute* protection levels, this partial convergence of global minimum standards presents great opportunities for innovative firms. Absolute increases in protection could afford a positive scale effect on all forms of IPR-sensitive activity. Further, the relative convergence implies that firms will no longer have to pay as much attention to localized protection and enforcement problems in safeguarding their proprietary information. In turn, they can focus their R&D programs on those areas with the highest global payoffs. Ultimately, however, this means that IPRs could play a smaller role in determining location choice.

As with international trade, this theoretical review indicates, that the relationships between IPRs and FDI are subtle and complex. While the weight of theory seems to lie on the side of a positive impact, overall it is ambiguous. Finding evidence on the nature of these relationships ultimately requires empirical analysis. Yet, despite the obvious importance that IPRs could play, few recent studies have included measures of their strength in different countries as a potential determinant of FDI.

Two early studies (Mansfield 1993, Maskus and Eby-Konan 1994) could not find any relationship between crude measures of intellectual property protection and the international distribution of FDI by US multinational enterprises. These articles suffered from limited specification of models and employed poor measurements of IPRs. Their results should be largely discounted. A more recent paper by Primo Braga and Fink (1998) could not find significant effects of patent rights on FDI in a gravity framework. This was a substantive piece of work, employing an extensive database and accounting for some determinants of investment other than patents. It raised doubts about the ability of econometric studies to find impacts of IPRs on FDI, or indeed whether such impacts existed.[24]

The results of two other recent studies bring this negative finding into question, however. Lee and Mansfield (1996) used survey results to develop an index of perceived weakness of IPRs in destination countries for US firms. They regressed the volume of US direct investment in various countries over the period 1990-92 on this index, along with measures of market size, the past investment stock, the degree of industrialization, a measure of openness, and a dummy variable for Mexico to control for its special investment relationship with the United States.

They found that weakness of IPRs has a significant negative impact on the location of American FDI. Further, in a sample of chemical firms, the proportion of FDI devoted to final production or R&D facilities was negatively and significantly associated with weakness of protection. The weakness of IPRs had much less impact on the decisions of firms with limited ownership (less than 50 percent) of local affiliates because such firms would be unlikely to transfer their frontier technologies in any case. From these results, it appears that both the volume and quality of investment are diminished in countries with limited property rights.[25]

Maskus (1998a) took an extended approach. It was argued that much of the prior literature is poorly specified in that it does not recognize the

---

24. See also Kondo (1995).

25. See also Moran (1999). Primo Braga and Fink (1998) discuss a number of shortcomings of the Lee and Mansfield approach.

interconnected decisions made by MNEs. In particular, MNEs may choose to export, raise sales from existing foreign operations, increase investment, or transfer technology directly in response to stronger patent rights. A simultaneous set of equations were to capture these joint impacts, controlling for market size, tariff protection, the level of local R&D by affiliates, distance from the United States, and investment incentives and disincentives provided by local authorities. This was done for 46 destination countries, using annual data from 1989-92. The index of patent strength was the corrected RR index, taken from Maskus and Penubarti (1995), and was interacted with a dummy variable selecting developing economies. The interaction term was included to examine whether IPRs affect FDI differently according to level of economic development.[26]

Table 4.11 lists the results from the preferred specifications. All four commercial flows—patent applications, sales by local affiliates, exports from the United States to the host country, and level of affiliate investment assets—are strongly attracted by large markets, as measured by real GDP. A high average tariff tends to diminish FDI, as measured by assets. Local R&D performance is positively associated with each commercial flow. It also appears from this specification that investment incentives have a positive impact and disincentives a negative impact on the level of FDI assets deployed across destination nations.

Average patent strength is strongly associated with patent applications, though the sum of the coefficients on Patent and Patent*DD suggests that the effect is rather weak in developing countries. Exports to affiliates are positively affected by patent strength in developing economies. While average patent strength has little apparent effect on affiliate sales across all nations, the effect is significantly positive in developing countries.

Taken together, these results suggest that if an average developing country were to strengthen its patent index by one unit, local sales of US affiliates would rise by $243 million, or about 2 percent of average annual sales. It is also interesting to note that the coefficient of the patent variable is negative and significant in the assets equation, but the impact in developing countries is significantly positive. Indeed, the results suggest that a one-unit increase in the patent index of the average developing economy would raise the asset stock of US multinational affiliates by $1.9 billion, or about 16 percent of average asset stock.[27]

---

26. The equations were estimated with corrections for unequal error variances within each year and for serial correlation over time (in order to account for temporal dependence in the observations). The equations did not include country fixed effects.

27. The elasticity of sales with respect to patents in developing countries was 0.05, while the elasticity of assets was 0.45. At the mean patent index, a one-unit increase would represent a 36 percent rise in the index number. Remaining elasticity estimates from this analysis are listed in Maskus (1998b).

Table 4.11 Simultaneous equations model of the impact of patent strength on the international exploitation of intellectual assets (46 countries, 1989-92)

Variable	Applications	Sales	Exports	Assets
Constant	0.27*	0.46*	0.60*	0.14
	(2.77)	(5.13)	(7.51)	(1.46)
GDP	3.66*	31.19*	1.07*	26.26*
	(26.79)	(27.23)	(10.02)	(10.13)
Tariff rate	−6.34*	−3.19	−3.95*	−108.88*
	(−4.89)	(−0.26)	(−4.92)	(-3.34)
Affiliate R&D	1.78*	42.80*	1.74*	40.76*
	(3.42)	(19.42)	(23.86)	(6.17)
Distance	0.012*	−0.057*	−0.008*	−0.95*
	(3.08)	(−2.32)	(-5.01)	(-9.02)
Patent	1703.15*	−76.05	−21.23*	−1,585.41*
	(10.24)	(−1.26)	(−5.19)	(−6.70)
Patent*DD	−1690.37*	319.53*	53.99*	3,516.62*
	(−10.13)	(4.50)	(8.63)	(11.62)
Incentives	$43 \times 10^{3*}$	$340 \times 10^{3*}$	$15 \times 10^{3*}$	$1,389 \times 10^{3*}$
	(12.2)	(13.85)	(11.14)	(16.29)
Disincentives	−3489.02*	$-23 \times 10^{3*}$	2423.17*	$-354 \times 10^{3*}$
	(−4.41)	(−2.32)	(4.29)	(−7.80)
R^2	0.90	0.97	0.97	0.90

Applications = Number of US patent applications filed in host country.
Sales = Total sales of foreign affiliates of US parents (US$ millions).
Exports = US exports shipped to affiliates (US$ millions).
Assets =Total assets, foreign affiliates of US parents (US $millions).
GDP = Real GDP in host country (US$ billions).
Tariff rate = Import revenues divided by total dutiable imports.
Affiliate R&D = Expenditure on R&D by foreign affiliates of US parents (US$ millions).
Distance = Distance from US to host country (kilometers).
Patent = Instrumented patent index.
Patent*DD = Index interacted with a dummy variable for developing countries.
Incentives = Number of affiliates that received tax concessions in host country divided
  by number of affiliates that received tax concessions in any of the countries.
Disincentives = Number of affiliates that employ a minimum amount of local personnel
  in host country divided by number of affiliates that employ a minimum amount of local
  personnel in any of the countries.
* = Significance at the 1 percent level.
Note: The equations are run in a SUR framework corrected for heteroskedasticity and
autocorrelation. Figures in parentheses are t-statistics.

Source: Maskus (1998a).

The finding that patent strength does not attract more applications in developing nations but does increase affiliate sales and asset stocks is intriguing. While precise interpretation is difficult, it is possible that MNEs, in allocating their investment funds, are sensitive to improvements in IPRs in developing countries, even if they choose not to incur the expense of applying for local patents to the same degree as in developed countries. However, the substitution effect between FDI and licensing noted earlier may become dominant once patent protection exceeds a particular level. In conjunction with the results in Lee and Mansfield (1996), these findings indicate that levels of FDI are responsive to IPRs in developing nations. It should be noted that these tentative conclusions are based on aggregate FDI data and may not pertain in some sectors in some countries.

To see whether such results carry over into other empirical modeling contexts, I performed the regressions reflected in table 4.12. The approach stems from a two-country, general-equilibrium theory of foreign direct investment, as detailed in Carr, Markusen, and Maskus (2000). In that model three fundamental determinants of FDI are emphasized:

1. The public-input nature of R&D, management, and marketing ("headquarter services") permits economies of scope in horizontal FDI. This encourages such investment in countries of similar size and income levels.

2. Differences in skills encourage parent companies in skill-abundant nations to invest in vertical FDI in labor-abundant nations.

3. Trade barriers in the host country should induce more FDI, other things being equal, for purposes of jumping tariffs, though the likelihood of this outcome would diminish with the technological sophistication of the commodities produced.

Various interaction terms are added to account for nonlinearities in the model. Geographic distance appears in the equations to account for monitoring costs, which should reduce FDI. Finally, the model adds a variable measuring how MNE managers perceive the adequacy of intellectual property protection in host countries. The notion is that weak intellectual property rights would deter FDI because they raise the costs of maintaining secrecy and of monitoring local operations. However, as we have discussed, the theory could support a prediction of higher FDI in nations with weak IPRs.

The dependent variable in the regressions is the real sales volume of majority-owned foreign affiliates of US manufacturing enterprises and, similarly, the real sales volume of foreign-owned US subsidiaries. These data are taken from the US Department of Commerce annual publications on activities of US affiliates abroad and foreign affiliates in the

Table 4.12   Estimates of the general-equilibrium knowledge capital model

Variable	GLS1	TOBIT1	GLS2	TOBIT2
Constant	−25,911* (−2.48)	−46,739* (15.9)	−17,093 (1.63)	−42,590* (13.7)
Sum GDP	13.56* (12.5)	15.65* (208.3)	12.98* (12.1)	15.66* (216.8)
(GDP differences)^2	−0.0013* (−10.6)	−0.0011* (71.4)	−0.0012* (-9.83)	−0.0011* (72.2)
Skill differences	49,048* (3.32)	60,682* (13.9)	26,001* (2.19)	56,002* (12.25)
Trade cost	13.77 (0.21)	142.6* (3.90)	43.83 (0.68)	132.9** (3.52)
IPR	−113.4 (−1.29)	−167.8** (3.23)	−199.1* (-2.57)	−163.2** (3.19)
(GDP differences) × (Skill differences)	−0.61 (−0.23)	−4.82 (2.57)	−2.83 (−1.24)	−4.67 (2.51)
(Trade cost) × (Skill differences)^2	−1,363 (−0.97)	−3,114* (4.23)	−1,237 (−0.89)	−2,593** (3.02)
Distance			−0.86* (−5.10)	−0.66* (15.41)
Number of observations	513	671	513	671
Adj. R^2	0.87		0.87	
Log likelihood		−5,496		−5,489

Notes: Figures in parentheses are t-statistics for GLS regressions and chi-squared statistics for TOBIT regressions.
*Significance levels of 5 percent or lower
**Significance at 10 percent.

Source: Author's calculations.

United States. There are 36 countries in the sample, with a panel of bilateral observations over the period 1986-94. Not all countries provided full data for each year. Independent variables include the sum of the two countries' real GDP, the squared differences in their GDP levels, a measure of skill endowment differences, and indicators of trade barriers and intellectual property protection. Labor skill is measured by the percentage of each country's labor force that is employed in managerial, technical, and professional occupations, with bilateral skill differences simply being the difference between the skill ratio of the parent country and that of the host country.

The measure of trade barriers is an index of national protectionism, defined as efforts to prevent importation of competitive products, constructed from a survey of MNE managers and reported in the World Economic Forum (1995). Finally, the index measuring the inadequacy of IPRs was taken from the same survey. These last two variables are transformed so that higher values indicate higher trade protectionism and weaker IPRs.

The regressions included country fixed effects and embodied two techniques. The first is a generalized least squares (GLS) procedure accounting for heteroskedasticity in the error terms. The second accounts for the fact that, for many small developing economies in the sample, the data do not list any foreign affiliate sales. It is likely that these cases reflect the absence of any investment. To incorporate these zero observations for FDI into the dependent variable, I perform Tobit regressions, thereby increasing the sample size and including more developing countries.

These results again are interesting. Joint market size, as given by the sum of GDP, exerts a powerful and positive impact on affiliate sales. In theory, the squared term in the difference in GDP levels should be negative, for as market sizes diverge, incentives for horizontal FDI fall.[28] The positive and highly significant coefficient on skill differences provides strong evidence of an endowment basis for FDI, referring largely to vertical investment. The trade cost variable, a measure of local protectionism, is uniformly positive but does not often attain significance in the GLS equations. However, it *is* significant in the Tobit equations, which embody more observations for developing economies. Thus, the tariff-jumping argument for FDI seems to hold more strongly for investment going to, and coming from, developing economies than for investment between developed economies.

As anticipated, the intellectual property coefficients are consistently negative and significant in three of four cases. For the GLS specification, adding distance raises the magnitude of the coefficient considerably and also its statistical significance. Thus, controlling for distance, which may act as a proxy for the administrative difficulty of monitoring and controlling foreign operations, MNEs pay significant attention to the local protection of IPRs in their decisions on sales volumes of foreign affiliates. Using the GLS2 estimate, a one-unit increase in the IPR index in the average country in the data sample would raise affiliate sales by $199 million. Since sales volumes correlate positively with FDI, this finding provides further support for the notion that direct investment reacts negatively to the weakness of intellectual property protection.[29]

---

28. See Markusen (1995) and Helpman (1987).

29. Again, such results raise as many questions as they answer. One fruitful avenue for further research would be to incorporate into the FDI equations measures for corruption and tax burdens across countries, because such variables have been found to matter in

IPRs and International Technology Transfer

Some of the discussion in the last section hinted at a theory of how IPRs affect the transfer of technology by altering incentives to choose between FDI and licensing contracts. The issue is far deeper than that, of course, and requires further discussion before we look at some basic evidence.

"Transfer of technology" covers a vast array of complex transactions that can only be summarized here. At the most basic level, it means the successful learning of information and the know-how to use it by one party from another party. The transfer may be unintentional and uncompensated, intentional and fully compensated, or somewhere in between.

The distinction between information and know-how is important. Gaining access to blueprints for a complex technology is of little competitive advantage in itself unless there is also a way to determine how to use it efficiently. Clearly, the ease of mastering production technologies varies considerably across products and sectors.

It is convenient to think of the channels through which technology may be transferred, for IPRs influence how these channels may be used. Technologies may be effectively misappropriated through straightforward imitation or copying without compensation to their developer. In this context, copying should be distinguished from reverse engineering. The technology for copying software or music is available to anyone with a computer and a supply of storage devices. Similarly, it is easy to produce toys, apparel, and related goods that copy the designs of trademark owners. Though little effective technology is learned this way, significant amounts of revenue may be generated.

Reverse engineering is more difficult. The classic examples are software and pharmaceuticals. Competitors may decompile computer programs in order to learn their structure; once learned, the program language may be used to launch competing products, but this process can be difficult and expensive. In pharmaceuticals it is typically neither costly nor difficult to determine chemical formulas simply by decomposing the drugs. It is then possible to sell competing compounds. Thus, it is difficult to protect the technical secrets embodied in these products through purely private mechanisms. More complex technologies, such as automotive engineering, avionics, and medical devices, bear their secrets more deeply; these cannot be duplicated without considerable cost. Still, the basic acts of exporting goods or producing and selling them locally through FDI risk imitation.

Even without literal attempts to copy technologies or products, there may be a remarkably rich flow of uncompensated information among potential competitors through trade shows, publications, patent applica-

---

investment decisions. IPRs may proxy for such influences, but that possibility has not yet been assessed.

tions, and movement of technical employees between firms. For example, the needs of a firm to share know-how with its suppliers could spill over into design improvements that are beneficial for competing firms using the same suppliers. Channels of this kind were found by Mansfield (1985) to be important in explaining the relatively rapid dissipation of US industrial technologies into public knowledge. Mansfield found that technological secrets leaked into competitors' hands typically within one or two years. Such diffusion also seems to be rapid across borders (Krugman 1987); it is likely that this transfer has accelerated with improvements in communications technologies.

However, even though such information may be available to competitors quickly, turning it into competing products may be costly and time-consuming. For example, another survey by Mansfield, Schwartz, and Wagner (1981) discovered that average imitation costs totaled some 65 percent of innovation costs and that imitation time equaled about 70 percent of innovation time. Again, however, these figures are likely outdated. They would, in any case, vary sharply by sector.

Intentional technology transfer comes through three channels: FDI, joint ventures, and licenses.[30] Because FDI aims largely to exploit proprietary technological advantages, it represents a critical source of technology trade. At the same time, intrafirm transactions complement the productivity advantages of MNEs and expand technology learning in host countries. MNEs may ship advanced material inputs to subsidiaries that help reduce production costs. They also share, in addition to blueprints and product designs, the inputs of skilled producer services, such as engineering and management. In typical production joint ventures, partners share technologies or provide technology in return for access to marketing networks or some other competitive advantage.

In arm's-length licensing one firm leases rights to another, unrelated firm to (1) use a technology that is protected by patents and trade secrets or (2) produce and market a copyrighted or trademarked good or service. Terms may include a fixed franchise fee, royalty payments based on sales volumes, or both. As discussed earlier, there are extraordinarily difficult problems in designing licensing contracts, not least of which is assigning a market-specific value to the patent or trademark being leased. The value depends on, among many other things, market size, demand characteristics, age of the technology, availability of substitute products, and the strength of local IPRs. Some of these variables cannot be known at the time contracts are made.

Whatever the form, technology transfer costs money (Teece 1986). The costs range from trivial, in the case of software and music piracy, to extensive, in the case of complex interrelated technologies. If there is considerable uncertainty about such factors as future demand and the

---

30. For an extensive review, see UNCTAD (1995a).

ability of licensees to absorb new technologies, and if information is weakly available or asymmetric between parties, the associated market imperfections will likely result in inefficient licensing. Such problems are magnified in the international context, where different legal systems and information reporting requirements may interfere.

IPRs have an important effect on the costs of transferring technology. At one extreme, strong IPRs eliminate the ability to copy products slavishly (or otherwise to develop functional equivalents) and significantly raise the costs of imitation through reverse engineering or inventing around patents. Thus, IPRs raise the costs of competing through uncompensated and unauthorized learning, thereby limiting information spillovers through those channels.

At the other extreme, IPRs tend to reduce the costs of *authorized* technology transfers. For example, patents and trade secret protection may encourage arm's-length licensing in two ways: (1) well-understood rights allow a clearer revelation of technological advantages and market size, permitting contracts to be struck more efficiently, and (2) strong IPRs make it more certain that the licensee will not misappropriate the technology or debase the trademark and that technical employees will not defect to form competing firms. As for FDI, there could be both an expansion effect as the costs of transferring and protecting know-how within the firm are reduced, and a substitution effect as MNEs shift away from FDI toward external licensing. The evidence in the previous section suggests that the expansion effect strongly dominates in developing economies.

Thus, IPRs play a role in international technology transfer that is parallel to their role in promoting innovation and limiting imitation within an economy. By providing additional certainty about the enforceability of contracts, IPRs could encourage firms to trade technology across borders through making costly investments in FDI and licensing.[31] And by raising the costs of imitation, IPRs might limit international diffusion through unauthorized means. As ever in this area, a balance must be struck in setting policies, a balance that would, other things being equal, favor weak IPRs in poor countries but continuously stronger IPRs in nations approaching the technological frontier.

Recent theoretical treatments of how IPRs affect technology diffusion bear mixed messages. In some models, technology is transferred through imitation by firms in developing countries. When the global IPRs system is strengthened by the adoption of minimum standards and as foreign patents are enforced, imitation becomes harder. As the rate of imitation declines, contrary to what might be expected, it slows down the global

---

31. IPRs may not be strictly necessary for this task; strong contract laws could in principle achieve the same purpose. However, the contracts would have to provide protection from imitation and defection that would be essentially equivalent to patent and trade secret rights.

rate of innovation. This outcome emerges because if innovative firms expected slower loss of their technological advantages they could earn higher profits per innovation, reducing the need to engage in R&D (Helpman 1993; Glass and Saggi 1995).

This result, which is sensitive to model assumptions, may not hold up to alternative specifications. Indeed, Lai (1998) found that product innovation and technology diffusion would be strengthened by tighter IPRs if production were transferred through FDI rather than through imitation. This points to the need for developing economies to remove impediments to inward FDI as they strengthen their intellectual property systems. Vishwasrao (1994) demonstrated in a game-theory setting that, while the mode of technology transfer is affected by IPRs protection, with internalization through FDI the preferred mechanism in countries with weak patents, the quality of technologies transferred would rise with stronger IPRs. Taylor (1994) also showed theoretically that technology transfer would expand with stronger patents when there is competition between a foreign and a domestic innovator. Failure to provide patents removes the incentive for the foreign firm to license its best-practice technologies. Rockett (1990) found that where local imitation requires knowledge that is available only through licensed technology, the foreign licensers make available lower-quality technologies. This reduces the licensee's incentive to imitate the technology, reducing both the quality and extent of knowledge transfer. Yang and Maskus (2000a, 2000b) developed dynamic North-South models in which the rate of technology transfer could be enhanced by stronger IPRs in the South to the extent that cost reductions in licensing contracts would outweigh cost increases in imitation. Markusen (2000) found a similar possibility in a duopoly setting.

Once again, empirical analysis must be brought to bear. Studies that ask a variety of questions are relevant. First, there is evidence that a policy of weak IPRs in technology-recipient nations reduces the quality of technology transferred. Drawing on a study of collaboration agreements between British and Indian firms, Davies (1977) concluded that difficulties in securing rights over the profits accruing to technical information raise powerful barriers to information trades between developed and developing economies. Contractor (1980) studied a sample of 102 technology licenses provided by US firms; his regression results supported the hypothesis that returns to a technology supplier increase with patent protection in the recipient nation. He found that technologies transferred to developing countries tended to be significantly older than those transferred to industrialized economies. While these findings may be dated, they point to the significance of patent regimes in attracting technology through licensing.

There is also evidence that the effectiveness of IPRs protection in inducing technical innovation and technology transfer depends on the trade orientation of an economy. In a survey of more than 3,000 Brazilian companies, Braga and Willmore (1991) found that the propensities of firms both to develop their own technologies and to buy them from foreign sources were negatively related to the degree of trade protection they enjoyed. Thus, in closed economies, protecting IPRs may not expand innovation much because the competitive conditions are inadequate to stimulate it. Gould and Gruben (1996) found in an econometric study that patent strength was an important determinant of economic growth and that this effect was stronger in relatively open economies. I return to this important finding in the next chapter, on IPRs and economic development.

Further, in an important study of international patenting behavior, Eaton and Kortum (1996) discovered that significant amounts of technology are transferred across borders through the patenting system. The value of patent rights varies by country and technology field but is typically significant in important developing countries, suggesting that stronger patents would induce further R&D, patent applications, and patent exploitation. There appear to be considerable spillovers of technological knowledge through patenting and trade in patented products. Indeed, Eaton and Kortum claim that, except for the United States, the OECD countries have derived substantial productivity growth from importing knowledge through patents.

The importance of technology transfer through trade in technologically advanced inputs (machinery, chemicals, software, producer services, and so on) should also be emphasized. There is evidence that such trade is responsible for significant productivity gains across borders and is a crucial part of technology convergence among the developed economies in recent decades and the diffusion into developing countries (Coe and Helpman 1995; Coe, Helpman, and Hoffmaister 1997). This suggests that emerging economies have a joint interest in trade liberalization and linking their IPR systems with those of the developed countries. The resulting productivity spillovers could easily outweigh the costs associated with additional market power.

Two studies have related data on US licensing receipts to the strength of IPRs in licensee countries. Ferrantino (1993) included memberships in the Paris and Berne Conventions along with duration of patent length in each of 75 countries as determinants of production and licensing fees of overseas affiliates of US MNEs in 1982. The results suggested weakly that stronger IPRs, measured in this way, favored local production over intrafirm exports from the United States and also expanded licensing payments by affiliates.

Yang and Maskus (2000c) regressed the real volume of license fees for industrial processes paid by unaffiliated foreign firms to US firms in 26 countries for the years 1985, 1990, and 1995. The measure of IPRs was the GP patent rights index. Other independent variables for licensee nations included real GDP, population, secondary enrollment ratio, and the

Sachs-Warner index of openness. In their preferred estimation, they found that with country fixed effects unaffiliated royalties and license fees were positively and significantly affected by the strength of patent rights. The coefficient suggested that a one-percent rise in the GP index would expand licensing volumes by around 2.3 percent in the average licensee country. To the extent that license fees reflect the value of underlying technology, this result supports the view that technology transfer would rise with stronger patent rights. However, despite its use of license volumes (values deflated by a price index) the approach does not adequately distinguish between the higher valuation associated with additional or higher quality technology flows and higher fees associated with additional market power for licensers.

Summary

As the world continues to undertake unprecedented policy changes in IPRs, economists strive to peel away the veil of darkness surrounding the likely effects on global economic activity. The evidence reviewed in this section is not definitive. It would benefit from further study and better measurement of IPRs. Nonetheless, I am sufficiently comfortable with the work to draw some confident conclusions:

1. There is no doubt that international differences in intellectual property rights have statistically and economically important effects on international economic activity.

2. Trade flows into large developing economies with significant capacities for imitation are restricted by weak IPRs. Adoption of the TRIPs standards bears the potential to raise their imports of technologically sophisticated goods by significant amounts.

3. However, as small poor nations strengthen their IPRs, they may find some of their markets becoming more monopolized by foreign exporting firms, a conclusion that holds as well for rich economies that are net importers of intellectual property. In this context, competition authorities may need to be more vigilant. Unfortunately, the poorest countries rarely have competition regimes in place; the process of installing them will be complex, as I discuss later. More fruitfully, such economies would do well to ensure that competitive processes thrive on their markets, so that the availability of substitute products can blunt monopoly pricing impacts.

4. FDI is also sensitive to variations in IPRs. The amounts of possible additional investment as a result of patent reforms could be large. Imports and FDI both embody technological advantages that can spill

over into domestic economies, even under strong patent regimes. Thus, a dynamic benefit from rising activity flows could outweigh losses in the terms of trade for such countries. The likelihood of such an outcome depends on complementary factors, such as the ability to absorb and commercialize technologies, openness to trade, and maintenance of competition. These observations are at the core of the discussion in chapter 7.

5. Finally, a feature of IPRs that is underappreciated, at least by economists, is that they can undergird an efficient system of contracts to promote formal technology transfer through licensing. Again, the potential increases in licensing volumes from strengthening such rights could be significant and the quality of the technologies should rise. Seen in this light, it is inevitable that technology importers will pay higher costs to absorb more and better technologies as a result of tighter IPRs. Note that this outcome would not be by any means universal. Stronger property rights could also permit firms to choose not to license their closely held technologies except in cross-licensing or patent-pooling arrangements. Thus, a trade-off likely will emerge between stronger licensing incentives and greater prerogatives to maintain technologies under close control. Such trade-offs are the essence of intellectual property rights and call for some balance in achieving an appropriate mix of incentives.

These conclusions are important for the ensuing discussion. However, keep in mind that they follow from limited econometric analysis. Two shortcomings of this analysis are particularly troublesome. First, either the studies adopt aggregate approaches, failing to consider impacts across sectors, or the sectoral approaches are partial equilibrium. It would be useful to estimate interindustry linkages through a computable general equilibrium approach, which has yet to be done. Such an approach would also permit consideration of international trade effects across countries more readily. Second, while the studies to date permit tentative conclusions about dynamic effects of IPRs, there are no explicitly dynamic analyses. This is unfortunate in light of the inherently dynamic trade-offs that IPRs embody. This oversight surely implies that the effects of stronger IPRs are being underestimated.

5

Intellectual Property Rights and Economic Development: Patents, Growth, and Growing Pains

In 1900, Korekiyo Takahashi, the first president of the Japanese Patent Office, announced during a visit to the US Patent Office:

> We have looked about us to see what nations are the greatest, so that we can be like them. We said, "What is it that makes the United States such a great nation?" and found that it was patents and so we will have patents.[1]

Japan did adopt a comprehensive patent regime, though its features were distinctive from the American and major European systems. It was designed to encourage industrial development through emphasizing technology acquisition from abroad, domestic information diffusion, and incremental innovation. In short, the system was developed with the interests of a technology *follower* in mind. The Japanese regime significantly limited patent scope and breadth. For example, pharmaceutical patents were not provided until the 1970s. Whether this system was important in making Japan a "great nation" is subject to debate, but I believe it played a positive role. As Japan matured into an industrial power and technological leader, features of its patent system attracted increasing complaints from both foreign and domestic enterprises, leading to its reform in 1994.

This story illustrates two important characteristics of intellectual property rights: (1) IPRs can be of material assistance in a country's attempts to encourage its own technological, industrial, and cultural development; failure to provide protection can be damaging for domestic inventive

---

1. Quoted in Heath (1997, 305).

effort. (2) The terms on which a country might wish to protect IPRs depend on, among other things, its position on the global technology ladder and on social concerns. For example, the United States progressively increased the strength of its patent system and protection for trademarks and trade secrets from the 19th century to the 20th century. The demand for protection rises with economic development and with technological change and entrepreneurship. Accordingly, IPRs are inherently dynamic, both in their formation and in their effects. The relationships between economic development and IPRs are complex, with causation surely running in both directions.

As demonstrated in the last chapter, the strength of IPRs appears to be a nonlinear function of economic development, at first falling as incomes rise and then increasing after that. Only at a per capita income of around $7,750 (in 1985 international dollars) do protection levels return to those of the poorest countries. It therefore seems that as incomes and technical capabilities grow to intermediate levels, adaptive innovation emerges, but competition remains focused largely on imitation, so that the bulk of economic and political interests prefer weak protection. As economies mature to higher levels of technological capacity and as demands for high-quality, differentiated products increase, more domestic firms favor effective IPRs. Finally, at the highest income levels the strength of IPRs shifts up sharply (Evenson and Westphal 1997; LaCroix 1992).[2]

Perhaps this finding suggests that the appropriate international policy is simply to wait until income levels rise enough that there is an automatic rise in standards, as has been suggested in the areas of environmental protection and labor standards. However, it is likely to take considerable time before many significant developing countries approach the necessary per capita income. External pressure from the United States for reform and the negotiation of TRIPs implicitly recognized this problem. In this regard, the world is undertaking an unprecedented experiment: to accelerate the introduction of higher standards into regions that would not ordinarily be expected to adopt them.

This policy shift raises fundamental questions about the role of IPRs in establishing conditions conducive to economic growth. The related issues are subtle and difficult; unfortunately, evidence remains scarce and fragmentary. In this chapter the analysis focuses on the causation chain from IPRs to development. What do we know about how IPRs affect economic growth and living standards? The evidence is not as clear as we would like, although economists have paid attention to the issue recently and some important studies shed light on the question. The

---

2. This description seems broadly accurate but is not a formal political economy model of the process. Whether governments would choose to provide an "optimal" level of IPRs, even if that could be identified at any point, would depend on the weights they assigned to consumer interests, producer interests, and intergenerational transfers.

basic conclusion from that work is that there is significant complexity surrounding this relationship. This is not surprising given the second-best nature of IPRs in addressing complex market failures: strengthening IPRs may expand growth prospects under certain circumstances but may offer no improvement, or even retard conditions for development, under other circumstances. Strong conclusions are subject to caveats. On both sides of the issue special cases abound.

The broadest conclusion supported by logic and evidence is that IPRs provide an important foundation for sophisticated business structures. While this argument holds at nearly any level of economic development, the function of IPRs as appropriate support mechanisms varies with income and technological capabilities. Structured so as to promote effective and dynamic competition within a context of strong competitive processes and appropriate and transparent regulation, IPRs can play an important role in enhancing technical change and growth.[3]

The remainder of this chapter analyzes mechanisms and evidence on IPRs and growth, setting the stage for the broader analysis in the next chapter. I often illustrate concepts with evidence from Lebanon and China, based on recent field research (Maskus 1997b, 1999, 2000a; Maskus, Dougherty, and Mertha 1998).

How IPRs Contribute to Development

Economists recognize several mechanisms through which IPRs may stimulate economic development and growth. These processes are interdependent, meaning that a broad view of the incentives associated with IPRs is appropriate.

Before turning to particular issues, consider the general proposition that secure property rights are a precondition for growth. While that may defy systematic empirical analysis, there is significant documentary evidence that ownership of rights (1) to exploit tangible property and (2) to exclude others from using such property without approval has played a positive role in the development of advanced economies (North 1981; Powelson 1994). These rights provide incentives to acquire property, improve it with productivity-enhancing investments, and maintain it for purposes of building asset value.

Societies limit the private exploitation of physical property to ensure public safety, provide public goods, and promote environmental, aesthetic, and public-health ends. The observation that limited but exclusive private ownership of rights promises growth-enhancing benefits pertains

---

3. For extensive reviews see Evenson and Westphal (1997), Maskus (1998b), and Primo Braga, Fink, and Sepulveda (2000). Enthusiastic arguments for a positive role for IPRs are offered by Sherwood (1990) and Rapp and Rozek (1990).

equally to land and physical capital. Perhaps more significantly, the ability to market one's skills freely as a human property right encourages the development of human capital as well. Such investments are critical drivers of growth.

Private property rights are meaningless if they cannot be enforced. Enforcement may range from informal mechanisms based on cultural norms or personal power relationships to fully articulated legislated remedies with legal representation of adversarial parties before an impartial judge. Many have argued that as societies build more complex social and business relationships among their members, informal mechanisms must give way to legal enforcement, both because informal systems become overwhelmed by complexity and because the legal system becomes economically feasible as its high fixed costs may be spread more widely. Those who favor a rule-of-law approach to economic development tout the greater legal certainty of well-specified rules of engagement, making businesses more willing to undertake additional investments.

A fascinating question, which has not been studied adequately in the broad sweep of history, is whether intellectual property rights have the same effects as general private property rights.[4] To a considerable degree the same arguments apply to property created by human inventiveness. Absent rights to exclusive use, the extreme problems of nonexcludability associated with some forms of intellectual endeavors would destroy incentives to create them. Equally, unless rights are well articulated and enforceable, their owners have few incentives to improve their creations through further investment. Thus, standard property rights theory applies in the main to intellectual creations and provides sound justification for the existence of patents, trademarks, copyrights, and trade secrets. Such rights are limited also for purposes of social regulation.

However, these conclusions require qualification. First, intellectual property has characteristics that distinguish it from tangible property. For example, excludability may be more readily achieved without protection than is commonly recognized. As discussed below, imitation costs are significant in many forms of industrial property, technologies evolve rapidly, and goods proceed quickly through product cycles. In this sense, IPRs may not be a necessary spur to investments in creation, except in sectors where imitation is easy and low-cost, and may only supplement extranormal profits from dynamic competition.

At the same time, the nonrivalrous nature of many intellectual assets poses an acute policy conundrum in the international (or interregional or even intersectoral) context. Unlike physical property, intellectual property is internationally mobile at relatively low cost. How can the government of a technology-importing country justify awarding to foreign interests the exclusive rights to exploit information on the local market, when

---

4. David (1993) provides an interesting historical perspective on the evolution of IPRs.

that information might be freely available through imitation and also might spread quickly within domestic borders?

Of course, this question lies at the heart of the long-running debate over IPRs. An affirmative answer must demonstrate that weak IPRs result in foreign owners not making the desired information available, thereby causing society to forego any benefits from its creation and transfer. The evidence reviewed in the last chapter suggested that it is common for MNEs to undersupply investment and advanced technologies to such countries, buttressing the case for stronger IPRs.

Invention, Innovation, and Diffusion

Traditionally, developing countries have established IPRs systems favoring information diffusion through low-cost imitation of foreign products and technologies, believing that domestic innovation was insufficient to warrant protection. However, inadequate IPRs can stifle technical change even at low levels of economic development because much invention is aimed at local markets and can benefit from local patent or utility model protection. Though in the overwhelming majority of cases invention is simply minor adaptation of existing technologies, the cumulative effect can be critical for growth in knowledge and activity.

To become competitive, firms in developing economies may need primarily to adopt new management and organizational systems and techniques for process and quality control, which can markedly raise productivity. Such investments are costly and likely will only be made when risks of unfair competition and trademark infringement are small. Adequate and enforceable IPRs also help reward new enterprises and entrepreneurs for creativity and risk taking. Countries that retain weak standards tend to remain dependent on uncompetitive firms that rely on counterfeiting and imitation.

Much learning and technical change occurs through adapting domestic and foreign technologies to particular applications. To absorb knowledge and know-how in advanced technologies requires considerable investment in such factors as process control and product quality maintenance. These investments tend to have high social returns in developing economies because they are crucial for raising productivity toward global norms (Evenson and Westphal 1997). Again, IPRs protect firms assuming those costs.

An example of this process is that protection for utility models has been shown to improve productivity in technology-follower countries. Recall that utility models are patents of short duration awarded to incremental inventions that build on more fundamental discoveries. In Brazil, utility models were important in permitting domestic producers to gain a significant share of the farm-machinery market by adapting foreign technologies to local conditions (Dahab 1986). Utility models in the Philippines encouraged successful adaptive invention of rice threshers (Mikkelsen 1984).

In perhaps the most systematic study, Maskus and McDaniel (1999) considered how the Japanese patent system (JPS) affected postwar Japanese technical progress, as measured by increases in total factor productivity (TFP).[5] The JPS in place over the estimation period 1960-93 was designed to encourage incremental and adaptive innovation and diffusion of knowledge into the economy. Mechanisms for doing so included early disclosure of, and opposition proceedings to, patent applications, an extensive system of utility models, and narrow claim requirements in patent applications. The authors found that this system promoted the development of large numbers of utility model applications for incremental inventions that were based in part on laid-open prior applications for invention patents. Utility models had a strongly positive impact on real TFP growth over the period; patent applications had a weaker though still positive effect. Maskus and McDaniel concluded that utility models were an important source of technical change and information diffusion in Japan, while patent applications had both a direct and an indirect effect on raising productivity. It is interesting that as Japan has become a global leader in technology creation, its patent system has shifted dramatically away from emphasizing learning and diffusion and more toward protecting underlying inventions through patents.

Innovation through product development and entry of new firms seems to be stymied in part by weak trademark protection in poor nations. A recent survey of trademark use in Lebanon provided evidence on this point (Maskus 1997b). Though Lebanon has extensive IPRs laws, they are weakly enforced. Firms in the apparel industry claim to have a strong interest in designing clothing of high quality and style for Middle Eastern markets. Their attempts to do so have been frustrated by trademark infringement by smaller firms in Lebanon and in neighboring countries, where protection is even weaker.

This problem is even greater in the food products sector, where legitimate firms suffer from considerable misappropriation of their trademarks. This misappropriation has limited the success of attempts to build niche markets for Lebanese foods in the Middle East and elsewhere. Similar difficulties plague innovative producers in the cosmetics, pharmaceuticals, and metal products sectors. The essential point is that local product development and entry of new firms may be restrained by trademark infringement targeted largely at domestic enterprises.

---

5. Total factor productivity refers to the ratio of GDP to primary inputs (capital and labor) weighted by their income shares. Thus it measures the additional output generated by the technological information embodied in primary inputs.

Similar problems exist in China, as evidenced in a recent survey (Maskus, Dougherty, and Mertha 1998). While the information is largely anecdotal, it seems that trademark infringement significantly and negatively affects innovative Chinese enterprises. In interviews many examples were cited of difficulties facing Chinese producers of their own brands of consumer goods, such as soft drinks, processed foods, and clothing. Establishing brand recognition in China requires costly investments in marketing and distribution. Enterprises that achieve this recognition quickly find their trademarks applied to counterfeit products, in the same or in other product categories. Products of lower quality damage the reputation of the legitimate enterprise, a problem so difficult that it has sometimes forced enterprises to close down or give up their trademarks.

This situation likely has an important deterrent effect on enterprise development in China. It effectively prevents marketing across the country, which would permit economies of scale. It is significant that Chinese trademark infringement currently is concentrated on products with low capital requirements and high labor intensity. These are sectors in which China has strong comparative advantages. Thus, on this evidence, trademark violations may be particularly damaging to enterprise development in poor nations.

Similar comments apply to copyrights. In developing countries copyright industries like publishing, entertainment, and software are likely to be dominated by foreign enterprises (which can absorb temporary losses and afford to deter infringers) and pirate firms. Though lower-quality copies may be widely and cheaply available, the economy's domestic cultural and technological development is slowed down. This process was clear in the Lebanese survey. Lebanon has a small but vibrant film and television industry that believes that with stronger copyright protection it would successfully export to neighboring economies. In China, the domestic software industry has grown rapidly in particular business applications that do not suffer much copying, but has faced obstacles in developing larger and more fundamental program platforms. Thus, domestic commercial interests in stronger copyrights are now playing a role in promoting enforcement. In contrast, India has long had a system of effective copyright protection, which is thought by many observers to have been important in growing and protecting its modern film industry.

These observations suggest that business formation, trademark registration, and simple innovation are elastic with respect to IPRs reform even at low levels of income. Controversy persists, however, over the innovation-inducing properties of IPRs at higher levels of technological sophistication. As noted earlier, survey evidence (Levin et al. 1987) suggests that patent protection is not considered critical by most US firms making decisions to market new products and processes. Exceptions arise only in a few industries, such as pharmaceuticals and chemicals, where fixed costs of R&D are high and imitation is fairly easy. More significant incentives for innovation come from competitive pressures, market growth, factor costs, and the like, while appropriation of profits relies on imitation costs and lags, product loyalty, maintaining trade secrets, and other mechanisms.

However, this evidence was assembled before the extensive globalization of technology in the late 1980s. Moreover, the potential importance of patents in inducing innovation under broader protection may well be larger than such surveys anticipate (Mansfield 1988). The general weakness of the global patent system before TRIPs, exacerbated by easy flows of technological information across borders, could have so limited the incentives for R&D as to induce a suboptimal level of new product development. Perceptions that protection will be more effective over time could raise inventive activity. Further, dynamic linkages or intertemporal spillovers between product generations might argue for strong protection.

Technology Transfer and Learning

IPRs also can play a positive role in the dissemination and acquisition of information. Patent claims published anywhere are accessible to all, allowing rival firms to use the information in them as a basis for further inventions. This dissemination process takes place in 10 to 12 months in the United States (Mansfield 1985). Knowledge formation is cumulative: as new inventions build on past practices, technical change accelerates (Scotchmer 1991). Patents, trademarks, and trade secrets also give firms legal certainty and should induce them to trade and license technologies and products, thereby expanding diffusion into the economy.

Turning to international transactions, in strengthening their IPRs regimes, either unilaterally or through adherence to TRIPs, developing countries hope to attract additional inflows of advanced technology from abroad. There are three important and interdependent channels through which technology is transferred across borders: international trade in goods, FDI within MNEs, and formal licensing of technologies and trademarks to unaffiliated firms, subsidiaries, and joint ventures. As discussed in the previous chapter, economic theory indicates that international technology transfers through each channel depend in part on local protection of IPRs, though in complex and subtle ways.

That imports of goods and services transfer and diffuse technology is widely accepted among economists. Imports of capital goods and technical inputs directly reduce production costs and raise productivity in the firms that employ them. The extent of this benefit depends on the technological sophistication of the imports, suggesting that close trade linkages to innovative developed economies engender considerable productivity gains.

As discussed in the last chapter, international trade in many manufacturing commodities, including high-technology goods, depends positively on the strength of the patent regimes in large developing countries. Consider an illustration that is highly speculative. Suppose that enforcement of China's new patent regime becomes strong enough to make patent rights 25 percent more effective than they are currently. According to the elasticity of imports of machinery with respect to IPRs that was implicit in table 4.8, there would be a rise in such imports of perhaps 0.3 percent of GNP ($2.8 billion in 1998 prices), other things being equal. This would represent a 5.6 percent rise in Chinese machinery imports. In terms of technology content, Coe, Helpman, and Hoffmaister (1997) found that a 1 percent increase in the share in GDP of imports of machinery and equipment from OECD countries tends to raise TFP in developing countries by an average of around 0.3 percent. In this context, assuming GDP otherwise rises by 4 percent per year, stronger patent rights in China could raise long-run TFP by as much as 0.48 percent annually over levels produced by standard determinants of TFP growth, strictly through the increase in machinery imports. To put this in perspective, the average annual increase in Chinese TFP over the sample period of 1971-90 was 3.5 percent. The additional imports would raise this average rate to 4.0 percent.[6]

A rise in TFP of this magnitude has important effects over time. Thus, for example, in 10 years' time Chinese GDP would be higher by 4.9 percent than it would be with existing factor accumulation and TFP growth. This would be a welcome productivity bonus. Yet I consider it a significant underestimate of the potential impact on productivity, given that the trade estimates are outdated and based strictly on a static model. A maximum estimate might be computed by applying Smith's result (1999); then such a change in patent rights would expand Chinese imports from the United States (and presumably from other technology-exporting countries) by around 15 percent. Assuming this percentage applied to machinery and equipment imports, it would imply in turn a long-run TFP bonus of 3.3 percent per year. Clearly, there is considerable uncertainty about this effect, but it would be positive in large economies and economies with significant imitative abilities.

More important channels of technology transfer are FDI, joint ventures, and licensing contracts. Empirical work demonstrates that the strength of IPRs and the ability to enforce contracts have important effects on MNE decisions on where to invest and whether to transfer advanced technologies. The estimates presented in table 4.11 demonstrated that American MNEs are sensitive to IPRs improvements in developing economies. The patent coefficient in the assets equation suggests that a 1 percent rise in local patent strength would raise asset stocks by 0.45 percent. Thus, let us assume that Chinese patents become 25 percent more effective. This

---

6. This calculation results from the formula: TFP growth = $(1.035)*(1.0048) = 1.04$.

change would imply, other things being equal, a long-run rise in the American FDI in China of around 11 percent.[7]

The impact of FDI on learning and technology diffusion in host countries has long been a subject of considerable controversy; it is impossible to review this enormous literature here.[8] In principle, FDI provides ample opportunity for productivity-enhancing learning and spillovers because it largely reflects the injection into an economy of an improved technology or other form of efficiency advantage. The essential question is whether such an injection raises productivity. MNEs often have been criticized as enclave producers that fail to integrate effectively with the broader economy in ways that would facilitate learning.

To the extent that additional FDI transfers more technology inward, there would be a positive direct impact on knowledge absorption in host economies. The subsequent diffusion of that knowledge into the broader economy is a complex process. IPRs could enhance that diffusion by ensuring greater contract certainty between enterprises and suppliers and by providing more protection for commercializing technologies in local markets. Further, enterprises would experience stronger incentives to train managerial and technical workers because the workers would feel more pressure not to misappropriate trade secrets. At the same time, IPRs raise imitation costs, thereby limiting diffusion of simple technologies at least temporarily. Learning by honest means could be slowed if the system were so protective that it markedly raised costs of inventing around patents. Finally, legal restrictions on defection of skilled workers would engender conflict between the objectives of training and diffusion.

Thus, two questions are significant here: Do FDI flows provide spillover benefits to the economy? How might IPRs influence this process? Recent empirical evidence supports the FDI learning-spillover hypothesis. There are numerous channels through which this might happen, including on-the-job training, expanded management expertise, other forms of human capital formation through learning of newer technologies, training of suppliers, labor mobility, and imitation. Competitive threats to domestic firms may induce them to adopt better techniques.

Romer (1993) claimed that cross-country evidence suggests that a country's growth performance is importantly associated with its utilization of ideas embodied in FDI. Aitken and Harrison (1993) discovered that, controlling for capital stock and other productivity determinants, higher foreign ownership in Venezuelan manufacturing plants was associated with higher plant-level TFP. However, this impact did not spill over into higher productivity of domestically owned firms, in part due to limited labor

---

7. This finding may not readily apply because it refers to majority-owned investments, which are controlled in China.

8. See Blomstrom (1989) and Caves (1996).

mobility between domestic and foreign firms. Aitken, Harrison, and Hanson (1994) found that Mexican manufacturing firms were considerably more likely to become exporters when foreign firms were located nearby, evidence of a spillover impact on productivity and quality. Aitken, Harrison, and Lipsey (1996) reported that high degrees of foreign ownership were associated with markedly higher wages in manufacturing industries in Mexico, Venezuela, and the United States, which they attributed to productivity enhancements associated with foreign technologies. Interestingly, higher wages existed mainly in foreign-owned firms: there was little evidence of wage spillovers into domestically owned firms in Mexico and Venezuela. In the United States, there was evidence that higher wages in foreign-owned firms induced rising wages in domestically owned firms because of competition for labor.

Feenstra and Hanson (1997) found that FDI in Mexico's maquiladora plants was associated strongly with rising wages of skilled workers and increased the wage disparity between skilled and unskilled workers. Dougherty's regression results (1997) indicated that, across manufacturing sectors, Chinese TFP growth among industrial enterprises was positively and significantly related to the extent of foreign direct investment between 1980 and 1995.

The conclusion to draw from this work is that FDI typically carries efficiency advantages through superior technologies, management skills, and marketing. These direct advantages introduced into host economies bear considerable potential for spilling over into higher productivity through learning and competition. However, the extent to which spillovers occur depends on other factors, such as labor mobility (that is, labor market flexibility), the human capital stock, and the structure of competition, as governed by openness to trade and entry of firms.

To illustrate the important linkages between FDI and local conditions for promoting growth, consider the regression results of Borensztein, De Gregorio, and Lee (1998). They discovered that inward flows of FDI from industrial countries to 69 developing countries over the period 1970-89 contributed positively to growth of the recipient nations, more powerfully than did domestic investment. However, the positive impact of FDI came through only in interaction with a human capital variable (male secondary school-enrollment ratios). That is, the positive contribution of FDI to growth was registered only for countries with human capital above a particular threshold. This threshold was exceeded by 46 of the 69 countries. The regression suggested that, at the average level of educational attainment in the sample, an 0.005 increase in the ratio of FDI to GDP would raise the annual growth rate of the recipient country by 0.3 percentage points. However, the estimated impact of FDI on growth in countries below the educational threshold was negative. The authors attribute this finding to the possibility that the relationship between FDI and growth is nonlinear and therefore poorly estimated at low levels of income.

The essential finding of these authors is that there is a strong complementary relationship between FDI and educational attainment in promoting economic growth. The explanation surely is that countries with greater skill endowments have stronger capabilities to absorb, use, and learn those technologies effectively. Thus, both the direct cost-reducing impact of FDI and the indirect spillover benefits for growth are more in evidence in developing economies with at least moderate levels of education.

In this context, IPRs could play an important role. As discussed in chapter 4, econometric evidence from Maskus (1998a) indicates that FDI reacts positively and elastically to stronger IPRs in large developing economies. Moreover, there is a positive correlation between human capital and the strength of patent rights. Virtually all of the countries in the Maskus sample have secondary enrollment rates in excess of the threshold in Borensztein, De Gregorio, and Lee (1998). Thus, it is reasonable to claim on this evidence that as these nations strengthen their patent regimes, the associated inflows of FDI will have positive growth effects. To illustrate, consider an increase in the GP patent index for Mexico from 2.29 to 3.25, roughly approximating the patent changes required between 1995 and TRIPs implementation.[9] Employing the implicit elasticity of US-owned asset stock to patent rights from table 4.11, this change would result in a long-run rise in these assets of perhaps $3.2 billion (1994 dollars). Assuming this process takes 10 years, there would be an implied increase in annual FDI of around $320 million, which would raise the average FDI-to-GDP ratio for the mid-1990s from 0.038 to 0.039.[10] The finding from Borensztein and his colleagues would then predict a long-run rise in Mexican growth of 0.06 percentage points, say, from 3.00 percent per year to 3.06 percent per year. Once again, this would be a significant growth bonus.

These results are buttressed by Park and Ginarte (1997), who focus on the relationship of patents, capital and R&D investment, and growth. They found no direct correlation between patent strength and growth but a strong and positive impact of patents on physical investment and on R&D spending, which in turn raised growth performance. Thus, it seems clear that IPRs, investment, and human capital accumulation work together to raise productivity and growth.

Turning from FDI to licensing, Mansfield's survey results, discussed in tables 4.9 and 4.10, point to the importance of IPRs in convincing MNE managers to transfer their most advanced technologies. There is practical evidence from China to support these arguments (Maskus, Dougherty,

---

9. In fact, because Mexico's IPR obligations under NAFTA are even stronger than under TRIPs, the ultimate change in patent strength will likely be even larger.

10. Figures adapted from UNCTAD (1998) and World Bank (1997).

and Mertha 1998). Managers of many foreign enterprises expressed great reluctance to locate R&D facilities in China, citing fear of misappropriation and patent infringement, even after the legal reforms in 1993. Nearly all reported that their enterprises transfer technologies that are at least five years behind global standards (unless other means can be found to protect them) or bring in technologies that will be obsolete within a few years. Note that the importation of lagging technologies is not necessarily inappropriate for a country with China's cost conditions; absorbing such knowledge can help motivate follow-on innovation. However, as nations like China move toward international best practices in several fields of technology the problem should become more restraining.

Note that the effective weakness of IPRs in China seems to affect market structure. For example, foreign enterprises are reluctant to license advanced technologies to unrelated enterprises, preferring instead joint ventures and majority-owned subsidiaries within which they maintain greater control of trade secrets. Importantly, concerns about weak IPRs have helped discourage both foreign-owned and domestic enterprises from fully integrating their Chinese operations. Instead they tend to divide production processes among facilities in order to avoid revealing all their technologies in any one location.

The practical implications of this are important:

1. Countries with weak IPRs are isolated from modern technologies; they must try to develop technological knowledge from their own resources, a difficult and costly task. In the terminology of development economists, they have large "technological distances" (Evenson and Westphal 1997).

2. They get fewer spillover benefits from new technologies in their economies.

3. The technologies that are available tend to be outdated.

4. Nations with weak IPRs experience both limited incentives for domestic innovation and depressed inward technology flows.

Building Markets and Improving Quality

IPRs do more than promote R&D and product innovation. They also encourage the interregional and international distribution and marketing that are important for achieving firm-level scale economies. Weak IPRs limit incentives for such investments because rights owners cannot prevent their marketing outlets from debasing the quality of their products, nor can they readily deter counterfeiting of their trademarks. Thus, IPRs permit effective monitoring and enforcement of activities throughout the supply and distribution chains, giving both innovators and distributors an incentive to invest in marketing, service, and quality guarantees. It is curious that, despite the obvious importance of these processes for business development, economists have paid little attention to them.

Among these issues, quality assurance is critical to safeguarding the interests of consumers. However, widespread sale of counterfeit products can ruin reputations achieved at considerable cost, especially for new enterprises, and the problem can be overcome only with additional costs. In principle, effective trademark enforcement both raises the average quality of products over time and provides a wider range of qualities from which consumers may choose.[11] This process is particularly important in food products, beverages, cosmetics, and medicines, where counterfeit products can be hazardous for consumers. Indeed, field research in China suggests that despite the advantages to poor consumers of having access to low-cost product knockoffs and unauthorized copies of entertainment products, they are becoming resentful that market saturation by unauthorized goods diminishes the range of legitimate goods available (Maskus, Dougherty, and Mertha 1998).

Global Research and Development

An important possibility is that consumers in nations with weak IPRs suffer because innovation is not aimed at their needs.[12] There is ample evidence that inventive firms in developed economies bias their research programs toward products and technologies for which they expect a large global demand and that may be protected through IPRs and trade secrets. This means that a disproportionately small amount of global R&D is focused on the needs of developing economies with low incomes and weak IPRs. For example, the World Health Organization (1996) claims that of the $56 billion spent globally on medical R&D in 1994, only 0.2 percent was aimed at pneumonia, diarrheal maladies, and tuberculosis, which together account for 18 percent of global illness. Virtually all of that research was undertaken by public agencies or military authorities.

However, the aggregate market for pharmaceuticals in the countries that will upgrade their patent protection as a result of TRIPs is sufficiently large that, even at current shares of drugs patented elsewhere, the rise in demand could be as much as 25 percent of global spending (Lanjouw 1997). This figure does not include China, which has already implemented product patents in pharmaceuticals. Thus, the incentives for R&D to focus on poor countries could be significant. While this is a crude calculation, it suggests that pharmaceutical firms could anticipate

---

11. While this statement is widely accepted by economists and business scholars and finds extensive anecdotal support, I have found no systematic econometric study of whether it applies in developing countries.

12. Diwan and Rodrik (1991) first analyzed this point.

higher profits in developing nations, some portion of which would be devoted to research on their endemic diseases. Note that it is likely that some of this additional R&D would take place in MNE research facilities in developing countries. Such decisions would depend on the strength of IPRs, local skill endowments, public infrastructure, and demand characteristics as markets grow.

While these salutary impacts are possible in principle, the likelihood of their emerging over even a long period of adjustment seems small. Pharmaceutical research aims at markets that not only are protected by patents but also provide sufficient demand. It will be a long time before consumers in the poorest countries, and the many impoverished citizens in middle-income developing countries, will be able to afford advanced therapeutic treatments.[13] Thus, additional research into cures for their ills may not be forthcoming if left to the private market.

How IPRs Hamper Economic Development

While strengthening IPRs has considerable potential for enhancing economic growth in the proper circumstances, it also implies important economic and social costs. Indeed, many developing economies and some rich countries may in the short run experience net welfare losses from global policy reform because many of the costs could emerge earlier than the dynamic benefits. This situation explains why it has proven difficult to organize interests to work for effective reform in many developing countries.

Closing Down Infringing Activities

There are likely to be significant amounts of labor employed in copying and retailing unauthorized products in most economies, though such activity is concentrated in poor countries. As nations introduce stronger trademarks and copyrights and expand their enforcement efforts, this labor must find alternative employment. This is the first challenge for policymakers dealing with stronger IPRs.

Some evidence on this point is available from a survey of the Lebanese economy in 1996 (Maskus 1997b). Lebanon is strengthening its legal basis for IPRs and increasing its enforcement activities in anticipation of a partnership trade agreement with the EU. (Because Lebanon is a small, relatively open economy, the illustration may not extend readily

---

13. This point has been made forcefully by Sachs (1999) and Sachs, Kremer, and Hamoudi (1999).

Table 5.1 Simulated static effects of stronger IPRs enforcement in Lebanon, 1996

Sector	Infringing employment	Legitimate employment	Net employment	Weighted price (%)
Software	−717	+426	−291	
Software				+18.5
Personal computers				+17.8
Printing & publishing	−642	+298	−343	
Printing services				+13.2
Books, etc.				+7.3
Music, video, & film	−500	+119	−381	
Music & video				+10.1
Film				+2.3
Food products	−2,681	−479	−3,160	+3.8
Cosmetics	−614	−119	−733	+4.3
Pharmaceuticals	−315	−235	−550	+10.0
TOTALS	−5,469	+10	−5,459	n.a.

n.a. = not available.

Source: Maskus (1997b).

to larger, more closed economies.) Lebanon's per capita real GNP in 1996 was $5,990, high enough to encourage emerging domestic interest in stronger intellectual property protection.

Table 5.1 presents simple partial-equilibrium calculations of the static employment and price impacts of stronger IPRs in several Lebanese industries. These calculations reflect the total effects of various aspects of IPRs. For example, copyrights in software were assumed to reduce piracy by 50 percent, which would lower infringing employment by 717 workers. However, it would shift demand toward products of legitimate producers and distributors, which claimed that they did not anticipate any rise in licensing costs from foreign software firms. As a result, legitimate employment would rise by 426 workers, leaving a net employment loss of 291 workers. However, workers in legitimate firms made far higher wages on average than those that would be displaced by copyrights. Moreover, it appeared that many of the skilled and partially skilled displaced workers would find employment in the noninfringing firms or would start their own enterprises.

The model also predicted a rise in software prices of 18.5 percent and in personal computer prices of 17.8 percent. These were sizable increases, reflecting rising markups to legitimate producers as copyrights become enforced. However, they are likely higher than they would be in large countries because Lebanon has a smaller market (preventing scale effects) and because it has quite restrictive sole distributorship laws. Thus, the additional market power generated in Lebanon by copyrights would be considerably stronger than might be experienced in larger countries, say, China or Brazil.

The remaining copyright sectors may be read similarly. As illegal copying is reduced, there would be net employment losses in printing and publishing and in music, video, and film. Book prices were predicted to rise only by 7.3 percent because the legitimate publishing sector is competitive in Lebanon; however, copyright enforcement would be expected to raise video prices by around 10 percent.

The situation is different in food products, cosmetics, and pharmaceuticals, which are subject to both trademark and patent regulation. The pharmaceuticals sector, for example, is built on copying and marketing active ingredients that may be patented elsewhere but are not currently patented in Lebanon. In the model, new patents were assumed to raise patent licensing fees by 50 percent and to remove imports and exports of infringing products, while trademark enforcement was assumed to reduce counterfeiting by 50 percent and to raise licensing fees by 20 percent. These effects not only would reduce infringement but also would raise costs for legitimate firms. Accordingly, employment would fall in both activities, with a total employment loss of 550 workers and a price increase of 10 percent. Employment effects in the food products sector were bigger because it is a larger industry, but price impacts were small because there are many competitive firms.

Overall, these static calculations suggest that employment in IPR-sensitive Lebanese sectors could fall by some 5,459 workers, about 0.5 percent of the formal labor force in Lebanon. In that sense the problem is small in relation to the overall labor market. However, it would be concentrated in areas where piracy is common or where industries built on copying are significant. Thus, there might be difficulties in providing alternative employment or cushioning adjustment costs. In general, such costs would be minimized in economies with flexible labor markets and rapid economic growth, making it easier to shift workers and firms into legitimate activities.

Market-Power Pricing

A major concern of technology importers is that strong patents and copyrights expand the market power of foreign providers of information and new products, permitting higher price markups. In turn, importing countries would experience losses in their terms of trade, while access to new products and key inputs could be diminished. The evidence on trade flows from Smith (1999), discussed in chapter 4, lends credence to this claim.

Though this basic view of IPRs has some grounding in fact, such fears may be overstated. Obviously, patents cannot apply to currently unpatented drugs, a fact that is often ignored in policy discussions. More fundamentally, the extent to which prices will rise in response to exercise of stronger market power is a function of several variables:

1. *Market structure* before and after the newer IPRs matters crucially. This area covers such elements as the number of firms (domestic and foreign) competing with rights holders, the type of competition, the ease of market entry and exit, quality differentiation among products, openness to trade, and wholesale and retail distribution mechanisms.

2. *Demand elasticity,* a key variable determining market power, may vary markedly across countries and over time.

3. *Pricing regulations,* particularly for pharmaceuticals, may blunt tendencies toward monopoly pricing, although at some potential cost in terms of reduced willingness of firms to supply markets that have such controls.

4. *Competition policies* may also limit monopoly practices. Examples are whether parallel imports are allowed and whether sole distributorship laws support market power.

Consider pharmaceutical patents. Under the TRIPs agreement, the nearly 50 developing countries in the WTO that did not provide patent protection for pharmaceutical products must do so by 2005. Indeed, many nations did so upon accession to the WTO. New entrants must also meet the requirements of TRIPs. No aspect of TRIPs is more controversial than the introduction of patents for medicines. The legislature of India, for example, found it difficult to establish the registration procedures and exclusive marketing rights required during the transition period. India has not yet implemented full patent protection.

It is remarkable how little is known about the potential effects of changing global policy regimes in this fundamental manner, despite the fact that the pharmaceutical sector is the most extensively studied of all IPR-sensitive industries. This information gap results from a scarcity of data to support estimation of key elasticities and market-structure parameters, and from uncertainty about the potential effects on prices, profitability, and innovation. However, several articles may help us understand the issues and get a sense of their tentative conclusions. The preponderance of conclusions is pessimistic about the net effects of drug patents on the economic welfare of developing countries (or, more accurately, of net importers of patentable drugs).

Nogues (1993) provided an excellent overview, listing a series of interrelated factors on which pharmaceutical pricing decisions depend. As noted originally by Maskus (1990), a key determinant is the structure of market competition before and after the introduction of patents for medicinal preparations.[14] Roughly stated, the more competitive the local pharmaceutical market before patents are awarded, the larger the prepatent share of drug production that consists of copies of patentable drugs, and the more inelastic the demand for medicines, then the higher will be the increases in prices associated with patents. Each of these factors depends on the strength of patent protection, of course, but also on collateral determinants of market structure, including trade protection, investment regulations, and marketing and entry restrictions.

The absence of product patents and the relative ease of entry into imitative production means that in countries without product patents significant numbers of small and medium-sized firms produce copies of drugs patented elsewhere. This prepatent structure characterizes (or has characterized) a wide range of countries, including Argentina, Brazil, Chile, India, Italy, Turkey, South Korea, Egypt, and Lebanon.[15] The Chilean study showed clearly that drug prices fell markedly in the presence of competing products (Coloma, Gabrielli, and Williamson 1987). The real price of Glaxo's aerolin fell by some 52 percent over the period 1983–86 as two competing copies came on the market; in the previous five years when aerolin was a monopoly, its real price rose by 45 percent.

Schut and Van Bergeijk (1986) presented evidence that, in a sample of 32 countries in 1975, a standardized pharmaceutical price index was much lower on average in countries without patents than in countries with patents. To isolate the impact of patents they econometrically related the price index to per capita GDP, per capita drug consumption, a dummy variable for the existence of patent protection (either process or products or both), a dummy variable for the presence of pharmaceutical price controls, and a dummy variable accounting for indirect price controls.

The results demonstrated that drug prices rose significantly with per capita income, fell with per capita consumption volume, fell with price controls, and rose with patent protection. The patent coefficient was insignificant, probably due to the inclusion of process patents and the inability to distinguish between enforced and unenforced product patents.

Thus, the preponderance of evidence suggests that preprotection market structures are relatively competitive in middle-income countries with significant imitative capabilities and that prices are sensitive to demand variables and patent protection. Further, there is likely to be a considerable element of oligopoly in the pharmaceutical industries in many developing countries after patents are recognized, because drug firms can differentiate their products through brand loyalty and marketing.

---

14. See also Subramanian (1995) and Maskus and Eby-Konan (1994), who develop numerous interesting extensions.

15. See Coloma, Gabrielli, and Williamson (1987), Katz and Groisman (1988), Kirim (1985), Lanjouw (1997), Maskus (1997b), and Scherer and Weisburst (1995).

In this context, it seems likely that the introduction of patents could place pronounced upward pressure on drug prices. As a crude indicator, for 20 products sampled in the United States in the early 1980s, the average gap between prices of branded products and of generic substitutes was 281 percent, with a range of 151 percent to 658 percent (Katz and Groisman 1988). This may overstate the potential effects of patents because the United States is a high-income economy with distinctive insurance markets. However, it may understate the effects because this comparison is between brand names and generics rather than between patented products and copies, which would present larger price gaps.

It is interesting that competition in prescription drugs increased dramatically in the United States in the 1990s, with the share of generic drugs rising from 19 percent in 1984 to 43 percent in 1996 (US Congressional Budget Office 1998). This competition stemmed from 1984 legislation permitting easier entry of generics, drug-product substitution laws permitting pharmacists to dispense generic drugs in place of prescribed brand-name drugs, and public and private cost-containment programs. In turn, manufacturers' discounts on brand-name drugs tend to rise with the number of generic substitutes and patented drugs with similar therapeutic qualities ("me-too drugs"). Thus, rigorous but honest competition can moderate the price effects associated with patents.

Anecdotal evidence compiled in Taiwan and China is consistent with the possibility that protection can induce significant price hikes. For example, it appears that uncontrolled prices of protected drugs at small pharmacies in Beijing and Shanghai have risen by a factor of three or four on average since the introduction of exclusive marketing rights in 1991 and patents in 1993.[16] Given the regression results reported above, such effects could be expected to be even larger in higher-income developing economies, though smaller in poorer nations.

The most extensive study I have come across is by Lanjouw (1997) for India. Her research showed that India currently has a highly competitive pharmaceutical sector: there are some 250 large pharmaceutical firms (12 of the 20 largest are Indian) and another 16,000 small producers. These firms are quite capable at product adaptation. For example, within seven years of its introduction in India, 48 firms were producing a version of Ciprofloxacin, which is patented in Europe and the United States. When Glaxo Corporation marketed a version of Zantac, it was quickly met with several local competitors who had already copied the drug, though Glaxo retained 40 percent of the market.[17] Interestingly, many of the companies competing with these patented drugs are foreign-owned MNEs.

Thus, competition is based essentially on product differentiation and brand recognition. In India brand advantages are important, reflecting

---

16. Based on interviews conducted in December 1997.

17. I am grateful to Jayashree Watal for this observation.

quality control, reputation, and physician prescription practices. Yet they seem to capture only perhaps a 10 percent price premium on uncontrolled products.

In such a setting, the introduction of pharmaceutical product patents could be expected to raise prices considerably if they are not controlled. Lanjouw (1997) compared the relative prices in 1995 of four patented drugs in India, the United Kingdom, and the United States.[18] The price of Ranitidine was 26 times higher in the United Kingdom and 57 times higher in the United States than in India. For Ciprofloxacin, the relative differences were 10 times and 15 times. Whatever the difficulties in these comparisons, it is clear that drug prices in India are very low in comparison with those in the United Kingdom and the United States.

As noted earlier, some of these differences are attributable to higher per capita incomes in the developed economies. Another distinction is that only about 4 percent of India's population is covered by medical insurance with prescription benefits, so that most consumers must buy drugs directly, making them more price sensitive. It seems that pharmacists are generally willing to substitute cheaper alternatives for prescription pharmaceuticals. Moreover, the Indian government subjects a large part of the pharmaceutical market to price controls. Finally, an important distinction between India and the United States is simply that the US provides product patents. For these reasons, India has drug prices that are quite low on a world scale.

Assessing these factors, it is likely that the most significant price-restraining difference is that India has not patented drugs since 1972, a fact that itself partially supports the competitive structure of the Indian market. Thus, as Indian patents are introduced in the next decade, prices are likely to be substantially higher on newly patented drugs than they would otherwise have been. Again, how much depends on numerous collateral factors. Much will depend on whether a new product dominates a therapeutic application or whether (and how quickly) alternative treatments (both on- and off-patent) become available. Put more simply, the larger the share of the drugs market that is patented, the higher will be the price impacts, which would vary also across therapeutic classes. The last point is important, for even though a relatively small share of overall registered drug sales in India in the 1990s were of products containing substances patented in Europe, the shares in particular therapeutic groups could be much higher. Note also that as incomes rise and as more consumers are covered by insurance, the demand for patented and branded drugs should become less elastic, supporting higher prices.

---

18. See also Danzon and Kim (1995), who documented carefully that international price comparisons in pharmaceuticals are difficult to make due to differences in price measures, dosages, and currency conversions.

This review suggests that the preponderance of forces will support markedly higher drug prices in economies like India as patents are introduced. Accounting only for static price impacts under elasticities assumed to vary by therapeutic class, Watal (1999) computed the potential price effects of introducing patents in India.[19] She assumed that patents would convert domestic pharmaceutical markets, currently highly competitive, into monopolies dominated by foreign patent owners. This assumption implied that price increases would be the maximum possible. Watal found that the weighted-average price increase for the patentable portion of the market would be 26 percent under linear demand and 242 percent under constant-elasticity demand from a 1994 base. Associated welfare losses amounted to between 3 percent and 8 percent of the total pharmaceutical market. These losses were much smaller than those simulated by Maskus and Eby-Konan (1994), Subramanian (1995), and Nogues (1993), because Watal took pains to characterize competition in the prepatent market more accurately.

Considering the qualifications mentioned earlier, Watal's estimate is probably conservative. Keep in mind that such increases potentially accrue only to new products that receive patent protection, not to existing products. Indeed, Rozek and Berkowitz (1998) could find no evidence of unusual price increases for pharmaceutical products already on the markets in South Korea, Mexico, Taiwan, and Hungary after they introduced patents. Factors that limited possible price hikes included competition within therapeutic classes, price regulation, monopsonistic (government) purchasing practices, and provisions in the patent laws aimed at maintaining competition.[20] Offsetting the potential for higher prices is the possibility of certain dynamic benefits that should not be ignored:

1. It is possible that a higher proportion of new drugs will be made available to countries as they protect patents, though product introduction in India seems to be not much different from protected markets.

2. Additional global research, as noted earlier, might be devoted to the diseases of poor nations, which currently attract a small proportion of global R&D funds.

3. Some of the additional R&D is likely to take place in MNE research facilities in developing economies. Market development activities could particularly be enhanced. Stronger patents (and trade secrets and brand

---

19. This is an update of an earlier study (Watal 1996).

20. As Watal (2000a) pointed out, the Rozek-Berkowitz results likely are biased because they did not compare baskets of patentable and patented drugs but included all drugs in particular therapeutic categories.

protection) should have the effect of lowering contracting costs and facilitating know-how transfers in the industry (Arora 1996; Yang and Maskus 2000a).

Finally, some observers argue that stronger drug patents will encourage local firms to devote additional R&D spending to developing patentable substances, a possibility about which Lanjouw (1997) is optimistic. In fact, the preponderance of evidence suggests that domestic pharmaceutical companies in developing countries are unlikely to marshal the considerable resources required to compete successfully at this end of the business. Evaluations of pharmaceutical stock prices in South Korea after patents were adopted suggest that investors expected drug firms to lose business and profits, though the situation was more positive in Japan (Kawaura and LaCroix 1995; LaCroix and Kawaura 1996). Nogues (1990) found no reason to expect increases in R&D by local pharmaceutical firms in Argentina. Similarly, survey results in Lebanon found no intention on the part of local drug firms to compete through product research (Maskus 1997b).

Finally, the establishment of product patents in 1978 in Italy was not accompanied by any increase in the inflation-adjusted trend of R&D expenditures or in the introduction of new chemical entities in that country (Scherer and Weisburst 1995). Some years after product patents came into force, there was, however, considerable consolidation of the Italian industry in terms of the number of firms, though employment and output have gone up faster there than in the general economy (Korenko 1999). Much of the consolidation was associated with takeovers by foreign enterprises. Moreover, real R&D expenditures have risen, but with a shift in their emphasis toward product development and marketing. Thus, the Italian evidence is not altogether clear on the innovation-inducing aspects of patents.

Another area of considerable concern in developing countries is the potential for IPRs to support monopolization of plant breeders' rights (PBRs). Under TRIPs, countries are obligated either to provide patents for new plant varieties and seed strains or to provide effective sui generis protection for inventors for minimum periods. Many developing countries have no protection for plant varieties. Patents give inventors exclusive rights for the production, sale, and import of seeds and varieties. The concern is that farmers in poor countries might not be able to afford key agricultural inputs priced under patent protection and would be forced to use older technologies. An environmental worry is that protection of breeders' rights could reduce genetic diversity over time. Questions are raised also about whether stronger protection will affect the ability of public research laboratories to develop and disseminate protectable materials.

In recognition of these problems, many countries have adopted other protections for plants, further limiting the exclusive rights granted. The farmers' privilege allows farmers, after buying protected seeds, to retain for their own use enough seed to plant the following year's crops. The breeders' exemption allows competing breeders to use varieties freely in conducting research leading to new plants. Neither limitation would generally be available under patent protection.

Unfortunately, there is virtually no empirical information available on the economic impacts of PBRs. One recent study in Argentina, Chile, and Uruguay, which have established such systems (Jaffe and van Wijk 1995), looked only at qualitative indicators of how PBRs affected private investments in plant breeding, plant breeding policies of public research institutes, international transfer of germ plasm, and seed diffusion among farmers. The systems of rights adopted have had mixed effects on these Latin American economies:

1. They have markedly improved the ability of private breeders to control local seed markets and prevent unauthorized trade in protected varieties. The controlled share of seed supply is above 55 percent in wheat and around 40 percent in soybeans, figures that compare favorably with those in the United States. As a result, market prices for seed have risen, though the extent of these increases was not reported.

2. These rights have increased access to privately developed foreign seed varieties, the developers of which are more willing to market their products in those countries.

3. The systems have well-defined farmers' privileges, which means that farmers have not been much disadvantaged. However, unauthorized seed dealers have seen their costs rise and some have been squeezed from the market. Over time increasing concentration of the market could result in further price increases.

4. It is interesting to note that government research institutes express strong support for the new systems because they can use the rights to protect the results of their research.

There are no systematic studies of how computer software prices vary across countries with differing levels of copyright protection and enforcement. It is often claimed that stronger protection would raise prices markedly in developing countries in light of comparisons between retail prices of legitimate and copied programs. For example, in December 1997 it was possible in Hong Kong to purchase a pirated copy of Microsoft Office 97 for approximately $6 (US), while the retail price for a legitimate copy was around $1,500. In the summer of 1998 the same product sold for around 8,000 RMB (approximately $1,000) in Beijing.[21] Thus, if

---

21. Field research done by the author. Prices are likely lower now.

strong enforcement were to support the substantially higher price of legitimate programs, the price impact on computer users would be severe. This is consistent with the static calculations for Lebanon reported earlier.

However, it appears that software firms prefer to sell in places like Hong Kong and China at low volumes with substantial markups, reflecting small markets with inelastic demand from corporate and government users. The markups accrue partially to local distributors, who may be protected also by restrictive distributorship laws. Thus, in a dynamic sense it is likely that as markets develop under copyright protection, authorized software firms will supply more copies of programs at considerably lower prices. Indeed, prices of copyrighted software have fallen sharply in Taiwan since the aggressive crackdown on counterfeiting in the mid-1990s, in part because of additional competition from local developers.[22] This is consistent with the fact that retail copies of Office 97 typically sell in the United States for $160-$200.

In summary, there are reasons to be concerned about elevated prices supported by the market power inherent in IPRs. However, if IPRs are introduced into competitive markets, these effects may be limited. Indeed, it makes little sense to protect market positions with both strong IPRs and barriers to competitive entry.

Higher Imitation Costs

One basic point of IPRs is to raise the costs of copying and imitation in order to expand innovation and learning through market channels. In nations where information diffusion comes largely through copying and imitation, growth prospects could be diminished. It should be noted that straightforward counterfeiting of copyrighted and trademarked goods is unlikely to achieve much technical progress, so raising those costs would not reduce growth.

The more fundamental issue is access to technological information. As suggested above, by raising imitation costs, pharmaceutical and biotechnological patents place considerable pressure on imitative enterprises in developing economies. Improving trade secrets protection will make it more difficult to acquire technologies through misappropriation, copying blueprints, and encouraging defection of technical personnel. Effective systems of PBRs could raise costs of developing similar plant strains. Copyright protection for software makes it more difficult to copy programs; if that change were accompanied by a ban on decompilation for learning purposes the ability of competing software firms to work on inventive applications would be diminished.

---

22. Interviews in Taipei, December 1997.

Such potential costs are real and explain the reluctance of many countries to improve their IPRs regimes. However, they must be put into broader perspective:

- These costs are counterbalanced by the potential for greater incentives to transfer technology through trade, FDI, and licensing. Indeed, it is likely that many pharmaceutical enterprises will find it necessary to achieve production and technology-sharing and marketing agreements with international pharmaceutical firms in order to survive.

- Stronger IPRs should improve prospects for innovative enterprises to enter markets with new products, a process that should accelerate with time and learning.

- Rising imitation costs need not be damaging if IPRs are introduced into a competitive economy in which firms can choose among many potential suppliers of technology and products.

Potential Abuses of IPRs

The essence of IPRs is to define the boundaries within which the creator of a piece of information with economic value enjoys exclusive rights to its use. These rights are limited by public policy interests in access, dissemination, and dynamic competition.

Abuses of the rights inherent in a patent, trademark, or copyright relate primarily to business strategy, including selling practices and licensing restrictions, that extend the scope of property rights beyond that intended.[23] There are few concrete guidelines because of the complicated nature of markets for information and technology. Vertical licensing agreements, for example, may ensure downstream product quality on the part of local vendors, which aids competition. However, tie-in sales to technology purchasers of unrelated products could represent an attempt to extend the scope of the initial property right, thus injuring competition.

In a later chapter, I discuss potential competitive problems raised by the exploitation of IPRs and appropriate competition policy approaches. Here it suffices to point out that the potential for competitive abuses is curtailed to the extent that competition policy is vigilant and, more importantly, to the extent that markets are open to both domestic and foreign entry. This observation points to the critical role of access to domestic markets in supplementing stronger IPRs.

---

23. There is a vast literature on the competitive effects of market power created by patents, trademarks, and protected know-how. Discussions may be found in OECD (1989), UNCTAD (1996), and Gallini and Trebilcock (1998).

Evidence on the Overall Impact of IPRs on Growth

Reforming IPRs could raise or lower economic growth, though the relationships would be complex and dependent on circumstances. Again, we are left with a difficult empirical question and only a limited body of evidence. One recent study considered the question empirically. Gould and Gruben (1996) related economic growth rates across many countries to the Rapp-Rozek index of patent strength, among other variables. They found no strong direct effects of patents on growth, but there was a significantly positive effect when patents interacted with a measure of openness to trade. That is, stronger patents in open economies raised growth rates by 0.66 percent on average, suggesting that market liberalization in combination with stronger IPRs tends to increase growth. The argument is that open economies experience greater competition, higher competitive FDI, and a need to acquire advanced technologies in order to raise product quality. Moreover, firms in open economies are more likely to undertake the costs of effective technology transfer and adaptation to local circumstances. However, such innovation will be more in evidence in economies with protection for intellectual property.

The growth impact of IPRs in open economies, associated with inward trade, investment, and technology flows, is significant. To illustrate, consider two economies with an initial real income per capita of $5,000. Over a 10-year period, if output in one economy grows 2.0 percent faster than population, real income per capita will reach $7,430. An identical (but more open) economy growing 2.66 percent faster than population would achieve real income per capita of $8,453. An important implication of this is that as developing countries strengthen their IPRs, accompanying market liberalization provides a more affirmative path to economic growth. Combining this outcome with the results in Park and Ginarte (1997), IPRs, openness, FDI, and human capital accumulation seem to work together to raise productivity and growth. To be sure, striking the appropriate balances among these complex processes is a considerable challenge.

Summary

Despite the complexity in the many relationships involved, empirical evidence supports an optimistic view about the potential impacts of stronger global IPRs on international economic activity, innovation, and growth and development. It is tempting to supplement these observations by pointing out that industrialized countries, which have strong systems of intellectual property protection, remain the overwhelming sources of new invention and artistic creation. Developing economies with weak IPRs generate few patentable inventions. These facts support the view that

IPRs and innovation go hand in hand and that IPRs are an important factor in technological and cultural development.

Or are they? The difficulty with strong conclusions is that counterexamples abound. As discussed in chapter 3, the United States refused to award copyrights to foreign authors until its own, highly competitive, authors were disadvantaged by an absence of reciprocity in Britain. Japan is commonly thought to have engineered its phenomenal technological "catch-up" by acquiring foreign technologies at concessionary terms, a process buttressed by a system of industrial property rights favoring dissemination of knowledge over its creation (Ordover 1991; Maskus and McDaniel 1999). Korea was able to absorb and develop considerable amounts of adaptive technological information in the absence of meaningful IPRs through the 1970s and early 1980s.

The role of IPRs in economic development is complex and multifaceted. Protecting intellectual property offers gains in innovation and market deepening but imposes costs through higher prices, reduced imitation, and potential abuses. I claim that IPRs can play an important and positive role in economic advancement, with the role becoming larger as economies grow richer. Even among poor economies, however, IPRs can be an important condition for business development, so long as they are well structured and accompanied by appropriate collateral policies. This is the essential challenge as economies adopt stronger IPRs under the new global system. It is the subject of the next two chapters.

6

The Global Policy Framework: Intellectual Property Rights and Wrongs?

As discussed in earlier chapters, the global regime of IPRs protection strengthened dramatically in the 1990s, primarily through TRIPs but also through unilateral initiatives and intellectual property chapters in regional trade agreements. I presented the legal structure of TRIPs in chapter 2, and defined the concepts in chapter 3 in order to set the stage for the positive economic analysis of international economic effects of IPRs in chapter 4 and of IPRs and economic development in chapter 5.

We are now ready to complete the circle by discussing important normative aspects of the new regime. This chapter focuses primarily on the TRIPs agreement itself, in terms of both its implementation and its potential effects on the international balance of costs and benefits. I also discuss the implications of differential standards for IPRs in regional trade agreements. The normative analysis, though grounded in data and economic logic, is necessarily rather speculative. I present it largely as a basis for wider discussion.

Putting TRIPs into Action

The TRIPs accord is still being implemented; it is also being reviewed for eventual revision. That makes it premature for us to make confident claims about how it will affect the well-being of people in particular countries. However, it is worth discussing in detail a number of important issues TRIPs brings up, among them problems in its implementation and administration. Moreover, it is important to understand that the minimum TRIPs standards still leave considerable flexibility for nations to select regulations promoting welfare-enhancing competition in their markets. Their decisions will be decisive in determining the ultimate distribution of gains and losses from the new global regime.

Implementation Issues

The TRIPs agreement is not solely about reform in developing nations. Several developed economies have changed their intellectual property laws in order to comply with TRIPs. For example, the United States, while retaining its unique system of awarding patents to applicants who demonstrate they were the first to invent a technology, now ensures that the term of patent protection is 20 years from the date of filing. Other countries award patents to the first to file successful applications.

Ireland has failed to adopt the EU's directive on rental rights, including rental rights for films, which complies with TRIPS.[1] The United States lodged a dispute at the WTO in May 1997 that is still pending. Thus, to an important degree the agreement updates protection even among those nations with strong prior regimes. To a far greater degree, the TRIPs requirements place significant demands for reform of the IPRs regimes in many developing countries. Primo Braga (1996) compiles some useful information: as of 1994, 25 developing nations (of 98 GATT contracting parties in this category) excluded pharmaceutical products from patent protection. Further, 13 of those countries failed to protect chemical products. In the full sample, 56 countries provided terms of protection for patents that were shorter than the 20 years required by TRIPs. Relatively few developing countries were members of UPOV and only six provided sui generis protection for plant varieties, although patent protection for plant strains was available in principle in a number of nations. Only 36 developing countries provided copyright protection for software as of 1994. Sherwood (1995) claimed that 8 of the 12 Latin American nations he studied would require changes in their compulsory licensing laws, as indeed would nearly any country that had adopted compulsory licenses before TRIPs entered into force. These figures point to the need for significant legal and institutional change in a broad sweep of the developing world.

Six years into the transitional periods, implementing laws and regulations are in place in a number of countries. Evidence of this may be seen in the significant increases in accessions to the WIPO Conventions and UPOV noted in table 4.1.[2] For example, Brazil passed new patent legislation in 1996 that was effective in 1997. The law extends the term

---

1. Rental and Lending Directive, 92/100/EEC.

2. TRIPs does not require entry into UPOV, though some countries find it convenient to do so as they implement plant variety protection.

of protection to 20 years from filing date, makes pharmaceutical products and agricultural chemicals patentable, and reverses the burden of proof in process patents. However, it retains fairly broad procedures for issuing compulsory licenses, subject to the limitations imposed by TRIPs. For this reason the Pharmaceutical Research and Manufacturers' Association (PhRMA), an international industry association headquartered in the United States, has called it inadequate.

As the Brazilian example suggests, implementation strategies adopted over the near term promise to be contentious. American trade authorities claim that adequate implementation and enforcement of obligations are US priorities that should be met before any further negotiations on IPRs.[3]

Administration and Enforcement

These expectations are likely to be disappointed for some time, for two fundamental reasons. First, it will take years for developing countries to actualize strong commitments to effective administration and enforcement of IPRs. The administrative mechanisms in many poor countries remain skeletal. The costs of establishing a system adequate to handling even counterfeiting cases, let alone complex conflicts over patent infringement, can be daunting. Institutional infrastructure has significant fixed costs in the form of examination and registration offices and equipment, drafting administrative procedures, and training examiners, judges, attorneys, and police and customs authorities. There are further recurrent costs for training, hiring new personnel, and upgrading IPRs systems—costs that will rise as IPRs come into greater use.

UNCTAD (1996) provides some rough estimates of the administrative costs of complying with TRIPs in various developing countries.[4] In Chile, additional fixed costs of this upgrade were estimated at $718,000 and annual recurrent costs at $837,000. An Egyptian expert thought fixed costs in Egypt would be perhaps $800,000, with additional annual training costs of around $1 million. Bangladesh anticipated one-time costs of administrative TRIPs compliance (drafting legislation) of $250,000 and over $1.1 million in annual costs for judicial work, equipment, and enforcement efforts. These estimates do not include training costs. Note that in Egypt and Bangladesh trained professional administrators and judges are extremely scarce, suggesting that these estimates may be low. One of

---

3. Interview with Joseph Papovich, Assistant US Trade Representative, *Inside US Trade*, 16 July 1999.

4. See also Finger and Schuler (1999) for a broader view of the costs of implementing the Uruguay Round in the least-developed countries.

the largest costs of implementing an effective administrative system is that it would divert scarce professional and technical resources into such administration and out of other productive activities. It should be noted that these estimates are based on survey responses provided by intellectual property experts in each nation, rather than on extensive studies using a standardized methodology. In that sense, they are questionable, if intriguing.

The existence of considerable fixed costs (in both a budgetary and an opportunity-cost sense) should mean that the demand for IPRs must be relatively large in order to induce a country to absorb these costs efficiently through the exploitation of economies of scale.[5] In itself, this means that small, poor countries are likely to have little commitment to adequate institutional reform.

Countering this problem are three factors. First, intellectual property offices may charge fees for examination and registration procedures to defray their costs. There is clearly a question of incentives here. The higher the fees, the lower the willingness of firms to apply for IPRs. Because such fees particularly disadvantage small start-up firms, some authorities have differential fee schedules depending on the size of the firm and the nature of the technology, potentially a useful prodevelopment strategy. Under TRIPS, such schedules must be applied on a national treatment basis, so it matters whether intellectual property offices are instructed to meet revenue targets or to facilitate applications and registrations.

Second, poor countries may petition for technical and financial assistance from industrial countries and WIPO and the WTO to help absorb the fixed costs of implementing new administrative and enforcement procedures. In practical terms, such assistance would need to come predominantly from the developed countries, because WIPO and the WTO have few resources for this task.

Third, developing country authorities may join cooperative international agreements to help cut their costs. Membership in the Patent Cooperation Treaty, for example, provides significant economies because examiners may read the opinions made by major patent offices about novelty and industrial applicability, rather than undertake such technical examinations themselves. Similarly, international trademark registries can cut the costs of looking for prior registration. These costs are further reduced by access to electronic databases on the internet. Thus, assistance in linking to these internet databases is useful.

Another difficulty lies in the straightforward political economy of IPRs. To enforce patents, trademarks, and copyrights is to shift market power from imitators to innovators. This has a number of subtle effects, but in

---

5. However, recall the econometric finding in chapter 4 that market size had little impact on the strength of patent rights.

the intermediate term the main effect is a transfer of rents, as amplified further in the next section. Owners of patents in developing countries are overwhelmingly foreign; there is little likelihood of that changing for a considerable period of time. The figures provided in table 3.2 attest to this situation. In Mexico, only 389 patent applications in 1996 came from domestic residents, while over 30,000 came from foreign residents. Brazil's domestic patent applications in 1996 amounted to just 8 percent of total applications. India's domestic applications were 20 percent of the total, but the absolute numbers were small in relation to India's size, reflecting its weak patent system. Canada and Australia also have low percentages of domestic patent applications; they remain significant net importers of intellectual property. South Korea and China are unusual in having experienced massive growth of domestic patent applications in the 1990s.

Countries in which patents and widely recognized trademarks are largely owned by foreign interests are unlikely to experience much domestic political pressure for reform or for effective enforcement. Instead, the profits and employment made from piracy and imitation constitute a powerful force against reform. As incomes grow and demands develop for higher-quality goods, and as firms are established and become more capable of innovation, interests in stronger rights emerge endogenously. But, as chapter 3 suggested, such processes in the patenting arena mature only at per capita income levels much higher than those found in most poor nations. Domestic preferences for protection of trademarks likely emerge at lower income levels, but those preferences must be strong enough to overcome the countervailing forces of infringement.

Copyright enforcement can be important for particular sectors in developing countries, such as boutique films and applications software for local markets, but such interests are faced with considerable consumer enthusiasm for pirated copies of music, films, and software platforms. These latter sectors often face significant entry barriers associated with high fixed costs of designing, producing, and marketing performances, films, and computer programs. Successful entry by information industries in many developing nations is difficult and probably far off.

Thus, domestic interests in developing economies are likely to oppose effective enforcement for the medium term. Continued external pressure and awareness campaigns may shift preferences marginally toward stronger protection but intellectual property owners in developing nations should expect infringement to continue in spite of new laws and regulations covering enforcement. Indeed, this view is consistent with American concerns about the potential ambiguity in the enforcement obligations in TRIPs.[6] For example, the requirement in article 42 that procedures be fair and

---

6. Papovich interview, op. cit.

equitable does not also require that they effectively deter counterfeiting. Judges must be given the authority to impose fines and sentences, but in practice they may not do so. These issues promise to engender disputes between intellectual property developers and industrial property authorities, even after TRIPs is fully implemented. It is likely that dispute settlement panels will be required to assess the true extent of the enforcement obligations over time.

Selection of Standards

Enforcement is important, but in dynamic terms the more critical question for the long term is whether the standards put forward in the implementation stage are appropriate for various countries. TRIPS sets out a list of minimum standards and countries cannot escape their obligations to implement them. However, these standards are generally quite broad, allowing considerable flexibility in their construction. This flexibility means that it is not necessary for countries to emulate the highly protective practices of the United States and the EU, which go well beyond those required by TRIPs in numerous dimensions. Rather, it is possible to select from a menu of IPRs standards and limitations with a view toward promoting certain economic and social objectives.

Designing and implementing appropriate standards is a complex business. In effect, TRIPs encourages nations to pursue their own goals in intellectual property rights, subject to two significant constraints:

1. The procedures adopted must meet at least minimum thresholds, which are considerably higher in some cases, notably in patents, than most previously in place in developing countries.

2. The regulation of IPRs cannot discriminate against foreign interests and cannot seriously prejudice the exploitation of IPRs by foreign firms. Either would invite the wrath of authorities in the technology-exporting countries and could backfire by discouraging the use of intellectual property assets in local markets.

Within this framework, it is possible to set out reasonable approaches to meeting TRIPs obligations while still paying attention to a country's needs. Economic development is a dynamic process; IPRs may be used fruitfully to push it forward. The dynamic shortcoming of absent or weak IPRs is that economies are liable to remain technologically isolated and increasingly to lag behind the information frontier. Such economies emphasize free riding on the technical advances of others, a strategy that has short-run competitive advantages but suffers from inadequate access to new technology and a growing inability to develop local strategies for fostering R&D and technical change.

The task in selecting IPR standards is to ensure that they promote dynamic competition, encouraging the transfer of technology from abroad that may be learned and diffused through the economy in acceptable ways. In short, TRIPs represents an opportunity to structure intellectual property rights to convert "free riders" into "fair followers" in Reichman's (1993) apt phrase. It is evident that countries at different levels of economic development would prefer to set standards of varying degrees of liberality.[7] The least-developed countries might opt for TRIPs-consistent minimal standards with wide limitations. Middle-income industrializing economies should see the value of more protective standards and firm recognition of trade secrets. Countries where most technology developers reside would prefer strict standards combined with regulation of competition. Given this variability in interests, definition of the word "fair" is problematic, depending on income levels, cultural traditions, and preferences.

A brief review of how standards may be varied is instructive.[8] First, consider patents, which must apply to all fields of technology for a minimum 20-year term under TRIPs. Yet countries may take advantage of exclusions from patent eligibility for purposes of maintaining public order, national defense, and environmental protection. They may exclude therapeutic, surgical, and diagnostic techniques, though not medical equipment.

Consistent with practice in many developed economies, patents need not be extended to scientific principles, mathematical formulas and algorithms, and discoveries of nature—a provision that could support excluding genetic discoveries. Patents need not pertain to higher life forms, nor must plant varieties be patented if they are protected by another system. Finally, the stipulation in TRIPs that computer programs be protected with copyrights as literary devices seems to envision that patent protection need not be extended to software. This exclusion appears in the patent laws of Brazil, Argentina, and China.

Beyond the eligibility question, countries have flexibility in defining the conditions for protection: Article 27.1 leaves the determination of these conditions up to each country. Developing countries could choose high standards of novelty and nonobviousness in order to certify an invention as patentable, though requirements much in excess of global practices would be of questionable utility. Patent authorities might be instructed to recognize only narrowly written claims, in order to promote the ability of competitors to invent around patents. In this context, a system of utility models or petty patents, with significantly lower thresholds defining the "inventive step," is procompetitive in principle, for it encourages domestic incremental innovation.

---

7. See Evenson and Westphal (1997) for a fuller explication of such strategies.

8. See also Oddi (1996), Watal (2000b), UNCTAD (1997), and Reichman (1993).

Authorities could also permit (1) opposition proceedings before the grant of a patent and (2) early disclosure of patent applications. So long as the right of priority is recognized and frivolous opposition is deterred, such procedures do not unduly prejudice the interests of applicants, and they encourage learning and information diffusion throughout the economy. Indeed, the United States has recognized the value in this approach by introducing legislation in 1999 to publish applications within 18 months of filing, consistent with European and Japanese practices, in order to promote dissemination of new information.[9]

Article 30 of TRIPs provides that member states may allow for unauthorized use of patented inventions under certain circumstances, so long as these exceptions do not unreasonably interfere with exploitation of the patent and do not unreasonably prejudice the legitimate interests of the patent holder. In practice, this allows countries to permit limited use for private and noncommercial purposes, for research and experimental or teaching purposes, and for preparation of individual medicines by pharmacies. It might also be invoked in the process of approving generic drugs, though a WTO dispute between the EU and Canada is testing this interpretation. Such limitations appear in the patent laws of many developed countries.

TRIPs places new limitations on the use of compulsory licenses of patented information but clearly recognizes their potential usefulness as competition-enhancing devices to ensure access to critical technologies. Indeed, on close reading Article 31 offers much leeway for specifying conditions under which compulsory licenses may be used (Watal 2000). It reflects a carefully crafted compromise between technology developers and potential users and does not unduly burden policymakers wishing to employ compulsory licenses in specified circumstances. Significantly, Article 31 does not limit the grounds for compelling licenses to abuses of patent rights, as some had sought. It is silent on how countries may define "working requirements." Nonexclusive and nonassignable licenses may be issued when patent holders have failed, within a reasonable period of time, to negotiate voluntary licenses with applicants offering reasonable commercial terms. Licenses must be used predominantly in domestic markets in order to protect the rights-holder's interests abroad. The rights holder should be paid adequate remuneration based on the economic value of the authorized use. Less stringent requirements pertain to compulsory licenses issued to correct practices that have been demonstrated by authorities to be anticompetitive.

The TRIPs language thus amounts to an increase in the cost of acquiring licenses but not a significant interference with conditions under which

---

9. This procedure would apply only to those inventions for which overseas protection is also sought, because those applications are subject to disclosure abroad in any event. Those applying only domestically could prevent 18-month disclosure.

licensing may be compelled. Recall, for example, that the new Argentine patent law expressly envisions the use of compulsory licenses, potentially permitting domestic pharmaceutical firms to retain relatively flexible access to foreign-owned patented drugs and chemical processes. It remains to be seen how sparingly such conditions will be applied.

As noted earlier, TRIPs requires member states to afford some protection for plant varieties, via either patents or an effective special regime. This is a new obligation. Such protection is not common in developing countries; and it is unlikely that many developing nations will provide patents for the foreseeable future. Rather, while countries are not required to join UPOV, they may be expected to follow its general framework of protection.[10] In particular, countries may provide for a breeders' exemption and a farmers' privilege. The farmers' privilege in particular, though unpopular among plant variety developers, is widely seen as an effective antidote to higher seed prices.

From the standpoint of dynamic efficiency and learning, it is sensible for technology-follower countries to encourage reverse engineering as an honest competitive practice, fully consistent with TRIPs. Such a right allows potential rivals to use unpatented information, but only at the cost of undertaking their own, potentially costly and time-consuming engineering and design efforts. While the issue has not been studied systematically, the procompetitive aspects of trade secrets in otherwise com-petitive economies has been supported analytically by Friedman, Landes, and Posner (1991) and advanced forcefully by Reichman (1994). Indeed, a regime protecting confidential information but with liberal treatment of reverse engineering could promise considerable dynamic benefits for industrializing economies.

For reasons discussed earlier, trademark protection can be similarly valuable in developing nations, for it provides incentives to develop brand recognition for domestically produced high-quality crafts, clothing, and foods, among other goods and services. It also could reduce the costs of transferring technology and monitoring licensees, tending to expand technology trade and franchising. Because the potential supply of trademarks is limitless, there is likely to be little effective market power associated with all but well-known international marks, which must be protected from speculative registration. To the extent that trademark owners impose

---

10. UPOV was originally negotiated in 1961 and revised in 1978 and 1991. Countries may adhere to either of the latter versions if they are members. UPOV 1978 requires provisions for the farmers' privilege (including the right to retain seed for own use and for noncommercial exchange or sale) and the breeders' exemption discussed earlier. However, UPOV 1991 disallows the exchange or sale of seeds and mandates that authorization of the rights holder be obtained for use of a variety that is essentially derived from a protected variety. Because of these and other less restrictive conditions, many developing countries have opted for UPOV 1978 over UPOV 1991. However, currently only the latter is open for accession (Watal 2000).

unreasonable or anticompetitive commercial conditions on licensees or engage in monopoly pricing, recourse may be made to competition policies and the international exhaustion doctrine.

In copyrights, TRIPs allows countries to set their own parameters of fair use or the unauthorized use of copies for achieving social objectives. Clearly, copying on a commercial scale cannot come under the rubric of fair use, for it would limit the value of the copyright. However, it is acceptable to allow limited copying for educational and research purposes; some countries extend the doctrine to a single "private use" exception. There are provisions in many countries, including the United States, for compulsory licensing of cable television broadcasts in order to serve remote areas. The scope of copyrights may also be limited by the first-sale doctrine and parallel imports.

In computer programs, wholesale copying must be prohibited, along with slavish copying of computer code. However, copyright by definition protects only expression; TRIPs therefore allows reverse engineering of software by honest means. In this context, programs that deliver essentially similar functional performance as original software are legitimate forms of competition, despite concerns about this standard on the part of major software developers in the United States. This ability to decompile software in order to understand the unprotected aspects of the code is partially responsible for the growth of applications software industries in numerous economies, developed and developing.

Copyrights and neighboring rights have considerable potential for encouraging cultural industries in developing countries, including film, broadcasting, literature, and music. To advance this potential, countries should establish an institutional framework, including national collection societies, to transfer consumer benefits to creators and performers. Finally, copyright protection should enhance the access of citizens and institutions in developing countries to electronic databases—at protected prices.

Beyond these and other functional areas of protection, both developing and developed countries must make choices about collateral regulations that bear directly on IPRs. Important among these policies are competition regulations and the treatment of parallel trade. Chapter 5 noted the strong implication that IPRs function best in open, competitive economies; competition maintenance is a crucial supporting mechanism. However, the issues are complex, as I discuss in the next chapter.

Within this broad milieu, nations have considerable latitude to set standards for IPRs and to regulate the behavior those IPRs engender. In principle, governments may be expected to establish standards that, while consistent with minimum TRIPs standards, could tilt the balance of competition toward technology users. It is evident that many choices made during the implementation period will not be to the liking of intellectual property developers in industrial nations. Their concerns will be reflected in diplomatic representations and WTO disputes lodged by trade authorities, claiming that particular standards counter the intentions of TRIPs or that enforcement efforts are inadequate. Such cases will clarify TRIPs over time as panel reports accumulate judicial interpretations. In this important sense, perhaps above all, the TRIPs agreement remains a work in progress.

The Balance of Advantages and Costs in TRIPs

With its enormous complexity and the uncertainty about its implementation and operation, it is too soon to be confident about how TRIPs will affect economic interests in various nations. However, the issue is so important that some form of preliminary assessment is required. To do so, it is informative to organize the discussion into a temporal framework and to clarify the costs and benefits, only some of which may be quantified even roughly, that might emerge.

Short-Term Effects: Whither the Rents?

Despite considerable enthusiasm for the long-run implications of stronger IPRs, it is impossible to escape the logical conclusion that, in the short run, the policy reform essentially creates more market power where there was less. Because the ownership and exports of intellectual property are concentrated in the hands of firms in a few developed economies, the effect of TRIPs will be to shift the terms of trade in their favor, away from intellectual property importers. In turn, profits will be shifted from both developing countries and developed countries with a comparative disadvantage in intellectual property marketing, toward a few developed economies, the United States in particular. This process has been characterized as "a form of disguised US strategic trade policy" (Harris 1996, 361). Rodrik (1994, 449) claims that "to a first-order approximation, TRIPs are a distributive issue: . . . the effect of enhanced IPR protection in LDCs will be a transfer of wealth from LDC consumers and firms to foreign, mostly industrial-country, firms."[11]

Indeed, this is essentially the point of partial-equilibrium analyses of the potential effects of stronger patents in pharmaceuticals (Maskus 1990; Maskus and Eby-Konan 1994; Subramanian 1995; Watal 2000a; Fink 2000). The conclusion from those analyses is that the rent transfers in awarding pharmaceutical product patents—assuming current patented market shares would continue as new products come on line but that market structure would be transformed—could range from small to large.

---

11. LDC stands for less-developed country.

This rather unsatisfying statement should be recognized for its qualitative importance. Additional market power awarded to predominantly foreign interests must reduce short-run welfare in technology-importing countries. If the market power is significant, as would be the case where initial market structures are competitive but the potentially patented share of the market is large, the transfers could be costly. Such calculations pertain strictly to monetary measures; they do not attempt to assess any spillover costs from reduced nutrition and health status as a result of higher-priced foods and medicines.

McCalman (1999b) made a more serious attempt to look comprehensively at the rent transfer issue. Rather than inferring the existence of market power indirectly from trade statistics, he followed Eaton and Kortum (1996) in looking at 1988 bilateral patent statistics for 29 countries, incorporating both industrial and developing nations. However, rather than assessing only the extent of technology transfers through the patenting channel, he also analyzed the implicit price of those transfers as it is influenced by patent rights. In particular, using an approach pioneered by Pakes and Schankerman (1984) he was able to infer the value of patent rights in each country by relating local parameters to the decision to patent. These parameters include the fiscal cost of patenting, the strength of patent protection, demand, and market structure variables that otherwise permit appropriation of the rents to an innovation. To make the idea concrete: an American firm, in deciding whether to patent in Mexico, would pay attention not only to patent costs and patent protection, but also to whether local imitation is likely to be effective without patents. If patents were costly or unnecessary for protecting the invention, the firm would choose not to absorb the cost and would supply the market through another channel, if at all.

McCalman used the Ginarte-Park (1997) index of patent rights, which is useful in this context for it decomposes patent laws into components reflecting specific characteristics. This permitted a closer attempt at capturing the patent changes TRIPs requires country by country. For example, Canada has strengthened patent enforcement by making infringement subject to criminal action and by providing for preliminary injunctions; it has raised the private value of patents by removing local production working requirements. Many developing countries must adopt similar enforcement mechanisms, remove working requirements, provide for reversal of burden of proof, and lengthen patent duration. Because each of these components, and others, may be identified in the GP index, their impact on patent value could be estimated econometrically using dummy variables. These coefficients are then applied to bilateral patent data to compute the anticipated rise in patent value, reflecting higher rents to domestic and foreign patent owners.

The econometric model was based on a theory that inventors license their technologies (intermediate inputs, which may or may not be patented locally) to domestic firms, who then compete with potential imitators. Inventors charge a price that leaves domestic firms just willing to use the technology, taking into account expected obsolescence from imitation. Thus, before imitation occurs, inventors earn rents to new technologies.

In essence, the effect of stronger patents is to reduce the likelihood ("hazard rate") that imitation will be successful at any moment in time. The extent of this reduction depends on institutional changes to the patent laws, in addition to local demand and market structure effects. By making imitation more costly, stronger patents permit higher license fees for inventors, which translate into greater net rent transfers abroad to the extent that licensers are foreign. In turn, the higher license fees on existing patents move licensees up the demand curve, generating some additional deadweight losses.

McCalman's results are sufficiently striking that I list in table 6.1 estimates that I have updated from his computations. Before discussing these, it is important to understand the basic calculations. The counterfactual exercise was to ask what the additional net present value of patents would have been in 1988, had each country in the sample provided patent rights that complied with TRIPs. Because innovation and patenting rates were held constant, it was inherently a static calculation and an exercise in shifting rents.

I have used national GDP deflators and exchange rates to update McCalman's figures to millions of 1995 dollars. The figures were updated solely to reflect price changes between 1988 and 1995. The experiment still was McCalman's calculation of patent-valuation changes. While the update increased the magnitudes of the estimates somewhat and changed the net rent transfer ranking of some countries, it did not affect the central message.

In table 6.1, the overwhelming share of rents transferred by stronger global patent rights would accrue to the United States. Because its patent policy was already essentially TRIPs-compliant in 1988, the US was not required to strengthen its laws more than marginally, implying only a small outward rent transfer on existing patents. However, its massive ownership of patents abroad, in conjunction with stronger aspects of patent laws, would have earned an additional $5.85 billion in inward transfers, for a net transfer of $5.76 billion. In the terms of modern trade theory, this is an example of strategic trade policy, par excellence. Of course, it is equally appropriate to consider the weakness of international patents pre-TRIPs as a strategic trade intervention of technology-importing countries.

Other developed countries that would receive net inward transfers are Germany, France, Italy, Sweden, and Switzerland. Though the United Kingdom would experience a sizable gross inward rent flow of around $588 million, it would have an even larger outflow of around $1.22 billion, because TRIPs required the UK to provide for preliminary injunctions, to establish reversal of burden of proof in certain process patent

Table 6.1 Estimated static rent transfers from TRIPs-induced strengthening of 1988 patent laws (1995 $ millions)

Country	Outward transfer	Inward transfer	Net transfer
USA	92	5,852	5,760
Germany	599	1,827	1,228
France	0	831	831
Italy	0	277	277
Sweden	13	230	217
Switzerland	474	510	36
Panama	0	0.3	0.3
Australia	177	154	−23
Ireland	71	12	−59
New Zealand	79	8	−71
Israel	125	32	−93
Colombia	132	2	−130
Portugal	138	0	−138
Netherlands	453	314	−139
South Africa	183	15	−168
Greece	197	2	−195
Finland	281	47	−234
Norway	277	25	−252
Denmark	330	77	−253
Austria	358	83	−275
Belgium	470	111	−359
India	430	0	−430
South Korea	457	3	−454
Spain	512	31	−481
Mexico	527	1	−526
Japan	1,202	613	−589
UK	1,221	588	−633
Canada	1,125	85	−1,040
Brazil	1,714	7	−1,707

Source: Author's update of McCalman (1999b).

cases, and to make willful patent infringement subject to criminal action.[12] In the econometric model, these changes combined to increase substantially the value of UK patent protection in an amount much larger than the rise in the value of foreign patents held by British inventors. The Japanese case is similar.

---

12. These calculations reflect McCalman's interpretation of how well the GP index captured both existing patent laws and those required by TRIPs. For example, it is questionable whether TRIPs in fact required the United Kingdom to adopt criminal enforcement in patent cases, as he claims. Thus the estimates could suffer from two sources of measurement error and, indeed, McCalman's point estimate of the net UK transfer had a high standard error (that is, a relatively low degree of confidence). Nonetheless, the central message is important and the relative ranking seems accurate.

Among developed economies, Canada would realize the largest net loss from net changes in patent values. Again, the reason is that Canadian patent changes would sharply increase the value of patents held there. However, because foreign patents held by Canadian firms are overwhelmingly located in the United States, their value would not increase by much.

Among developing countries, the gross outward transfer would rise with the size of economies and the extent to which patents were strengthened. Because it owns so few patents, India would receive negligibly higher inward transfers, but the value of foreign-owned patents would rise by $430 million. The result for South Korea is similar, but outdated. Since 1988 South Korean firms have been granted far more patents abroad, suggesting that in current terms, the gross inward transfer could be much larger. Brazil would experience the largest net outward transfer among all countries in the sample.

These rent transfers are significant in both statistical and economic terms. McCalman compared these magnitudes to the benefits from liberalization of goods trade reported by Harrison, Rutherford, and Tarr (1996). That report used a computable general-equilibrium (CGE) framework to compute the international distribution of benefits from tariff cuts on manufactures, liberalization of agricultural protection, and elimination of the Multifiber Arrangement, as negotiated in the Uruguay Round.

Comparisons of the results of these two papers are questionable, though interesting. Harrison and colleagues found that the short-run gains for the US from multilateral trade liberalization were about $14 billion (in 1995 dollars).[13] Thus, the rent transfer gain on patents of $5.9 billion would raise this benefit by 42 percent.[14] Canada's short-run gains would be cut by 94 percent, from $1.106 billion to $66 million, and Brazil's by 76 percent, from $2.239 billion to $532 million. Accounting for the patent-valuation aspect of TRIPs, Mexico would actually experience a net welfare loss in the short run.

McCalman went on to compute the deadweight losses in each country from stronger patents. As discussed in chapter 3, these deadweight losses refer to the surplus lost when technology purchasers move up their demand curves. Net static welfare impacts would be the sum of net rent transfers in table 6.1 and deadweight patent losses. In his calculations, only the United States, France, Germany, and Italy registered net welfare gains from this effect of TRIPs. For all countries, the additional deadweight losses induced by stronger patents amounted to as much as 20

---

13. These gains comprised both efficiency effects and the recapture of rent losses on agricultural and textile quotas.

14. McCalman's static calculations are not meaningful in the long run, so I do not provide a comparison to the long-run results in one study by Harrison's group.

percent of the global efficiency gains from trade liberalization. These are big impacts, with benefits accruing largely to the United States.

The way to think about these results is that, as Eaton and Kortum (1996) demonstrated, there are technology spillovers across borders through international patenting. The bulk of those spillovers were channeled from American R&D to foreign competitors. The point of McCalman's analysis is that patent rights in many countries were inadequate to allow American inventors to extract more than partial rents from this licensing. Thus, TRIPs clearly shifts the rules of the game to favor US inventive firms. The net static result is losses for countries that are essentially technology importers or must strengthen their patent rights, or both, but gains for technology exporters with strong patents. As a whole, the world must lose in static terms because the effect of stronger patent rights is to raise global market power, engendering deadweight efficiency losses.

Moreover, similar processes would apply when other IPRs, including copyright and trademark enforcement, are strengthened. Careful analysis has yet to be done, but given the substantial sales of software, recorded entertainment, and consumer goods in developing countries, the transfer effects could be significant. Again, the conclusion is inescapable: the short-term impact of TRIPs is redistributive, with profits being shifted from imitative interests largely but not solely in developing economies to a few developed countries.

Long-Term, Will TRIPs Lift all Boats?

It follows that advocates of stronger IPRs in technology-importing countries must rely on claims that dynamic long-run benefits will emerge that outweigh the short-run costs. Economic analysis is less amenable to quantifying such gains because they are inherently uncertain. Significant shifts in policy, as represented by TRIPs, engender more than just price effects on existing volumes of goods, services, and technologies. They also change the structure of market competition and alter the payoffs on innovation and technology transfer.

As I indicated in chapter 4, there is considerable evidence that trade, FDI, and licensing react positively to the strength of IPRs. By themselves, increases in such activities do not imply increases in welfare in the host country, though there may be a presumption in that direction associated with competition, learning, and skill acquisition. It does seem that at least FDI is positively correlated with growth processes in economies that strengthen their IPRs.

In this context, it is interesting to compute the potential long-run effects of stronger patent rights on trade, FDI, and licensing volumes in selected countries (see table 6.2). The first column lists the GP index values as of 1995. Those in the second column are my rough estimates of what those

Table 6.2 Estimates of how TRIPs patent changes affect international flows of economic activity for selected countries (1995 $ millions)

Country	GP1	GP2	Mfg. imports[a]	High-tech mfg. imports[a]	FDI assets[b]	Unaffiliated royalties & license fees[c]
USA	4.86	4.90	308	−3	n.a.	n.a.
Canada	3.24	4.30	2,713	−42	−7,873	227
Germany	3.86	4.60	2,823	−64	−3,781	322
UK	3.57	4.60	3,726	−68	−17,229	351
Ireland	2.99	4.30	656	−14	−1,609	n.a.
Netherlands	4.24	4.60	109	−2	−1,133	24
Switzerland	3.80	4.60	880	−24	−2,382	60
Spain	4.04	4.60	2,734	422	−413	56
Portugal	2.98	4.00	1,973	309	290	n.a.
Greece	2.32	4.00	2,637	365	327	n.a.
Australia	3.86	4.30	338	−7	−846	44
New Zealand	3.86	4.30	80	−2	−135	7
Japan	3.94	4.50	1,610	−37	−4,078	1,261
Israel	3.57	4.30	971	149	200	19
Mexico	2.52	3.80	7,349	1,942	4,068	174
Brazil	3.05	3.75	1,351	271	1,391	49
Argentina	3.20	3.75	719	123	414	37
Chile	2.74	3.75	1,056	144	510	n.a.
Panama	3.53	3.75	7	na	134	n.a.
Colombia	3.24	3.75	417	68	156	n.a.
South Africa	3.57	3.75	184	25	27	24
South Korea	3.94	4.30	2,072	446	188	271
China	2.00	3.25	16,020	2,693	657	n.a.
Thailand	2.24	3.25	6,384	1,390	1,017	n.a.
Indonesia	2.27	3.25	3,163	318	861	79
India	1.17	3.25	6,552	653	573	260
Bangladesh	1.99	3.00	145	15	n.a.	n.a.

mfg. = manufacturing.
n.a. = not available.
a. Updated from Maskus and Penubarti (1995).
b. Computed from Maskus (1998a).
c. Computed from Yang and Maskus (2000c).

values would be after full TRIPs implementation. In brief, these estimates cluster countries at particular index levels, depending on prior existing protection and per capita income. For example, within the EU, low values are assigned to the poorer member states in recognition that their standards and enforcement efforts will continue to lag those of the richer states. Mexico is assigned a higher index than the other middle-income Latin American nations by virtue of its membership in NAFTA. The minimum index is 3.0, which is calibrated to a lower-bound implementation of TRIPs standards.

Some of the hypothesized changes in the GP index are quite large, such as those for Greece, Mexico, and India. In such cases the application of elasticities estimated from an econometric model is particularly questionable because the underlying relationships are not likely linear. Thus, large changes in the policy variable may not engender changes that are consistent with the linear model. In the present case changes in the patent index have large impacts on predicted activity flows. In consequence, the estimates for countries with big index shifts are likely overstated.

With this caveat, consider the changes in imports of manufactures that could be induced by tighter patent regulations after TRIPs is phased in completely. These calculations, listed in the third column of table 6.2, result from applying the elasticities estimated by Maskus and Penubarti (1997) to 1995 imports. The volume effects depend on patent revisions, market size, and the extent to which the imitation threat would be relaxed by TRIPs. Results range from a small impact in the United States, which is not required to undertake much legal revision, to substantial increases in imports in China, Thailand, Indonesia, India, and Mexico, which must make significant changes.[15] Mexico has accelerated updates of its IPRs regime in part because of NAFTA commitments. The result here suggests that a substantial component of Mexico's increase in manufacturing imports in the 1990s may be attributed, other things being equal, to stronger patent protection.

It is instructive that many of the largest predicted impacts are in nations with strong imitative capacities. In contrast, Bangladesh would experience relatively weak impacts, though still positive.

The fourth column of table 6.2 reports similar computations for imports of high-technology manufactures, defined as pharmaceuticals, electrical machinery, and professional instruments. The sectoral regression estimates from the Maskus-Penubarti study implied that stronger IPRs in developed economies would actually reduce such trade because of a market-power effect and a diversion of trade to developing countries, which had strongly positive import elasticities in these goods.

Overall, the trade volume effects estimated here are significant for developing economies that undertake extensive patent revisions. For example, the increase in manufactured imports for Mexico of $7.3 billion would amount to 12 percent of its manufactured imports in 1995. Though this is likely an overestimate because of the large increase in patent rights entertained in the calculation, it does suggest that the effect of stronger patent rights could be important. This effect would take years to emerge because the patent obligations would be phased in over time.

---

15. China has largely met TRIPs requirements in anticipation of joining the WTO.

The increase in China's high-technology imports of $2.7 billion would amount to 2.5 percent of its manufacturing imports in 1995. Applying again the result from Coe, Helpman, and Hoffmaister (1997), this finding suggests that the stronger IPRs required by TRIPs could raise Chinese TFP by perhaps 0.25 percentage points per year, a significant productivity impact.

Consider next the potential impact of TRIPs on the international distribution of FDI. The figures in the fifth column of table 6.2 result from applying the elasticities of asset stocks (majority-owned by US-based MNEs) to changes in patent strength, taken from Maskus (1998a). Recall that the assets equation generated a negative coefficient on patent rights, suggesting that on average stronger patents would diminish local asset stock. However, there was a large positive coefficient on patents interacted with a dummy variable for developing countries, resulting in a positive elasticity. This result likely means that at low protection levels internalization decisions encourage FDI as patents get stronger, but that as protection exceeds a particular level, a substitution effect favors licensing over investment. In brief, there is negative elasticity of FDI with respect to patent rights in high-income economies but strongly positive elasticity among developing economies.

Using these estimated elasticities in conjunction with anticipated changes in patent rights engineered by TRIPs predicts the effects on asset stocks indicated in table 6.2. Reductions in asset stocks in the United Kingdom, Canada, and Japan would be large in absolute terms, around 2 or 3 percent of 1995 FDI assets. However, FDI is predicted to rise significantly in Brazil, Mexico, Thailand, and Indonesia as a result of stronger patents. Indeed, the increase in Mexican FDI assets would be 7.1 percent of US-owned assets in that country; in Brazil it would be 3.2 percent.

Turning finally to licensing, the figures in the final column of table 6.2 update results from Yang and Maskus (2000c), who estimated the effects of international variations in patent rights on the volume (in 1990 dollars) of unaffiliated royalties and licensing fees (a proxy for arm's-length technology transfer) paid to US firms. The elasticity of licensing with respect to patent rights was estimated to be 2.3, suggesting a significant sensitivity of technology trade to IPRs protection. Applying this elasticity to anticipated changes in patent rights, using existing fees in 1995, generates the predicted changes in volume. Japan would have a large absolute response, reflecting the importance of licensing in the Japanese economy. However, large responses, relative to prior licensing fees, were also predicted for South Korea, Mexico, India, and Indonesia. Indeed, the analysis suggests that arm's-length licensing volume in Mexico would rise by a factor of nearly three and in Indonesia would more than double.

Recall that this analysis cannot distinguish between a higher technology content of licensing contracts and higher costs of acquiring technology licenses. To the extent the predictions relate to the former, there would be additional technology learning available in recipient economies.

The findings just reported predict long-run impacts of the TRIPs patent provisions on imports, FDI, and market-based technology transfer. These figures may be uncertain but they are sufficiently robust for us to conclude that stronger IPRs could have potentially significant positive impacts on the transfer of technology to developing countries through each of these channels, especially in large developing countries with significant imitative capabilities. The results are less striking for the least developed economies, where the effects, though positive, are smaller.

Perhaps it is a leap of faith for poor countries to trust TRIPs to enhance their growth. However, there is a substantial body of anecdotal evidence that points to growth-enhancing structural changes in competition as various IPRs are strengthened. The strongest advocate is Robert Sherwood (1990, 1997), who has extensively studied these processes in Latin America. He cites an interviewee in Mexico, for example, who claimed that small companies developing a process or product innovation found it easier to attract investment after the new Mexican patent law provided greater certainty about its exploitation. Others have claimed that there was a significant increase in biotechnology patent applications after the 1991 patent law came into effect and that larger Mexican companies stepped up their internal R&D programs.[16]

In a similar vein, the interviews we conducted in Lebanon (Maskus 1997b) and China (Maskus, Dougherty, and Mertha 1998) provided evidence that product development and firm entry are elastic to the protection of trademarks, even in widely disparate markets. Further, trademark and trade secrets infringement was at least as costly to domestic as to foreign firms, who had greater resources to deal with it and more options to withdraw from the market.

Of course, anecdotal evidence does not demonstrate robust correlations across countries and time periods. Indeed, for every country that has been pushed forward by IPRs, it is possible to identify countries that engineered effective technological catch-up behind weak intellectual property protection. Japan, for instance, had a diffusion-oriented patent system after World War II and a policy of encouraging technology transfer on concessional terms; South Korea offered wide exclusions from patent eligibility until the late 1980s. Arguably, this also characterizes the United States, which provided no copyrights to foreign authors in the 19th century and until recently had weak trade secrets protection in many states.

Thus, as is typical in the intellectual property arena, it is difficult to make strong claims about the overall net distribution of gains and losses that could emerge from implementation of TRIPs. It seems clear that, in

---

16. Despite this claim, Mexican nationals have not appreciably increased their propensity to patent in the United States (www.uspto.gov).

the short run, countries that provide weak protection for imported technology, software, and entertainment products will find it more—perhaps significantly more—costly to acquire these items. The problem may be particularly severe for the poorest countries, though there are reasons to question how much more effective their IPRs will become as a result of TRIPs. In those countries, prospects for greater domestic innovation and enhanced dynamic competition seem remote. Their chances of benefiting from TRIPs stem mainly from its inclusion in the Uruguay Round agreements, which offer scope for effective compensation through greater market access abroad in textiles, apparel, and agriculture.

The potential rent loss extends to larger, semi-industrialized developing economies. However, in such countries domestic interest in advancing IPRs protection is emerging and might successfully transform their imitative skills into effective technical capabilities for legally adapting foreign technologies. Improving IPRs in a competitive and open economy could not only attract markedly more investment and technology licensing from abroad, it could also provide important incentives for domestic entrepreneurs to build new firms and market new products.

Net technology importers even among developed countries, such as Canada, Australia, and New Zealand, will find costs rising as a result of TRIPs. These negative effects stem not only from somewhat stronger domestic patent rights but also from the fact that the large potential increase in IPRs among industrializing, middle-income countries could reduce the relative attractiveness of such countries for investment. However, these are two-edged swords: markets in these countries are rapidly moving toward the home development of advanced technologies and new products in niche markets, as recent evidence suggests in Australia (Maskus 1998d). Such technologies and goods will also find expanding markets in developing countries as those nations strengthen their IPRs.[17]

The essential message from this analysis is that the economic implications of TRIPs will be different in each country, depending on a variety of complex factors. Among these are each nation's means of implementing TRIPs and its management of IPRs within its broader economic policy. At least as important are competitive market structures and endowments of human capital and technical skills. Thus, it is possible to be optimistic about the potential long-run effects of TRIPs, even in countries that currently lag well behind the technological frontier, as long as nations surround their IPRs with growth-enhancing supplemental policies. I return to this subject in the next chapter.

---

17. McCalman's bilateral results indicated, for instance, that TRIPs would result in a net rent transfer from India to Australia of $16.4 million and from Mexico to Canada of $5.5 million.

TRIPs as an Economic Optimizer

Is TRIPs a movement toward a global economic optimum? This is a difficult question—perhaps even an unfair one. In theoretical terms, one could imagine a global economic planner setting policies to maximize net consumer surplus, with utility depending negatively on prices and positively on the introduction of new goods and cost-reducing innovations. Maximization would be subject to resource constraints and production functions, including those for developing and commercializing new knowledge. The solution to this problem would be to set IPRs (and other policies, such as tax incentives for R&D or human capital subsidies) so that the marginal benefit of additional products exactly balances the marginal cost of enhanced market power and induced investment in R&D. If the marginal gains to new products were larger than the marginal costs, it would be appropriate to tighten global IPRs protection. In the full economic solution, the planner would ensure Pareto efficiency by directing some compensatory payments (market access commitments) to individuals or countries because of the redistributive impacts associated with asymmetric comparative advantages in knowledge creation.

Such arguments support including TRIPs in the multilateral trading system. Intellectual property protection left entirely to national discretion suffers from two externalities, in principle: (1) Weak and variable patents could generate international spillovers from innovation with inadequate compensation, tending to reduce global growth. (2) The ability of domestic enterprises to free ride on international inventive activity could translate into policy competition that keeps national protection levels below what they would be in a globally welfare-maximizing configuration. The need for policy coordination provides a primary justification for a multilateral agreement on IPRs.[18]

In reality, things are not so neat. IPRs are by nature second-best solutions to the problem of static and dynamic failures in markets for information. They seek to provide adequate incentives for creators to invest in new information and to ensure users reasonable access to it. Necessarily this requires creating market power. Market failures often are magnified in an international context, where preferences vary across borders and over time. No instrument like TRIPs can be expected to operate efficiently on all margins in creating and disseminating information and, indeed, no such set of policies could be designed or negotiated. Unlike the competitive ideal of free trade that drives trade liberalization, there is no clear benchmark against which to assess the efficiency of a global IPRs agreement.

---

18. One model making this case is put forward by McCalman (1999a). The arguments have not been tested empirically.

TRIPs may be expected to promise important dynamic global benefits if three questions are answered affirmatively:

1. Has the world been underinvesting in R&D, in the sense that socially valuable innovations have not been developed?

2. Does TRIPs set up sufficient incentives to induce significantly larger amounts of R&D?

3. Would there be adequate distribution of the fruits of this R&D across countries and regions?

On the first point, surveys suggest that there are high returns to private R&D in many developed economies and that the social returns considerably exceed the private returns.[19] Evidence on whether this is true globally is scarce, but given the findings in developed countries there may be a presumption in that direction. If so, the argument for stronger global IPRs through a mechanism like TRIPs is supported. To the extent that TRIPs promotes harmonization of technology protection policies at high levels, it would have the dynamic advantage that R&D resources would be aimed at projects with the highest global payoff, rather than toward projects only in countries with existing protection. If more innovation were targeted at developing countries with currently weak IPRs, they would achieve a dynamic benefit as consumers, providing a partial affirmative answer to question 3. Thus, TRIPs presents some promise of increasing the dynamic efficiency of global R&D allocation over time.

It is possible also to anticipate a positive answer to question 2. With TRIPs, major net exporters will reap greater returns on their intellectual property. According to McCalman's calculations (1999b), the additional returns could well be large enough, even in static terms, to induce further innovation. Moreover, because TRIPs improves the appropriability of future inventions, uncertainty in making such investments should be diminished. As markets expand in the presence of higher average levels of intellectual property protection, it is plausible also to expect increased innovative activity.

This positive view must be tempered by two observations. First, the survey evidence mentioned in chapter 4 indicated that, except in a few sectors, firms did not consider patents important stimulants to investment in R&D. Rather, imitation lags and marketing advantages provided sufficient lead time for first movers to extract most of the rents from innovation. If so, strengthening patent protection abroad would add market power generally but would induce more R&D only in such industries as pharmaceuticals, agricultural chemicals, and biotechnology. While promoting innovation in those sectors is important, the broader outcome

---

19. See the articles in Griliches (1984).

would be disappointing. However, this evidence is likely outdated. International imitation lags have fallen and second-comer firms in more countries have become effective competitors in many sectors.

Second, firms endowed with greater market power may optimally choose to earn higher rents without necessarily investing them in product innovation. It is possible to doubt, for example, whether Hollywood film production or American software innovation needs the stimulus of stronger foreign copyrights to induce them to market more products.[20]

As for whether TRIPs effects a reasonably broad distribution of gains across countries in the long run, an affirmative answer would require belief in the ability of IPRs to induce more rapid growth in developing nations. A number of mechanisms could support this possibility. Surely, however, the likelihood of such positive outcomes varies sharply by country.

It is therefore not surprising that developing nations insisted that TRIPs require only partial harmonization of IPRs by specifying minimum standards with a number of exceptions and limitations. Thus, while TRIPs clearly will upgrade protection around the world, it affords flexibility in designing national IPRs regimes.

The question of whether TRIPs will achieve a global economic optimum cannot be answered because we cannot identify the optimum. However, it moves incentives toward greater protection of new information, which could expand innovation and open new channels of technology acquisition. Recognizing the clear redistributive effects that would emerge from strong harmonization, it retains some flexibility for nations to choose their own regimes. By encouraging countries to recognize IPRs as fundamental conditions for promoting business, it should improve prospects for growth in many parts of the world.

Nonetheless, these beneficial impacts could be offset by exercises of market power on the part of IPRs holders and by arbitrary and excessive use of regulatory powers by government authorities. Thus, the answer to whether TRIPs moves the world closer to an optimum must be that it depends on the reactions of participants. Moreover, TRIPS is at least as much a political-economic equilibrium as it is an attempt to promote dynamic efficiency. Thus, it remains a work in progress and subject to additional reforms, as analyzed in the next chapter.

Regional Initiatives

The negotiation of TRIPs has not precluded the emergence of regional agreements on intellectual property protection, typically within the con-

---

20. This possibility is consistent with the finding by Mutti and Yeung (1997) that the enforcement of Section 337 by US trade authorities tended to raise complainant profits without increasing their R&D.

text of broader preferential trade areas (PTAs). Taking a page from the extensive policy coordination among countries of the EU through the Single Market Program, PTAs increasingly aim at deep regulatory integration. IPRs lead this integration. To the extent that regional standards become more protective and more harmonized than global standards under TRIPS, some interesting analytical questions emerge. In this section I address these issues qualitatively. To illustrate the concepts, consider the North American Free Trade Agreement: chapter 17 sets out substantive requirements for minimum IPRs standards that must be pursued by member nations. There is broad overlap between NAFTA and TRIPs; indeed, provisions in the former accord at times served as inspiration for provisions in the latter. Nonetheless, NAFTA standards are stronger in several important areas (Maskus 1997a). For example:

- In copyright NAFTA declares illegal the use of decoding devices for intercepting satellite transmissions.

- NAFTA requires pipeline protection for pharmaceuticals in the process of achieving regulatory approval, rather than the exclusive marketing rights provided in TRIPs.

- NAFTA establishes a five-year exclusive-use provision for confidential test data, which is absent from TRIPs.

- NAFTA sets out somewhat stronger protection than TRIPs for computer chips and trade secrets, and has tougher enforcement requirements.

- Finally, NAFTA gives participants less leeway in national implementation. For example, Mexico would find it more difficult to adopt fair-use exemptions and compulsory licensing procedures under NAFTA than under TRIPs.

The region that has advanced most toward international harmonization is the European Union. Membership in the EU requires the adoption of a series of policy directives issued by the European Commission on treatment of areas as diverse as database protection, confidential information, and biotechnological inventions. Moreover, the widespread membership of EU nations in the European Patent Office provides considerable uniformity in patentability standards. Given the EU's high average incomes, it is no surprise that EU standards are typically stronger than those of TRIPs.

There are also less extensive regional agreements on IPRs in the Andean Group and among several African nations.[21] In negotiating its Euro-Med trade agreements with several Mediterranean and North African nations,

---

21. On the Andean Group see Correa (1999).

the EU requires the partner country to adopt standards that are at least consistent with those in TRIPs. Similarly, the United States has actively pursued stronger standards in developing countries through bilateral investment treaties. For its part, the Asia Pacific Economic Cooperation Forum (APEC) typically exhorts its members to establish schedules for improving their intellectual property regimes.

The interesting point here is that in significant ways the IPRs provisions are stronger in NAFTA and the EU than in TRIPS. This situation raises questions about the efficiency implications of strong regional standards. Any answers would be only speculative at this point, and may always be, because identification of the effects would likely be impossible.

The issues relate to the inherently second-best character of both regional trade preferences and IPRs. The essence of PTAs is to provide discriminatory treatment in commercial policy; thus, there could be intellectual property *creation* (IPC) and intellectual property *diversion* (IPD). The former occurs when more intellectual property is created and marketed within a region strictly due to the expansion of regional demand and the replacement of inefficient local technology developers with more efficient ones. More fully integrated North American markets for technology and product development plus harmonized IPRs should help rationalize R&D programs in all three NAFTA member countries. For example, in some industries, such as chemicals, food products, and advanced textiles, plant-level scale economies tend to be high relative to firm-level scale economies. Given high transport costs to Mexico in those sectors, this situation could induce North American MNEs to transfer some of their R&D to Mexico. At the same time, in sectors with high firm-level economies associated with knowledge capital, such as transport equipment, machinery, and telecommunications, the effect should be to concentrate R&D efforts in the United States. Such rationalization impacts should provide long-term dynamic efficiency gains for the member nations, though perhaps at the expense of medium-term transition costs.

Perhaps more interesting is IPD, which occurs to the extent that less intellectual property owned by nonmember firms is exploited within the PTA. This could take the form of reduced demand for the products of those firms, reduced FDI within the region due to investment diversion, and market-based exclusion of foreign firms from regional technology development programs. This could happen even if the intellectual property standards within the PTA do not discriminate against nonmember countries.

Ultimately the question is whether the emergence of more and larger trading blocs sustaining regionally distinctive IPRs regimes would add to or subtract from the movement toward global uniformity implicit in TRIPs. Thus, while TRIPs is likely to offer more incentives for innovation aimed at global demands, those incentives could be offset by the skewed incentives created by regional trading arrangements. Such a system could result in significant structural inefficiencies in many countries.

Summary

This chapter discussed the potential implications of the intellectual property norms emerging under TRIPs, arguing that the agreement will significantly upgrade global protection. As many countries are still in the implementation stage, decisions on the standards to be implemented could be contentious in trade policy terms. Nonetheless, countries at varying levels of economic development should recognize that the agreement is essentially a compromise between preferences of technology developers for strong standards and the needs of technology followers for flexibility. Countries should opt for standards that, while fully consistent with the requirements and spirit of the agreement, can promote dynamic competition in and reasonable user access to their markets.

The short-term effect of TRIPs should largely be to redistribute innovation and imitation rents away from intellectual property users to intellectual property developers. What is remarkable is that these benefits would accrue so heavily to the United States, while the net outward transfers would come from a broad swath of nations.

Nonetheless, there is reason for optimism about the longer-term effects of stronger IPRs on a global scale. Particularly in the markets of middle-income developing economies, stronger IPRs could have significantly positive effects on imports of high-technology goods, FDI, and inward technology transfer.

The evidence presented here also sets out a framework for thinking about how such gains in international economic activity could spill over into higher growth. It must be recognized, however, that the likelihood of such gains emerging depends strongly on the competitiveness of economies that strengthen their systems and on broader, collateral, regulatory systems. Thus, while it is important that TRIPs provides flexibility for countries to implement standards, they should be complemented by measures that set the stage for dynamic benefits.

7

Benefiting from Intellectual Property Protection: Take the Medicine, but Get Some Exercise, Too

Governments in many developing countries justify stronger IPRs by claiming hopefully that this policy reform will result in greater inward flows of technology, a flowering of local innovation and cultural development, and a faster ability to close the gap in technological sophistication between themselves and rich countries. But improved IPRs by themselves are highly unlikely to engender such salutary effects. One need think only of the differences between countries in sub-Saharan Africa, with long-standing and relatively strong laws (though limited ability to enforce them), and countries in East Asia, many of which reformed their regimes only in the 1990s. The first group attracts little FDI and registers few patents at home or abroad. The latter group attracts the bulk of FDI in the developing world and is experiencing rising intellectual property protection (Maskus 1998d; Maskus, Dougherty, and Mertha 1998). Expectations that stronger IPRs alone will bring technical change and growth are likely to be frustrated.

A close reading of chapters 3 and 4 indicates that empirical claims that IPRs can generate more international economic activity and greater indigenous innovation are conditional. Other things being equal, such claims may be valid—but other things are not equal. Rather, the positive impacts of IPRs seem stronger in countries with complementary endowments and policies. Countries must ensure that their new IPRs regimes become a positive tool for promoting beneficial technical change, innovation, and consumer gains. In this chapter I consider these interactions.

While national action to complement stronger IPRs is critical, it is also important for the world as a whole to undertake initiatives that could expand the global gains from intellectual property protection and effect a more equitable distribution of those gains. Thus, the second point of departure in this chapter is to discuss global policy questions that link tightly to IPRs. Each of these issues, such as how to encourage further technology transfer and promote research into diseases endemic to impoverished nations, may be addressed on the grounds of both efficiency and equity. Ultimately, the objective is to strike a balance between the needs of information developers and of information users, with due regard to market externalities that may not be well managed, and could be exacerbated, in a framework of strong IPRs.

National Policies to Optimize IPRs

Implicit in some of the earlier discussion in this book is the claim that intellectual property protection works best in an environment of open competition, risk taking, and adequate engineering and entrepreneurial skills. Further, the inherent market difficulties of providing incentives for invention and innovation are only partially addressed by IPRs, leaving a role for public policy. Accordingly, governments could be advised to complement their intellectual property regimes with policy reforms along the lines of those listed here.

Human Capital Development

Perhaps the most important complementary factor is a firm commitment to education, training, and skill development. The positive role of educational attainment in economic growth is well established. Although no systematic econometric study has looked for a significant interaction between education and IPRs in growth equations, it is plausible that one exists given the results of Gould and Gruben (1996), Borensztein, De Gregorio, and Lee (1998), and Park and Ginarte (1997). The obvious argument is that an economy with greater skills is likely to invest more in innovation and product development, but such investment is more likely where IPRs are protected.

There are other strong arguments. Smith (1999) found that foreign exporters trade more with countries that have strong imitative abilities as they improve their IPRs, because the threat of imitation is reduced. An equally plausible interpretation is that IPRs are a stronger stimulus in countries with adequate skills than in countries where skills are scarce. One reason is that a nation with a greater supply of technical and managerial skills is more capable of successfully adapting foreign technology to local conditions. Teece (1977, 1986) found that the costs of transferring technology decline with increases in the supply of technical and professional workers. As discussed earlier, strengthened IPRs also may reduce transfer costs as licensers and licensees operate in an environment of freer information flows and greater certainty.

Finally, economies with stronger educational attainment and skill endowments are more capable of diffusing technical information into competitive uses through honest discovery and competition. Nelson and Pack (1999) point to the importance of learning and technical adaptation as critical in fostering structural change in East Asian economies. While this may have happened in an environment of permissive imitation and copying, the abundant formation of human capital was an important factor. With stronger IPRs it becomes yet more important that a sound basis of education and skills be built for competitive purposes.

Factor Market Flexibility

Stronger IPRs are likely to raise pressures for structural adjustment in many economies. Counterfeiting activity will be reduced significantly over time by copyright and trademark enforcement. The task of reallocating toward legitimate activities the jobs engaged currently in piracy will be easier the more flexible the labor market is in terms of internal migration and employment costs. Field evidence suggests that a significant number of pirate firms continue producing similar goods legitimately under licensing agreements after IPRs are enforced (Maskus 1997b). In this sense, the adjustment problem may be less difficult than envisioned. However, net job losses from formerly infringing firms could be significant in countries that rely extensively on counterfeiting. Countries may wish to establish training and assistance programs for displaced workers, an effort that conceivably could be advanced by technical and financial assistance from abroad.

It is also important to foster flexibility in the market for technical and managerial personnel, because they are important conduits for learning and adapting technologies to new uses—being careful not to interfere with the legitimate protection of trade secrets through nondisclosure requirements, however.

The issue of capital markets may be more one of scale than flexibility. In particular, the ability of local entrepreneurs to undertake R&D and to commercialize new products is greatly constrained when capital is limited. The problem is compounded if investment resources are allocated for political purposes, preventing the funding of new products. Thus, countries may wish to liberalize restrictions on international and interregional capital flows, recognizing that foreign investors may be willing to take risks on new enterprises.[1] Establishing venture capital markets may

---

1. Field research found anecdotal evidence that foreign venture capitalists are actively seeking new projects in Taiwan, Hong Kong, and China to the extent they are allowed to take equity positions (Maskus, Dougherty, and Mertha 1998).

be appropriate in some circumstances. It is also advisable to move toward market allocation of investment and away from public direction of capital, which is liable to be distorted by political imperatives.

Technology Infrastructure

While IPRs are an important encouragement for technology development, acquisition, and adaptation, they may be usefully supplemented by programs to promote national technical change. Developed countries and many higher-income developing countries have extensive systems of such support, ranging from public assistance for basic R&D in universities and research institutes to extension services in agricultural science. They also provide incentives for commercialization of the fruits of public research and encourage collaboration among private firms and between private and public enterprises for the development of new technologies and products. Such models might be usefully adopted in many developing countries if they are tailored to specific circumstances and are procompetitive.[2] However, there is an opportunity cost to the allocation of scarce budgetary resources to collaborative R&D programs. For example, the social returns to such programs in the least-developed countries likely would be small in relation to those from further improvements in primary education and other pressing development needs. Thus, the expected benefits of this approach would vary with the level of economic development.

No country has developed the relationships among government, university researchers, and the private sector further than the United States. There is a moral hazard problem associated with university inventions (Jensen and Thursby 1999). The practical development and commercialization of such inventions is unlikely to occur unless the inventor's income is tied to its sales, that is, to sales of a license via royalties or equity. Thus, in the absence of commercialization incentives university inventors would tend not to focus on inventions with marketable applications. In recognition of such problems, the Bayh-Dole Act of 1980 gave universities the right to retain title to and license inventions resulting from federally sponsored research. In response, research-based universities have established extensive offices for acquiring and managing patent rights. Licensing of university-discovered inventions, which mushroomed in the 1990s, now accounts for a significant portion of the use of patents in the United States.

The American model is inappropriate for most developing countries, whose educational resources would be better devoted to improving

---

2. See UNCTAD (1995b) for a full discussion.

primary and secondary instruction. Nevertheless, this experience suggests that in many countries technology development processes could benefit from greater incentives to bring publicly sponsored inventions to the marketplace. Survey evidence claims that public research institutes in developing countries often create useful inventions that languish without commercialization (UNCTAD 1995b). This problem is common, for example, in state-run academies of science in China, as readily admitted by Chinese officials engaged in fostering domestic technical change (Maskus, Dougherty, and Mertha 1998). Finding mechanisms for public agencies and private enterprises to cooperate in such commercialization could bring a number of new technologies to the market, with benefits for consumers. Intellectual property protection would play an important role in sorting out the appropriate claims to the returns from commercialization.

The issues go beyond public-private research partnerships. To the extent that the private market does not provide enough investment in product development, there would be a rationale for public assistance. Limited R&D could be associated with factors such as an inadequate environment for risk taking, taxation systems that fail to recognize R&D as a business cost, and weak information flows about technological opportunities. Policies could remove such impediments, especially by ensuring competitive prospects for small and medium-sized enterprises, which remain the source of much innovation in both developed and developing countries.

One strong reason for encouraging R&D by local enterprises is that it is an important condition for effectively absorbing technologies transferred from abroad. One clear example is the finding by Dougherty (1997) that in Chinese manufacturing enterprises TFP growth induced by foreign licensing contracts is significantly higher in sectors where domestic partners were engaged in R&D programs of their own.

These examples point out, again, that strengthening IPRs alone is not likely to generate much incentive for additional domestic innovation and inward technology transfer. Governments should also pay attention to mechanisms for improving the local environment for technical change.

Open Market Access

It is not difficult to understand why, relative to closed economies, economies that are more open to trade and FDI experience a growth premium from strengthening their IPRs. Stronger property rights create market power, which is more easily abused in economies that are not open to foreign competition. Perhaps the most significant effect of trade liberalization is the injection of foreign goods and techniques that compete with previously protected oligopolies. These procompetitive gains have been shown to be significant in a variety of contexts and at different levels of development.[3] In that sense, to strengthen IPRs, on the one hand, while maintaining closed markets, on the other, is to work at cross-purposes. For example, a patent takes on greater market power if there is an import quota on similar goods that limits consumer substitution choices. Competitive markets help limit the effective scope of IPRs to their intended function, which is to foster investments in competition but not to prevent fair entry.

There are other reasons why IPRs and open markets are complementary. First, a liberal stance on inward trade and FDI improves a country's access to international technologies, intermediate inputs, and producer services—all items that can raise domestic productivity. However, our evidence demonstrates that such flows are deterred by weak patent rights and trade secrets protection. Second, a critical purpose of IPRs is to encourage investment in improved product quality, which is often a precondition for breaking into export markets. Similarly, IPRs can support marketing investments that raise product demand and permit economies of scale in production. These processes pertain as much to domestic entrepreneurs as they do to incoming foreign competitors.

These observations support certain policy prescriptions for nations as they strengthen their IPRs. First, it is important to complement the new policy regime with continued efforts to remove restrictions against trade, investment, and market access in services. Second, while authorities should remain vigilant about the potential for licensing abuses, the intrusive practice of inspecting all proposed licensing contracts and requiring costly modifications and disclosure clauses seems largely to limit access to advanced technologies. Thus, it may be advisable to adopt a liberal stance toward technology agreements and to replace technology-monitoring offices with a reliance on competition policy.

As a corollary, it is evident that IPRs have the potential both to expand access to new technologies and to raise the cost of that access. Higher costs may be alleviated by reducing import restrictions on critical technologies, such as telecommunications equipment and services, and computer hardware and software. Widespread adherence to the WTO information technology agreements is a useful complement to stronger copyrights, trademarks, and patents. These agreements aim at establishing tariff-free trade in critical products that support the information technology industry.

For their part, the rich countries that stand to gain considerably from stronger global IPRs must recognize their obligations to provide liberal access to their own markets. If IPRs are to support more advanced production structures in developing countries, those countries cannot be denied the ability to compete abroad. Countries adopting new IPRs regimes have a long-term interest in promoting free trade in goods for which

---

3. See Harris (1984) and Rodrik (1988), for example.

their own emerging intellectual property advantages will support exports. For example, poor countries could develop advantages in such goods as textiles and apparel, handicrafts, local cultural products, and prepared foods. To ensure such gains, developing countries should push their richer counterparts to implement the agreement to phase out the Multifiber Arrangement, avoid the use of arbitrary and protectionist technical product standards, continue to liberalize agricultural protection, and exercise restraint in the use of antidumping restrictions.

Competition Policy

A controversial issue is the specification and use of competition rules to discipline anticompetitive IPRs practices.[4] The essence of IPRs is to define the boundaries within which the developer of a piece of information with economic value enjoys exclusive rights to its use. These rights are limited for reasons of public policy interests in access, dissemination, and dynamic competition. To abuse an intellectual property right is to try to extend one's exploitation beyond the limitations established. Claims that a rights holder has exceeded the scope of protection by engaging in anticompetitive activity are often complex and require significant judicial and legal expertise in their interpretation. There is a strong link between IPRs and competition policy, with regulatory authorities and the courts empowered to manage this linkage.

Though several developing countries and countries in transition have recently upgraded or adopted competition regimes, this policy area is open to considerable transformation (OECD 1996). The implementation of TRIPs affords an opportunity for considering the intimate linkages between intellectual property protection and competition policy. An extensive discussion is beyond my scope here but it is instructive to set out the major issues in order to understand the trade-offs and complexities they pose.[5] Three general issues dominate discussion over competition and IPRs.

Regulating Monopoly Prices

Concern about monopoly pricing reflects fear of one such potential abuse, though it is rarely the focus of competition policy per se and more often the subject of regulation for purposes of public health and nutrition. Competition policy tends to ignore the pricing decisions of firms protected by IPRs, because those decisions relate solely to the covered technologies

---

4. This section borrows from Maskus (1998c) and Maskus and Lahouel (2000).

5. The papers in Anderson and Gallini (1998) provide an excellent and comprehensive overview.

or products. The basic view is that property rights provide the mechanism for firms to extract some portion of consumer surplus as the reward for innovation. Firms set prices in recognition of market substitutes that are rarely absent (in both a static and a dynamic context), suggesting that policy concern over monopoly pricing is misplaced. One exception is the perceived need in most nations to regulate prices of prescription drugs in order to limit patient costs and budgets of public health authorities, an issue discussed further below.

Interpreting Licensing Restrictions

Abuses of the rights inherent in a patent, trademark, or copyright often relate to business strategies, including selling practices and licensing restrictions, that extend the scope of property rights beyond that intended. There is a vast literature on the competitive effects of market power created by patents, trademarks, and protected know-how (see OECD 1989 and UNCTAD 1996).[6] There are few concrete guidelines because of the complexity of markets for information and technology. Vertical licensing agreements, for example, may ensure downstream product quality on the part of local vendors, which aids competition, but tie-in sales of unrelated products to technology purchasers could be an attempt to extend the scope of the initial property right and be injurious to competition.

Consider the potential competitive problems raised by the exploitation of IPRs. The first general concern is cartelization of horizontal competitors through licensing agreements that fix prices, limit output, or divide markets. Actual and potential competitors can be both licensees and licensors, either in the market for the product or technology itself or in extended markets. For example, patent-pooling and cross-licensing agreements between competing licensors may reduce competition in downstream product markets that use the licensed technologies as key inputs, particularly where the agreements set prices or restrict territories, customers, and fields of use (OECD 1989).

Competition authorities have found it difficult to set rules for such licensing agreements. Instead, the focus has been on whether the agreement presents the potential for cartelization of a significant share of a market (which requires definition of "significant" and "market," including whether there are competing products and technologies). Concerns also arise over agreements between licensors and licensees that require resale price maintenance of distributors' prices. Such agreements would have the effect of vertical price-fixing that would not necessarily be related to needs to monitor and enforce quality. Such risks are greater the

---

6. The OECD also publishes reviews of competition policies in its member countries; these are useful sources of information on how competition authorities define and deal with IPRs abuses.

more regulated is entry into distribution contracts, a common problem in many developing countries.

A second general difficulty relates to the exclusionary effects of license agreements. Such agreements could anticompetitively exclude other firms from competing in particular markets by raising barriers to entry. One means is tie-in sales, in which a licensor gains a dominant position in the market for the tied good. Potential competitors would be forced to enter the markets for both the technology and the tied good, raising their entry costs. Similar problems emerge if licensees must use only the licensor's technology, which could relate both to the subject of the license and future technologies. If a licensor succeeds in so restricting a significant share of licensees, it gains a dominant position in secondary markets, making competitive entry difficult.

A third concern arises when licensors, either individually or in patent pools, seek to hinder the entrance of competing new technologies through exclusive grant-back provisions and exclusivity arrangements in future technology purchases.

Again, competition policy must attempt to assess the potential anticompetitive effects of such arrangements if they are to be regulated, modified, or banned. These effects depend critically on the structure of the markets in which the agreements operate, the share of markets covered, and the difficulty of entry for licensors and licensees.

Another general class of problems relates to attempts to acquire market power beyond a firm's own protected technology or product by purchasing exclusive rights to competing technologies and products. Such efforts are effectively horizontal mergers, which may be analyzed in terms of their impact on current and future market concentration.

A final problem is nonprice predation, in which IPRs may be used to bring bad-faith litigation and opposition proceedings in order to exclude and harass competitors. This may be particularly troublesome where potential rivals are small and new, with insufficient resources to defend themselves. In turn, this problem could stifle the introduction of competing technologies by raising entry costs. Other policies also deter entry; the challenge to competition authorities is to distinguish predation from legitimate enforcement of IPRs. For example, if firms refuse to license technologies in particular markets or to certain firms, this could be construed either as legitimate business practice or unfair predation.

The basic message is that there are complex relationships between IPRs and their potential abuse. Property rights support market power, the exercise of which does not automatically constitute abuse of position. Competition authorities must learn to distinguish how various forms of behavior might affect static and dynamic competition. In this view, it is probably advisable for countries to adopt the US "rule of reason" approach, rather than the EU approach of attempting to codify rules covering specific actions.

Further, it is important to recognize that the anticompetitive effects of licensing and sales agreements depend heavily on market structure, including the potential for competitors to enter. In many developing economies, entry is impeded by monopoly-distributor laws, an absence of parallel imports, general trade and investment protection, and inadequate financial markets (limiting the evolution of venture capital and other risk-taking markets). In such circumstances it is important to consider the wider relation of business regulation to the development of stronger IPRs.

Treatment of Parallel Imports

Policy regarding exhaustion of IPRs is central to a country's regulation of those rights. Because exhaustion is among the most controversial aspects of international trade, it calls for extensive discussion here. Parallel imports (also called "gray-market imports") are goods brought into a country without the authorization of the patent, trademark, or copyright holder after those goods were placed legitimately into circulation elsewhere. For example, suppose that an authorized dealer of compact disks in Thailand produced under license to EMI sells them locally at a wholesale price below the retail price in Japan. The dealer or a third-party parallel trader could ship the disks to Japan and make a profit net of tariffs and shipping and distribution costs. These goods are legitimate copies, not pirated copies or knockoffs. Thus, parallel imports are identical to legitimate products except that they may be packaged differently and may not carry the original manufacturer's warranty.

Policies regulating parallel imports stem from the territorial exhaustion of IPRs. Under national exhaustion, rights end upon first sale within a nation but IPRs owners may prevent parallel trade with other countries. Under international exhaustion, rights are exhausted upon first sale anywhere and parallel imports are permitted. A third option is regional exhaustion, by which rights are completed within a group of countries, thereby allowing parallel trade among them, but are not exhausted outside the region.

A policy of national exhaustion amounts to a government-provided international restriction on vertical distribution. Each country adopting this approach declares itself a separate market with respect to goods and services traded with IPRs protection. Thus, rights owners retain full rights to distribute goods and services themselves or through authorized dealers, including the right to exclude imports. In contrast, countries permitting parallel imports provide no such territorial segmentation, effectively invalidating any right to control imports of goods in circulation abroad.

Because IPRs are stipulated on a national or territorial basis, traditionally each country has established its own policy for parallel imports. Despite efforts by US negotiators in the Uruguay Round to incorporate a global standard of national exhaustion into TRIPs, it was impossible to reach an agreement. Rather, Article 6 simply states that:

> For the purposes of dispute settlement under this Agreement, subject to the provisions of Articles 3 and 4, nothing in this Agreement shall be used to address the issue of the exhaustion of intellectual property rights.

This clause means that no violation or limitation of a TRIPs obligation beyond national treatment (Article 3) and MFN (Article 4) may be invoked to challenge the treatment of parallel imports, although there is legal debate about this interpretation.[7] It reflects a compromise that preserves the territorial prerogative to regulate parallel trade, rather than mandating a harmonized approach. The compromise was critical in securing the adherence to TRIPs of numerous developing countries, which maintain the right to set specific exhaustion regimes.

Considerable debate persists over whether to amend TRIPs to achieve a global approach. Some analysts advocate a global ban on parallel trade as a natural extension of the rights of intellectual property owners to control international distribution. For example, Barfield and Groombridge (1998) set out comprehensively the case for restraining parallel trade, though they recognize a collateral need for competition policy to discipline particular anticompetitive practices.

The need to ban parallel imports is advanced forcefully by representatives of copyright industries and the pharmaceuticals-biotechnology complex (Bale 1998). Others prefer a consistent rule of international exhaustion, placing no restrictions on parallel imports, in order to further integrate markets (Abbott 1998). In this view, proscribing parallel imports amounts to a nontariff barrier to trade, which is counter to the basis of the WTO. This notion is sometimes modified by recognizing the value of exemptions in particular sectors, such as pharmaceuticals, that may experience price differentials for regulatory reasons.

Exhaustion policies vary widely, even among developed economies (see table 7.1). The EU adopts exhaustion in all fields of intellectual property but bars parallel imports coming from outside the Community. The European Court of Justice (ECJ) consistently has upheld the right to resell legitimately procured goods within the Community as a required safeguard for completing the internal market. There are two important exceptions: (1) Countries may preclude parallel imports in pharmaceutical products that were placed on the market as a result of a compulsory licensing order. (2) The first showing of a theatrical movie or television broadcast abroad does not exhaust international distribution rights because of the need to make repeated showings under copyright.[8]

---

7. See Abbott (1998), Cottier (1998), and Bronckers (1998).

8. *Coditel SA vs. Cine-Vog Films,* Case 62/79, 18 March 1980.

Table 7.1 Summary of IPRs exhaustion regimes

Country	Trademarks	Patents	Copyrights
European Union	Community exhaustion	Community exhaustion	Community exhaustion
USA	National exhaustion, common control and no consumer confusion	National exhaustion	National exhaustion
Japan	International exhaustion, unless agreed by contract or original sale is price-controlled	Same as trademarks	International exhaustion, except for motion pictures
Australia	International exhaustion	National exhaustion, unless sold by patent owner without clear restrictions	National exhaustion, except for compact disks and books

Sources: National Economic Research Associates (1999) and International Intellectual Property Association (1998b).

American policy on parallel imports is mixed. Within its borders the United States enforces the first-sale doctrine, under which rights are exhausted when the product is purchased outside the vertical distribution chain. Accordingly, US companies cannot prevent purchasers from reselling goods anywhere within the country. This is viewed as an important policing mechanism for exclusive territories, which are permissible under antitrust law subject to a rule-of-reason inquiry.

The United States maintains a "common-control exception" for parallel imports in trademarked goods. This principle permits trademark owners to block parallel imports except when both the foreign and US trademarks are owned by the same entity or when the foreign and US trademark owners are in a parent-subsidiary relationship (Palia and Keown 1991; National Economic Research Associates 1999). This doctrine was upheld in a recent Supreme Court ruling.[9]

In addition, blocking parallel imports requires demonstration that they are not identical in quality to original products and cause confusion among consumers. Owners of US patents are protected from parallel imports by an explicit right of importation. Finally, the Copyright Act of 1976 bars parallel importation of copyrighted goods. A recent Supreme Court case rejected an attempt to extend this treatment

---

9. *K Mart Corporation vs. Cartier*, 486 US 281 (1987).

to inherently trademarked goods by claiming copyright protection for labels.[10]

Japan permits parallel imports in patented and trademarked goods unless they are explicitly barred by contract or unless their original sale was subject to foreign price regulation. Under its case law, Japan is considerably more open to parallel imports than is the United States (Abbott 1998). Australia generally permits parallel imports in trademarked goods but allows patent owners to restrict them. Australia removed protection from parallel trade for copyrighted compact disks in late 1998, complementing its earlier limited deregulation of book imports.

Few developing countries restrict parallel trade in any field. To some degree this reflects the general absence of competition policies and the existence of limitations on IPRs. Some nations substitute laws mandating a sole national distributor for products imported under trademark or copyright, effectively banning parallel imports. However, in other countries parallel imports are widely seen as a useful policing device against the price collusion emanating from exclusive territorial restraints, while parallel exports are viewed as a channel for penetrating foreign markets (Maskus and Chen 1999).

This wide disparity in policies and attitudes toward parallel imports suggests accurately that there is no obvious answer to whether they are beneficial or harmful, although they are certainly detrimental to the interests of IPRs owners. The economic literature on the subject, though limited, provides useful insights.

Three arguments are advanced in favor of permitting parallel trade. First is the view that restrictions on parallel imports amount to nontariff barriers to goods that have legitimately escaped the control of IPRs owners. Such barriers run counter to the WTO principle of liberal trade and sacrifice consumer gains from market integration. That international price differences may emanate from manufacturers' attempts to set market-specific prices is no less a source of comparative advantage than other demand or supply characteristics, including regulatory policies.

A second argument is that parallel imports play an important policing role against abusive price discrimination and collusive behavior based on private territorial restraints. Here, allowing parallel imports is a form of competition policy that acts as an important limitation to the scope of IPRs.[11] The notion that complementing exclusive territories with protection from parallel imports and domestic gray-market trade could induce collusion finds support in US economic history (Tarr 1985; Hilke 1988).

---

10. *Quality King Distributors vs. L'anza Research International*, 96-470, March 1998.

11. A regime of restricted parallel imports combined with appropriate competition regulation might be more appropriate in many circumstances. In practical terms, however, many developing countries do not have adequate competition policies.

Because the colluding firms could well be foreign in the case of parallel imports, the loss to consumers is not balanced by a gain in local profits.

The final argument is that government enforcement of territorial rights invites rent seeking on behalf of firms that claim they need relief from free-riding competitors but are actually interested in setting collusive prices. In this view, it is best to rely on private enforcement of contractual exclusive territories while permitting parallel trade.

Many arguments are made in favor of banning parallel imports. First, as is well known, price discrimination need not be harmful and under certain circumstances can raise economic well-being (Varian 1985; Schmalensee 1981). At the international level, banning parallel trade would result in perfect discrimination in the sense that one price is set per market (Malueg and Schwartz 1994). In contrast, full parallel trade requires uniform pricing by the IPRs holder, subject to differences in transport and marketing costs.

This comparison sets up several trade-offs. Economies with inelastic demand would face higher prices under price discrimination than under uniform pricing, harming consumers. This surely explains the limited permission of parallel imports into the United States, where demands for trademarked goods might be expected to be relatively unresponsive to price. To the extent that countries are not significant developers of intellectual property, they are made worse off by price discrimination. This logic underlies the favorable treatment of parallel imports in Australia, Japan, and elsewhere.

Countries with elastic demand, typically developing economies, would face lower-than-uniform prices under price discrimination. If they allow parallel trade, foreign rights holders may choose not to supply such countries because local demand is insufficient under uniform pricing (Malueg and Schwartz 1994). In this view, international exhaustion would lower the welfare of developing economies through higher prices and lower product availability.

However, most developing countries are opposed to restricting parallel trade (Abbott 1998). In part, this reflects concern that domestic prices under price discrimination could actually be higher for imported goods.[12] This concern is registered most often in the context of pharmaceuticals trade. More fundamentally, many nations see opportunities for achieving export and industrial growth through being parallel exporters, discounting the likelihood of their markets going unserved. Indeed, many view potential restrictions on parallel trade as back-door attempts by industrial countries to close their markets through nontariff barriers.

---

12. Recall the finding that major software firms tend to set higher prices for legitimate copies of their programs in developing countries with significant piracy than in the United States. However, it appears that legitimate copies of compact disks are markedly cheaper in developing countries than in developed countries, so the software example is not representative.

Thus, whether price discrimination harms or helps particular nations depends on circumstances. There are no robust predictions about global welfare rankings with and without parallel trade. Malueg and Schwartz (1994) argue for banning parallel imports on the grounds that perfect price discrimination would result in net global output expansion and raise global welfare, while ensuring further that low-price markets are provided goods. This result is sensitive to assumptions of the model, but is an important insight.

A second argument is that parallel traders free ride on the investment, marketing, and service costs of authorized distributors. Because these distributors incur costs of building their territorial markets through advertising, discounting, and postsale service maintenance, they require protection from competition by parallel importers, who can procure the goods without incurring similar costs. Indeed, this is the primary motivation for permitting privately contracted exclusive territories in the first place. That restrictions on parallel imports are a natural extension of the right to control vertical markets is espoused by the World Intellectual Property Organization (1993, 10). It claims that, for copyrights, "The principle of territoriality provides security for the chain of authorizations that permit [an] orderly supply of copies for international distribution." Such restrictions may be procompetitive, both through enhancing interbrand competition and through offering incentives to build markets and provide services. Inadequate protection risks the dynamic problem that markets may be underserved due to slower rates of product introduction and more limited service contracts. Thus, the regulation of parallel trade, like IPRs generally, involves a tension between the short-run static costs of market power and the long-run dynamic benefits of faster product introduction.

A third argument is that efficient distribution requires significant vertical control within an enterprise and that private contracts may be inadequate for this purpose. MNEs increasingly build production and marketing networks to extend their reach across borders. Such firms typically find it advantageous to build markets through exclusive territorial dealership rights. Exclusive rights make it easier to monitor marketing efforts and enforce product quality in order to deter local erosion of trademark value. However, it may be difficult in foreign markets to enforce private contracts prohibiting sales outside the authorized distribution chain. In this view, therefore, restrictions on parallel trade are a necessary complement to exclusive territories (Chard and Mellor 1989). This claim is a direct challenge to the idea that regulating IPRs is a matter of national choice rather than a shared international obligation based on universal principles.

A powerful counterargument to the vertical control idea is that a combination of private exclusive territories and parallel trade regulation could invite collusive behavior among exclusive dealers in products protected by IPRs, a particularly nettlesome problem in developing countries. In this regard, note that some firms may prefer to allow parallel trade as a way to discipline collusion among their dealers (or monopoly behavior by single distributors) that would limit their sales (Hilke 1988).

Maskus and Chen (1999) put forward a simple theory of parallel imports and vertical price control: a manufacturer protected by IPRs in both a home and a foreign market sets sufficiently low wholesale prices to distributors to induce profit-maximizing retail prices, which vary according to demand elasticity. This sets up an opportunity for the distributor to sell the product profitably outside the authorized channels in the other country.

Banning parallel imports always benefits the manufacturer, but has ambiguous impacts on social welfare in the two countries. On the one hand, parallel trade reduces the markup accruing to manufacturers and benefits consumers from integration. On the other hand, parallel trade wastes resources through cross-hauling goods between countries. Indeed, it is possible in the Maskus-Chen model for goods to be traded in both directions and for parallel exports to flow from high-retail-price countries to low-retail-price countries. One significant policy conclusion is that parallel imports are likely to be beneficial when trade costs (including tariffs) are low but harmful when trade costs are high. It follows that regional trade agreements permitting parallel trade may be welfare-enhancing. However, no general proposition about global welfare emerges.

A fourth argument is that efficient recovery of R&D costs might require setting different prices in different markets when R&D costs are joint in the sense of producing goods and services that are sold across borders. Intellectual property is typically produced in one location (a headquarters or research facility) but exploited globally through exports, licensing, and FDI. In principle, a global planner could treat firms as regulated monopolies with an allowable return on R&D. This approach would suggest following a global Ramsey pricing rule, which means setting prices according to demand elasticity in segmented markets (Danzon 1997). Restricting parallel trade supports such pricing schemes. However, the assumptions underlying this model are of questionable relevance in the context of profit-maximizing competitive rivals. Moreover, this model ignores the redistributive effects among countries and between producers and consumers, rendering its practical significance questionable.

A fifth argument is that international price differences may be the result of national price regulations established in order to achieve social objectives, an issue discussed further in the next section. The most prominent example is the global pharmaceuticals industry, in which virtually all nations regulate prices in order to limit consumer costs or health procurement budgets. Such regulations differ widely across countries and account for significant price variations (Danzon 1997). Permitting parallel trade could then defeat the purposes of regulation as distributors in more regulated (lower-price) markets export to less regulated (higher-price) markets. In this context, some observers think it appropriate to ban parallel exports from regulated markets on the theory that regulation amounts to a sector-specific export subsidy (Abbott 1998).

Finally, it is often claimed that permitting parallel imports invites consumer deception and piracy. The argument is of dubious validity. Deception would occur if lower-quality parallel imports were marketed as legitimate versions of higher-quality products. Piracy is trade in unauthorized versions of products, which is a different concept from parallel trade. In either case, customs authorities are empowered to act against such trade without restricting legitimate parallel imports.

Given this multiplicity of causes and ambiguous results, the question of whether regulating parallel imports is beneficial or harmful is ultimately an empirical question that depends on circumstances. There is not much systematic evidence to inform the discussion, not least because data on parallel imports are rare and often anecdotal. Tarr (1985) and Hilke (1988) found that parallel imports of high-end goods into the United States in the 1980s essentially followed retail price differences associated with lagged responses to exchange-rate changes, supporting a price-discrimination interpretation ("pricing to market"). They found little support for the notion that parallel traders free ride on the investment of distributors, despite consistent complaints of this kind by authorized distributors. The NERA study (1999) estimated that parallel imports within the EU in selected trademarked goods ranged from less than 5 percent in domestic appliances to 10-20 percent in musical recordings. The latter trade flows largely responded to wholesale price differences, consistent with the Maskus-Chen model. Unfortunately, there are no studies of parallel trade to or from developing countries.

Neither are there studies of the fundamental question of whether market segmentation encourages collusive behavior or monopoly pricing that could be effectively disciplined by parallel imports. This view, held widely in many countries, seems to rely on faith rather than sharp analysis, though it is not difficult to understand its source. Unambiguously, restrictions on parallel trade raise the profitability of intellectual property developers, which are overwhelmingly located in a few developed countries. The possibility that price discrimination could cause lower prices in developing countries, in the face of this enhanced market power, must seem a leap of faith to those unschooled in industrial organization theory. Moreover, it is reasonable to anticipate that, even in relatively low-income economies with large markets, such as India, there may well be lower-priced sources of goods in regional trade. For example, if the introduction of pharmaceutical patents were to raise prices in India by the ranges suggested in the Watal (2000a) study, Indian authorities might take advantage of potentially cheaper drugs marketed in Bangladesh.

Given this situation, it is impossible to have confidence either in the prescription for banning parallel imports or in mandates that there be free global parallel trade. More study is needed of the experiences of countries with varying policies on product prices and availability. The best advice seems simply to permit the status quo to continue, with each country or region selecting its own policy.

IPRs and Social Regulation

The private exploitation of any property right can, in principle, interfere with the attainment of social, noneconomic objectives. In the case of IPRs, two issues dominate discourse:

1. In all nations the maintenance and improvement of public health is viewed as partially or wholly a government responsibility. Governments are interested in making sure that patients have access to medicines on reasonable terms and in limiting their budgetary exposures in public procurement of health care.

2. The use of an economy's natural resources and indigenous genetic materials may have cultural and environmental costs. Governments are concerned with managing the speed of such exploitation and the technologies used for it.

Clearly, an externality argument is used to justify both these objectives. Many private consumers are incapable of paying the true cost of their health care, choosing to consume less than they need for health. Inadequate health reduces productivity. As for environmental resources, private development may proceed faster than would be socially optimal if the true costs of the resources were not borne by developers or consumers. For these reasons, each area is extensively regulated, with public provision of health care and various taxes on environmental use and land development.

It should be no surprise, then, that IPRs, themselves a suboptimal solution to externality problems, could make these social regulations either more or less effective. In medicines, the obvious problem is access, a worsening of the static distortion. If pharmaceutical patents support monopoly pricing, fewer patients could afford the protected drugs and public budgets would be stretched. Over the long term, however, the patents could result in new drugs coming onto the market, a dynamic gain.

In the environmental area, exclusive rights to market or use a bioengineered plant variety could squeeze out traditional agricultural techniques, raising concerns about reductions in biodiversity. Similarly, patent races to develop new disease therapies or cosmetics based on indigenous plants could accelerate their exploitation beyond socially preferred levels.

However, newer technologies also may make agriculture more productive, reducing the land required to meet nutritional demands. And IPRs may provide incentives for contracts that result in more rational and equitable development of resources.

It is evident that IPRs and systems of social regulations may either be at odds with one another or be mutually complementary. Undoubtedly, as IPRs are strengthened, nations will consider alterations to their regulatory positions in order to manage the new rights. This issue is again broad, multifaceted, and complex. It can only receive an airing here through two examples: pharmaceutical price controls and biotechnology regulation.

Regulating Pharmaceutical Prices

Virtually all countries have some regulation of prescription drug prices and budgetary costs. For example, prices and price increases in France, Italy, and Spain are tightly controlled for drugs reimbursed by social insurance (Danzon 1997).

- Canada abandoned compulsory licensing in 1993 but retains a vigilant pharmaceutical price review board.

- Germany strictly limits the pharmaceutical budget of doctors and health institutions.

- The United Kingdom limits the allowable rate of return on capital to pharmaceutical firms, while not restricting individual drug prices.

- Germany, the Netherlands, and New Zealand set reference prices defined across all effective formulations within a therapeutic class, including generic drugs, in order to keep down the prices of patented and prescription medicines.

- Japan sets reimbursement prices for each drug but permits physicians to prescribe and dispense essentially without limits, resulting in huge numbers of prescriptions being written per patient.

- Though prescription drug prices are largely uncontrolled in the United States, managed care organizations have used their buying power to extract price reductions. The pharmaceutical industry in the United States has expressed fears that expanding Medicaid benefits to cover prescription drugs would usher in price controls.

Throughout the developing world, such regulations are extensive. Indeed, the unwillingness of many nations to provide drug patents may be seen both as a form of industrial policy (to encourage local imitative industries) and as implicit price regulation. However, layered onto patent limitations are detailed rules covering pricing formulas and markups, which stem from negotiations among public health authorities (and often other ministries, such as labor, industry, and trade), hospitals, pharmaceutical suppliers (manufacturers and wholesalers), and retail pharmacists. Regulations typically extend to regional distribution requirements, packaging and labeling, and the size and strength of dosages.

Public policy may also require pharmacists to engage in cost-reducing practices. A common example is generic substitution, whereby retailers are required to sell generic versions of drugs so long as those drugs provide adequate therapeutic benefits and patients are informed of the availability of branded alternatives. On top of all this are extensive regulatory approval procedures and safeguards against the dispensing of ineffective or harmful formulations.

An instructive example is the South African Medicine and Related Substances Control Act Amendments enacted in November 1997. The law permits the health minister to revoke any pharmaceutical patents in South Africa if he deems the associated medicines to be too expensive. It also permits parallel importation of drugs and allows the health minister to override regulatory decisions concerning the safety and registration of medicines. It requires pharmacists to employ generic substitution unless the doctor or patient forbids it, sets limits on pharmacy markup rates, and bans in-kind inducements from drug manufacturers to physicians.

The law was immediately challenged in court by US drug makers, while Merck and Company dropped a planned $10 million investment and Bristol-Myers Squibb, Pharmacia and Upjohn, and Eli Lilly all closed South African factories. Application of the law was suspended by the South African government, pending negotiations with the United States, which claimed that it would nullify the advantages provided under TRIPs. An oral agreement between the two governments was reached in September 1999 under which South Africa would implement the law but would amend it in early 2000. In return, American trade authorities suspended their pressure on the South African government. In December 1999, the United States Trade Representative Charlene Barshevsky announced that the application of American trade law to intellectual property issues would pay more attention to the need of foreign countries to address health crises. She also removed South Africa from the Special 301 "watch list."[13]

Few developing countries seem willing to abandon their price control schemes. In light of extensive and similar regulations in many rich countries, the research-based pharmaceutical companies have little ground on which to demand a policy change. Rather, countries need to consider the benefits and costs of price regulation on its own merits. It may be that such controls are effective in managing the exposure of patients and

---

13. See "The Protection of Intellectual Property and Health Policy," USTR press release, 1 December 1999.

health expenditures to the higher prices associated with new patent regimes. At the same time, they may be counterproductive if they discourage entry of new products or joint ventures and licensing agreements between local and international pharmaceutical firms. Again, there is tension between static needs for access at reasonable cost and dynamic needs for product innovation.

Danzon (1997) argues persuasively that controls have restrained prices considerably in France and Italy, which had the lowest outpatient drug prices among nine developed countries in 1992. As economists would expect, however, the controls had a number of unintended behavioral responses:[14]

1. Because price increases were held to the rate of inflation, French and Italian consumers shifted health expenditures sharply away from other forms of therapy into drugs. In consequence, the increase in real drug expenditures per capita in Italy and France was the highest in the sample, suggesting there was little real budget saving.

2. Limited prices reduced incentives for the entry of generic drugs that would otherwise compete with expensive branded drugs, as they do in the United States. The lack of generic competition implied that the price differences between France and the United States in patented, branded, and generic drugs combined were not as great as the other figures would suggest.

3. The French market had a relatively small share of active ingredients that were available also in the United States. This suggested that a disproportionately high percentage of drugs on the French market were either too ineffective to meet the stiff US regulatory requirements or not economically valuable enough to make American sales worthwhile. In fact, French pharmaceutical R&D is largely aimed at small modifications of existing drugs rather than at new discoveries. Although France ranked third in the number of new chemical entities introduced between 1975 and 1989, none were global products (defined as those launched in all seven major developed markets) over that period (Danzon 1997, 62). Rather, discovery of global products was concentrated in the United States (45 percent), the United Kingdom (14 percent) and Switzerland (8 percent). Prices are least controlled in the United States and the United Kingdom.

4. Finally, French productivity in making drugs, measured by value added per employee, was far below that of American pharmaceutical firms in 1990.

---

14. Danzon's figures are persuasive but no attempt has been made to demonstrate causation or to hold other important economic variables constant in discussing these responses.

These findings support the claim that, if an economy wishes to increase productivity and encourage fundamental invention in its pharmaceutical sector, price controls are counterproductive. Developing countries may not share these objectives, of course. In many countries, imitative R&D among reasonably competitive firms in the absence of patent protection has brought major international therapies onto the market with a relatively short lag.[15] This imitation flourished even under the threat of price controls. Controls do not necessarily mean that manufacturers and distributors lose money; they may be constructed to ensure stable markups or rates of return.

Controls do mean that price-controlled firms in developing countries are not likely to engage in fundamental R&D that could produce global discoveries and win major patents abroad. In fact, however, the controls themselves may not serve as binding constraints to this. Few, if any, firms in developing countries are likely to find it attractive to engage in fundamental R&D in competition with the major international research-based pharmaceutical companies, which have expertise in research and marketing and benefit from significant economies of scale. Developing countries may therefore wonder what advantages could accrue from abandoning or weakening their control regimes.

The effectiveness of price and expenditure controls in developing economies has attracted little study. Lanjouw (1998) described India's price regulation and the problems it has encountered. Since the system was modified in 1995, approximately 50 percent of the Indian pharmaceutical market has been controlled (Watal 1999). The system is based on a straightforward cost-plus formula, with allowable retail price ceilings (including excise tax) calculated as markups over material costs, production costs, and packaging charges. The markup, which is divided between wholesale and retail margins, is set by the health authority. Prices are controlled in products with high volumes and moderately concentrated market structures and in products with low volumes and heavily concentrated market structures.[16]

As might be anticipated, such a thorough scheme has a number of problems. The domestic pharmaceutical industry is not cooperative in negotiating these controls. Disputes arise over the criteria for defining costs, what data to submit, the levels of wastage to count, and the like. The administration and enforcement costs are high and the system lacks transparency.

---

15. Lanjouw (1998) reported that certain drugs on patent elsewhere were imitated effectively in India within three years, sometimes even before foreign regulatory processes were completed and patents granted.

16. As Watal (1999) pointed out, this system automatically would subject any patented drugs to controls.

Beyond such structural problems, administrative price ceilings raise three additional interesting complications:

1. Companies that are awarded patents may choose not to supply particular markets at the regulated prices, suggesting that a balance must be struck between public-health needs and access.

2. As in India, price regulations are typically stated on a cost-plus formula, which encourages firms to set high transfer prices on imported ingredients (Lanjouw 1998). As a result, formulaic price ceilings might actually raise prices higher than they would be if prices were not controlled unless transfer prices are otherwise controlled.

3. Price ceilings set in some developed countries, such as Canada and France, seem to be tied increasingly to comparative indices of prices in other markets (Danzon 1997). Multinational firms thus have an incentive to bargain for the highest possible prices in low-price economies like India in order to gain a higher set of global reference prices. This issue, which is becoming increasingly important in the international pharmaceuticals markets, promises to be controversial in low-cost countries as patents are adopted. Rather than having firms set country-specific prices according to local demand and market structure characteristics (price discrimination supported by international proscriptions against parallel imports), markups could be a function of public-health concerns in developed economies, biasing prices upward in the larger poor economies.

Given these problems and the available evidence, developing countries might be advised to employ price ceilings with caution, perhaps limiting them to patented products with high market concentration, and accounting for the disincentive effects they imply. Innovative forms of procurement might include forgoing price controls in favor of prices negotiated between firms and public-health authorities. The buying power of such plans could extract price concessions without arbitrarily restricting returns to pharmaceutical companies. Health authorities could then limit costs to patients through rebates or discounts built into co-payments. If negotiations fail to restrain monopoly pricing, compulsory licensing under transparent conditions and demonstrated need might be an option.

Countries may perceive that, among the dangers of introducing pharmaceutical patents, the largest is that they would place competitive pressures on imitative local industries. However, pharmaceutical markets are not generally monopolized by patents. Rather, patents provide market power for new products but leave room for generic entry (post-patent), competitive inventing around the patent, and the promotion of brand recognition. An exception is pharmaceutical classes where patents provide considerable price-setting power, as in the case of treatments for AIDS. Overall, however, the danger of monopolization is weakened in open and competitive markets, which again points to the desirability of liberal trade and investment regimes as patents are introduced. Indeed, there is evidence that competent and competitive imitators may readily link up with foreign pharmaceutical firms through production agreements, technology licensing, and joint ventures in order to exploit patents and marketing rights through a local presence.[17] Thus, neither the threat of market-power pricing nor major industrial restructuring is likely to be a significant problem in open and competitive economies.

Biotechnology, Genetics, and the Environment

Nothing is more controversial in the IPRs area than the treatment of biotechnological inventions and plant varieties. The development, use, and protection of life forms bring up issues of science, law, economics, environmental conservation, and ethics. Since such technologies promise unprecedented advances in pharmaceutical therapies, industrial processes, food production, and nutritional status, all countries would seem to have strong dynamic interests in linking themselves to these advances. Yet there is concern about possible environmental degradation, the diversity of natural biological resources, food safety and human health, and the viability of traditional farming. Many of these concerns are likely based on exaggerated views of the likelihood that genetic engineering could result in mutant strains that might escape their intended uses and destroy or modify traditional organisms. In principle, effective regulation in the name of protecting biological safety would provide adequate safeguards against such low-probability, high-risk events. Other concerns are not misplaced, however, being firmly rooted in the economics of intellectual property exploitation.

The traditional view around the globe was that to patent living organisms in any form was unethical, for it would provide incentives to engage in the questionable practice of inventing life. The advent of the biotechnology industry greatly stressed this approach because, to move forward, its inventions required protection from misappropriation. Biotechnological inventions, like pharmaceutical products (these days, the latter often stem from the former), require substantial investments in R&D but are easily imitated. The US Supreme Court considerably advanced protection for biotechnological processes with its celebrated decision in 1980 awarding a patent for an invented microorganism that could ingest spilled oil. The court recognized the industrial utility of the invention

---

17. See Maskus (1997b) for Lebanon and Maskus, Dougherty, and Mertha (1998) for China.

and saw no reasonable bars to patenting, providing the organisms met all criteria for eligibility.

Practices in this area vary considerably around the world. The United States recognizes patent eligibility in all life forms save cloned human beings. This broad standard permits patenting of genetic research tools, gene sequences, and, since the 1988 granting of a patent on the Harvard oncomouse, higher-order (multicellular) life forms resulting from genetic manipulation. The United States permits broad patent claims covering all potential products from genetic engineering of a particular plant. It also recognizes patents for research tools, such as a genetic sequence for one drug that could be required to effectuate other pharmaceutical products. The later drugs would be subject to the initial patent, requiring licensing agreements (Barton 1995). Such a highly protective approach raises difficult questions regarding how to commercialize dependent patents if the patentee refuses to license. These standards for protection are thought by many to be excessive; debate continues within the United States, where a public agency, the National Institutes of Health, is attempting to fund the mapping of the human genome in order to place the genetic sequences into the public domain.

As clarified in the July 1998 directive on the Legal Protection of Biotechnological Inventions, the EU patents microorganisms and microbiological processes as well as plant and animal inventions that result from microbiological processes, though in general animal and plant varieties are excluded from protection. Many upper-income industrializing economies, such as South Korea and Singapore, patent biotechnological inventions and plant varieties, having a dynamic interest in these technologies themselves. Others, such as Brazil, Argentina, and nations of the Andean Group, provide wide exclusions, refusing to patent genomes from all life forms and excluding all or any part of living things found in nature (Watal 2000b).

Setting aside the ethical issues, the proper scope of patents for biotechnological inventions is widely debated on legal grounds. Because biotechnological research is expensive but its therapeutic and genetic results are easily imitated, patents are considered crucial for promoting the industry. However, it is possible to question how patents apply when products stemming from recombinant DNA techniques may be more the result of luck and patience than of originality: it is not clear whether under classical terms particular products are "inventions" (and therefore patentable) or "discoveries of nature" (and therefore not patentable).

The TRIPs agreement clearly reflects different preferences, both among developed economies and between developed and developing countries. For example, Article 27(2) allows countries to exclude from patent eligibility any inventions that might threaten human, animal, or plant life or health or might result in "serious prejudice to the environment." This exclusion is limited by the requirement that any such inventions may not otherwise be put into commercial use on the market, rendering it of dubious practicality. While all countries must patent microorganisms and microbiological processes, the definitions they choose for these terms and also for "nonobviousness" and "inventive steps" may sharply limit protection, as they do in Brazil and Argentina. There are likely to be many disputes in the biotechnology area as standards are implemented.

Two issues dominate international debate about the implications of protection for life forms in specific countries. First, because countries must now protect plant varieties either through patents or PBRs, there is concern that small farmers and farmers in poor countries will be unable to afford the technologies. Plant variety patents preclude the breeders' exemption and, unless explicitly allowed for in the law, also the farmers' privilege. Accordingly, most developing countries are adopting PBRs with both exceptions. As may be expected, plant developers in the United States and elsewhere who consider such protection to be inadequate are pushing for a revision of TRIPs to require patents. However, a proposal to require patent systems in PBRs, to the extent they preclude the use of retained seeds by farmers, would be questionable economics in its own right and would be widely resisted without some other mechanism for the diffusion of seed technologies.[18]

Developing countries are unlikely to agree to a patenting requirement in plants or plant varieties for the foreseeable future. Rather, they will implement and refine their PBR systems and monitor the costs to local farmers. If such costs are high, governments might consider public purchase of seeds for dissemination to farmers at discount. Purchasing programs by public authorities can put downward pressure on prices, though a balance must be struck to accommodate the needs of plant developers.

A second concern is that providing patents in biotechnology encourages firms to locate genetic materials around the world for purposes of testing them as sources for new drugs, food products, and cosmetics. Such materials include plants and animals that often do not carry adequate private property rights in the source countries. That is, plants may be extracted from public lands or from farms and villages that are incapable of representing their own interests. In consequence, such resources may be taken without adequate compensation.

Although many pharmaceutical and chemical firms remain opposed to attempts to share the rents from such exploitation, a few have undertaken voluntary programs to do so. Moreover, it makes economic sense to ensure that compensation is paid. It is disingenuous of authorities in developed countries to oppose such systems, which some do on the questionable grounds that it would slow down new product development,

---

18. The recent decision by Monsanto to forgo commercialization of the so-called "terminator gene" is eloquent testimony to the controversy.

because those same governments charge fees for exploitation of their own public resources and the environment.[19]

In principle, this problem calls simply for contracts that value the resources appropriately and effect payments that both conserve the materials and give incentives for innovation. In practice, the prescription is fraught with difficulties, including finding and paying for effective representation of resource owners in source countries. The owners may be indigenous tribes, farmers, local villages, regional governments, or other actors that cannot adequately represent their own concerns. It is important for international authorities to provide legal and technical assistance. The Convention on Biodiversity, signed at Rio de Janeiro in 1992, provides some guidance. Unfortunately, it is a vague and confusing document with strictly exhortatory powers.

International Initiatives

While the previous discussion provides a broad blueprint for policy in specific nations, strengthening IPRs globally also calls for international approaches to particular problems. These approaches come in two general categories: those that fit naturally into the WTO framework and those that go beyond it.

Extending the WTO Approach

While TRIPs is a comprehensive agreement, it remains in flux. Certain issues were left unresolved, while much of the compromise language on flexible interpretation of standards remains to be tested. This raises questions about the effectiveness of the agreement as it stands and about avenues for its extension.

Technology Transfer Commitments

Governments in many developing countries remain suspicious of the proposition that the intended benefits of TRIPs, especially technology transfer on reasonable terms, will be forthcoming. Articles 66 and 67 commit industrial nations to use their best efforts to identify measures they could take to encourage such transfers, in particular to the least-developed countries, and to promote mechanisms to build a sound and viable technological base in the recipients. To date those best efforts have been nil, generating concerns that technology exporters do not intend to use TRIPs

---

19. The argument is questionable on economic efficiency grounds to the extent that the issue is the split of inframarginal rents to resource exploitation.

in a manner that would be seen as equitable by technology importers. Concerns are mounting that firms owning critical technologies for the management of important public health and environmental problems could choose to use TRIPs to support highly restrictive licensing arrangements or not to license them at all (Watal 2000b).

The omission may well induce technology importing countries to mount an effort to roll back some of the TRIPs standards. It certainly could diminish the support for TRIPs in many parts of the world. Thus, an important initiative for enterprises and agencies in developed countries in the near term would be to announce a program to make the technology transfer commitments more effective. That could remove any impediments to outward transfers that persist in the developed economies. The program might also incorporate a fund to finance considerably more technical and financial assistance to poor countries as they implement and administer IPRs. Thus, within the context of TRIPs as it currently stands, developed countries could do much to raise enthusiasm for it by working harder to find ways to enhance technology transfer and to provide additional technical assistance to poor countries. Such programs could be viewed as investments in raising local awareness and support for IPRs, with potentially fruitful payoffs.

A Future Competition Agreement

TRIPs invites regulation of competition as a way to discipline anticompetitive abuse of IPRs. It remains to be seen how aggressively such authority will be used and how well the positive comity approach TRIPs envisions will function. However, its introduction into the WTO raises the issue of multilateral coordination in competition regulation. There are grounds for working toward a multilateral accord on competition policy (Maskus and Lahouel 1999; Graham and Richardson 1997a). As regulation increases, concerns will mount about cross-border jurisdictional and review questions, policy coordination, asymmetric enforcement, competitive aspects of parallel trade, and other problems that could justify a trade agreement in this area.

My view about the form of a desirable WTO agreement supplements that in Fox (1995). Nations would negotiate shared competition principles for the trading system, including a commitment to increase market accessibility. Enforcement would consider harm to foreign interests with the same gravity as harm to domestic competition. Members damaged by the actions of another member could petition for enforcement in the other country and, failing satisfactory resolution, have access to dispute resolution within the WTO. Cooperation and transparency would be emphatically emphasized. Most important for IPRs, nations would agree on principles recognizing that some licensing arrangements potentially enhance efficiency while others are presumptively anticompetitive. This could do much to resolve uncertainty for both licensors and regulators about protecting intellectual property.

IPRs in Cyberspace

The rapid expansion of the internet makes increasingly important the treatment of IPRs for electronic commerce and databases transmitted electronically. Numerous complex issues can only be mentioned here.[20] For example, the interests of firms and individuals that produce content (transmittable products and services) often differ sharply from the interests of content carriers, such as telecommunications companies and internet service providers. The former group would prefer strong copyrights and encryption devices that prevent unauthorized downloading; the latter group might find that such devices restrain the growth of demand for their services. Among related issues are ways to safeguard privacy on the internet.

The economics of IPRs within network providers is only now being analyzed. While many classical principles still apply, new questions have emerged. For example, in certain circumstances it may be beneficial to issue defined licenses to use IPR-protected technological standards in order to promote network development.[21] Similarly, because interoperability is critical to the growth of networks and the diffusion of their benefits, international variability in standards for protecting software and protocols could erect roadblocks to efficient cross-licensing.

International policy responses are in their infancy. It is unclear, for example, how responsibilities for promoting network growth using standards and licensing parameters should be allocated. In some circumstances, product and technical standards set by private associations have been efficient; in others they exclude competition. There could be scope for multilateral monitoring of standards and licensing, or even for public intervention to alleviate failures to achieve network gains across borders. Such an approach would incorporate elements of technology management, competition policy, trade policy, and IPRs, making problematic the assignment of responsibilities among such agencies as WIPO, the WTO, and the International Telecommunications Union.

Despite the uncertainty, some policy conclusions may sensibly be put forward. TRIPs could be extended to incorporate the evolving copyright rules that govern electronic transmissions over the internet (WTO 1998). Vigorous international growth in electronic transactions requires enforceable copyright laws and protection of trademarks and electronic domain names. The expanded use of electronic information networks is important

---

20. See Shapiro and Varian (1999) for extensive analysis.

21. Recall the earlier discussion that the United States effectively has a policy of compulsory licenses to ensure that rural areas receive cable and satellite transmissions.

for developing countries in administering their own IPRs regimes and in promoting technology diffusion through access to international databases.

Standard copyright principles apply to electronic transmissions under TRIPs. Therefore, rights to copy and distribute products over the internet extend to computer programs and recorded entertainment. However, enforcing these rights in digital products is extremely difficult, and TRIPS itself says nothing about how countries may deter their unauthorized downloading and distribution.

The 1996 Copyright and Performances and Phonograms treaties call for measures to protect against circumventing technical devices that limit access to, or control copying of, digital works. They also facilitate licensing and collective management of copyrighted materials on the internet by permitting identifying watermarks on materials and making unauthorized removal of those marks illegal. The treaties amplify the rights of performers, authors, and producers to authorize electronic communications of their works. These new treaties extend the frontiers of copyright protection, as is appropriate in light of the technical changes in copying associated with digital transmissions.

However, some observers argue that strict anticircumvention rules and extension of copyrights to databases unreasonably penalize those who need access to information for scientific and educational purposes. Developing countries and other technology importers should be leery of accepting the strong property rights accorded to databases adopted in the EU and pending in the United States. Electronic access on reasonable terms to the fruits of international scientific discovery will be critical in permitting technology followers to learn new technologies and adapt them to local needs. Thus, it will be important for countries to determine the scope for fair use of internet materials, balancing desires for access and learning against the needs of providers. It is inadvisable to undertake international negotiations within the WTO or WIPO that would extend strong database protection.

Trademarks are recognized on a territorial basis and support licensing restrictions on distribution, including restrictions against parallel trade. However, internet commerce inherently operates without borders. True, merchandise bought over the internet must be shipped, so that regulatory restraints (taxes and import barriers) are feasible. Yet imposing tariffs on products and services traded electronically would slow development of cross-border electronic commerce. Adoption of proposals to ensure free trade in internet transactions would be desirable.

Downloadable materials and services are less subject to border control. One challenge will be to devise mechanisms for identifying the true origin of products, enforcing permissible territorial restraints (a problem for which there may be private solutions), and defining the exhaustion of rights. These will be important for the evolution of TRIPs.

Beyond the TRIPs Framework

The advent of stronger global IPRs under TRIPs and other agreements offers an opportunity to consider international initiatives lying outside the purview of trade rules that could manage difficult aspects of intellectual property protection. The main problems relate to international market failures that could be exacerbated by stronger patent rights.

A Vaccine Fund for the Diseases of Poverty

As discussed in chapter 5, the amount of global R&D aimed at finding treatments or vaccines for diseases endemic in poor countries is minuscule. The problem largely reflects a substantial market and policy failure. It is conceivable that the stronger patent protection required by TRIPs could expand demand sufficiently to overcome this difficulty and direct adequate resources to finding cures for such diseases. However, this seems quite unlikely over the medium term as long as disease sufferers in such countries remain impoverished. The available evidence is not persuasive that patent protection in poor countries would make much difference.

In writings directed at this issue, Sachs cited a study by Wellcome Trust claiming as little as $80 million per year is devoted to malaria research and little of that to developing vaccines.[22] Similar difficulties plague research in tuberculosis. Further, virtually all the global research into treatment for HIV infection is devoted to the strain affecting people in developed countries. Almost none is aimed at the strains endemic in sub-Saharan Africa and South Asia, where the great majority of cases exist. These three diseases—malaria, tuberculosis, and AIDS—currently account for perhaps 5,000,000 deaths per year and considerably reduce productivity among the living sufferers.

The Sachs proposal for a public international fund to reward R&D in designated diseases presents an intriguing mix of private and public incentives. Private firms that develop an effective vaccine for any of these maladies would get a guaranteed payment per dosage sold to the fund. The payment would be calibrated to cover anticipated costs of developing the vaccine and could be adjusted upward if needed. For example, a malaria vaccine procured at $10 per child for the 25 million children born each year in sub-Saharan Africa would achieve $250 million in revenue. Given current costs of developing a new medicine,[23] this might not be sufficient. However, a price of $20 per unit would achieve $500

---

22. "Helping the World's Poorest" by Jeffrey Sachs, *The Economist*, 14 August 1999. See also Sachs, Kremer, and Hamoudi (1999).

23. These cost estimates may be excessive if the costs of clinical trials in poor countries are lower than those in developed countries.

million, which should be attractive for research-based pharmaceutical firms, while further revenues would come from immunizing children in Asia. The fund managers would then transfer these dosages to health authorities in target countries at low cost, perhaps incorporating a co-payment.

Sachs and his colleagues (1999) calculate that the maximum annual cost of a vaccine program against each of these three diseases would be $6.4 billion—a small portion of total development assistance to the least-developed countries. Moreover, it could have an important long-term benefit in terms of health status, productivity, and growth. In short, such an approach would be an effective and low-cost public health intervention.

With these payments as an inducement, it would be considerably more likely that pharmaceutical firms would see potential gains from engaging in such research than they do now. The proposal needs to be fleshed out to examine its feasibility and cost. It is not clear, for example, whether any firm developing a vaccine would be eligible for the funds or whether a patent-like "winner-takes-all" approach would be optimal from a procurement perspective. The former method could generate too little research if firms saw potential for competition; the latter could result in wasteful duplication of research. Ensuring efficient distribution of the vaccines would be necessary. Moreover, extensive controls on parallel exports of dosages would be required to support low pricing regimes, unless a (presumably suboptimal) decision were made to distribute in all countries at the same price.

Despite such difficulties, the Sachs proposal is an example of a sweeping and positive idea for addressing a critical need that is only partially addressed by IPRs. Determination to go forward with such a system could do much to restore confidence among developing countries in the new intellectual property system.

Managing IPRs to Improve Environmental Protection

A number of problems arise in the treatment of international environmental externalities that may be affected by stronger global IPRs. These complex issues should occasion serious thought, though they can only be mentioned here.[24]

It remains unclear how stronger patent rights, trade secrets, and protection for plant varieties might affect international environmental use. There are many cross-currents. For example, it is conceivable that some natural and genetic resources are being extracted at rates beyond those that would be nationally or globally optimal due to a lack of adequate property rights in those resources. If IPRs were attached to the products

---

24. Although he does not consider the role of IPRs, the discussion here complements Esty's proposal (1994) for a World Environmental Organization.

of those resources, there would be derived demands for the inputs that could help sort out competing demands in an orderly and efficient way. On the other hand, it is also possible that the promise of patents on the products of environmental resources could induce excessive exploitation at the research stage. In principle, contracts could be devised to manage this resource extraction, keeping both private incentives and public objectives clearly in mind. Considerable expertise in defining such contracts would be required, which again points to the need for technical assistance in many countries. Moreover, because these are issues of common use of resources with international spillovers, a role could arise for an international organization to assist in setting the parameters of rights and obligations.

A second issue is biodiversity, or the worry that widespread introduction of a few new and genetically manipulated plant strains could replace the great variety of traditional strains, with unforeseen consequences for the environment and human health. The rapid penetration of genetically modified plants in producing American crops attests to their advantages in terms of enhanced disease resistance, reduced use of chemical inputs, and higher yields. It also lends credence to the view that traditional varieties could be pushed out of the market, for these are powerful economic forces. Again, IPRs cut both ways, providing incentives for producing better crops and higher yields but potentially limiting consumer choice.

Governments in many countries, particularly in the EU, express reluctance to permit consumption of food products that are genetically modified through biotechnological techniques. This policy preference has so far resulted primarily in trade restrictions designed to keep out potentially unsafe foods, though there may be a protectionist element as well. However, interested observers are pushing for a rollback in the patent protection provided the biotechnological inventions of foods and plants, hoping to forestall widespread development of such products in the future.

From an economic standpoint, it makes little sense to retard incentives for plant development and food products by restricting IPRs beyond the usual public-interest limitations. Rather, the solution lies in labeling programs that allow consumers to express preferences for traditional crops and produce and also provide market incentives to sustain their production. Further, if the disappearance of plant varieties were seen as potentially damaging in environmental terms, a solid externality argument would exist for domestic and international public agencies to stockpile such strains to keep them alive as a form of social insurance. Because this would clearly spill across borders, the effort should be collaborative.

A significant and contentious question is whether stronger IPRs are likely to induce additional international transfer of cleaner technologies and products. The incentive effects of patents should do so in light of rising global demands for environmental protection. However, if adoption of new technologies becomes more costly, local firms could be slower to abandon polluting technologies, while inventors of environmentally friendly technologies could use their market power under TRIPs to choose not to license them in particular markets or to do so at high royalty rates. This could be particularly likely where there are few substitute technologies. However, as discussed earlier, stronger IPRs also provide incentives for efficient licensing.

Where a new technology might reduce environmental damages, with spillover international benefits, the inability of recipient countries to access the technology on reasonable terms is globally costly. Such situations could support public intervention to ensure both effective international access and adequate remuneration to the inventor. In particular, it should be possible to design a system of licenses of right in which critical environmental technologies would be supplied to national authorities in return for a negotiated schedule of royalties. These authorities would also guarantee that the technologies would not find their way into competing innovations for a certain period. So long as those technologies are protected in recipient markets inventors should have little concern about accelerating competition from second comers.

Such a scheme would offer a guaranteed market position to firms with technological solutions to global environmental problems in return for a compulsory right of license to ensure their diffusion. Given the incentives to free ride that could emerge, some multilateral agency would probably be necessary at the negotiation and transfer stages and to monitor the use of the technologies.

This proposal is purely preliminary. It would need to be fleshed out considerably, with due regard for its budgetary costs and the disincentives it might create, before it could be advanced seriously.

Summary

Adequate and effective intellectual property protection can be an important spur to competition at all levels of economic development. However, simply erecting a system of IPRs and expecting extensive gains in investment, technology acquisition, and growth as a result is unrealistic. The system needs to be accompanied by comprehensive policies that promote dynamic competition and technical change. Important among such initiatives are programs to build human capital and technical skills, ensure flexible factor markets, and liberalize restrictions on international trade and investment. The evidence seems clear that the payoffs to stronger IPRs are higher in countries with a strong skill basis and reasonable openness.

Some vigilance may be required to manage the costs that could emerge from the exploitation of stronger property rights. Each of the major policy concerns—competition policy, price regulation of pharmaceuticals, and management of biotechnology and plant protection—is complex and demands care in designing an appropriate yet competition-oriented program. The difficulties point to the importance of providing adequate technical and financial assistance to developing nations.

Finally, implementing stronger IPRs on a global scale raises issues regarding coordinated international policies to deal with externalities that might be accentuated. These are new and complex issues that require serious study into appropriate mechanism design, but their resolution could materially assist IPRs in advancing widespread sustainable growth.

8

Conclusions and Policy Recommendations: Are We There Yet?

It is not surprising that the 1990s ushered in unprecedented advances in global protection for intellectual property. The process is still ongoing. The powerful forces of economic globalization and technical change demand the ability to exploit innovations on a world scale, tapping the ever broadening circle of countries that are integrating more tightly with the international economy. As investments in new technologies and products rise, the costs of imitating or copying many of them fall. Rising incomes throughout the world are creating vast numbers of consumers with tastes for differentiated, high-quality goods and services. Producers in those economies increasingly are recognizing interests in protecting the fruits of their innovation. In short, we are in the midst of a significant increase in both the demand for and supply of intellectual property protection.

Where We Are

While these processes are by no means uniform across countries and the mechanisms for achieving policy changes have been difficult and contentious, the global result is dramatic. In 14 years, since the Uruguay Round began, IPRs moved from obscure background regulations that seemed only tangentially related to trade to a leading concern for global reform. Many countries, developing and developed alike, undertook upgrades in their systems. Regional trade agreements routinely included major provisions on intellectual property. The global trading system itself agreed to respect minimum standards for IPRs, an unprecedented injection of disciplines and regulatory obligations into the WTO. The TRIPs agreement is all the more significant for the impending entry of China and Russia, which also observe the IPR standards.

Unquestionably the status of intellectual property protection in the world has been strengthened markedly by these changes. Consider the most important of these shifts: countries are committed to take action against copyright and trademark piracy, even where this activity is economically significant and an important employer. This change alone is a major victory for intellectual property developers in the United States and other advanced nations, though it should also materially assist business development in the reforming countries as well. Patents must be provided for pharmaceutical products, agricultural chemicals, and many kinds of biotechnological inventions, while the scope of patents generally must be increased. These changes are supplemented by patents or effective protection for plant varieties. Thus, leading-edge technologies will reap higher returns to R&D on a global scale, even as countries affording new protection determine how they might benefit from the reforms.

The TRIPs agreement ushers in global copyright protection for computer programs, electronic transmissions, broadcasts, and phonograms. It requires countries to prevent the use of integrated circuits that infringe protected designs. It advances protection of trade secrets (confidential information) to the center of business law.

These are significant modifications in policy, even though stronger IPRs may be attenuated by competition rules and limitations on the scope of protection. They offer entirely new opportunities for MNEs to earn greater returns on their intellectual assets. The new IPRs truly represent the globalization of policy and may be only the vanguard of future harmonization of standards.

Economic analysis demonstrates that such a fundamental change in policy norms should have a host of complex effects. IPRs operate in a world of market failures and imperfections. Thus, it is impossible to guarantee as a matter of logic or fact that stronger IPRs will generate economic gains for all countries. Indeed, the implementation of stronger IPRs alone could make some nations worse off. In this sense, reforming IPRs is very different from liberalizing trade barriers.

Economics can point to relevant trade-offs, however, and inform empirical analysis. The evidence reviewed in chapters 4 and 5 largely supports the view that stronger IPRs have considerable promise for expanding flows of trade in technical inputs, FDI, and licensing. These in turn could expand the direct and indirect transfer of technology to developing nations. Such gains may not be uniformly available to all developing countries, of course. The poorest nations in particular may find little benefit in terms of greater economic activity as they absorb negative changes in their terms of trade. But more advanced developing nations could well benefit from the new policy regime and its ability to shorten technological distances between core technology providers and technology followers.

Long-run gains would come at the expense of costlier access in the medium term. Technological learning must shift from uncompensated imitation of lower-quality techniques to compensated acquisition of higher-quality techniques. The source of information spillovers should move from copying by free riders to incremental innovation by fair followers.

This transition could be difficult. Thus, the great challenge facing countries upgrading their IPRs systems is to establish procedures that, while fully consistent with both the letter and the intentions of TRIPs, maximize their dynamic gains over time. The challenge refers both to IPRs themselves and to the extensive complementary policies that make them effective.

Thus, for example, the least-developed countries, many of which are still in the implementation phase, are likely to select standards that meet only the minimum TRIPs obligations. Implementation could assist them in improving their abilities to engage in learning and adaptive, incremental innovation. These countries require considerable assistance in revising and administering their intellectual property systems. That assistance could be extended to broader help in managing any dislocations that could emerge, thus promoting stronger competitive processes in their markets.

For their part, higher-income developing countries could choose stronger standards to favor a mix of invention and adaptive learning. They have dynamic interests in acquiring and developing technology through compensated means, buttressed by enforceable contracts and supported by intellectual property protection. These countries are also in a position to establish an effective infrastructure for promoting technological change, exploiting synergies between research institutes and private enterprises. Again, such processes would operate more efficiently with open competition and transparent regulation.

Finally, developed countries generally have intellectual property standards that exceed the minimum levels required by TRIPs. With deep and competitive economies, they find that the gains from IPRs substantially outweigh the costs in most circumstances. Where the exercise of IPRs threatens to be anticompetitive or excessively costly in social terms, they have mature legal systems of corrective interventions.

Nonetheless, views on further investing private rights in information are by no means uniform among, or even within, rich nations. There are legitimate reasons to be concerned about the highly protective standards that have emerged recently in the United States and the European Union. These laws and judicial interpretations provide broad patent protection for software and biotechnological inventions. They also promote extensive rights in the formulation of databases, which could have a negative effect on scientific research. It remains to be seen whether such standards excessively tilt the balance within those jurisdictions toward the private rights of inventors and away from the needs of competitors and users. It is not too early to claim that they are inappropriate for developing economies and net technology importers.

Where We Are Going

Despite considerable institutional reform, the global IPRs system is still in flux. Over the next few years attention will focus on the implementation of TRIPs and on the new administrative and enforcement procedures in many countries. Here it is again appropriate to mention the need for effective technical assistance and to work toward effectuating the TRIPs language on technology transfer commitments. Further, TRIPs has a built-in review agenda that is to be invoked soon. Much of that review will consider the operation of Article 27 protecting biotechnology. There are good reasons to doubt the wisdom of strengthening these provisions markedly in the near term. It could backfire into an attempt by many developing countries to roll back the entire agreement.

TRIPs may well come up for discussion in the next round of trade negotiations. Among the contentious issues that would emerge, three stand out:

1. There is little scope in economic theory or evidence for a global policy banning parallel imports.

2. Because Article 40 of TRIPs explicitly invites countries to invoke antitrust rules to discipline abuses of IPRs, it raises some scope for multilateral consideration of an agreement on competition policy.

3. Attempts to extend the database protection laws of the EU and the United States across the world should be resisted. Protection on that scale is unlikely to serve the legitimate needs of researchers and competitors in many developed countries, much less in the developing world.

In my view, TRIPs is a delicate compromise among international competing interests. Despite the positive evidence presented earlier about its potential implications, there is much that we do not know about how it could affect competitive processes in different countries. It seems appropriate to let these new processes settle in and begin working on markets before considering extensive new multilateral obligations.

Does TRIPs Belong in the WTO?

An important question is whether the WTO risks being overburdened by the introduction of IPRs into its scope of authority. There are important systemic issues here (Maskus 2000b). For example, many TRIPs standards are expressly about production processes, which could open the WTO to further process-oriented rules. Further, the need to monitor and adjudicate TRIPs practices in member states could be problematic for the WTO Secretariat.

Nonetheless, there are valid reasons for its inclusion. First, international variations in IPRs clearly and directly influence trade flows, suggesting they fit within the purview of the trading system. Second, weak IPRs generate international static and dynamic externalities that are best addressed globally. Finally, the international policy coordination problems in the IPRs area seem particularly acute. Thus, I disagree with recent criticisms from trade economists that including TRIPs in the WTO is inappropriate (Panagariya 1999).

The Way Forward Is to Be Forward-Looking

With the negotiation of TRIPs and the strengthening of standards in regional and unilateral initiatives, considerable machinery will be in place to promote international technological dynamism. Like any other major set of rules, this machinery must be managed effectively for it to achieve its desired goals. For IPRs these goals include greater incentives for invention and innovation, more opportunities for compensated and effective transfers of technology, modernizing of the business sectors in developing countries, and tighter integration of poor nations into the global system of technological evolution.

Perhaps it is not widely appreciated, but the failure of the Seattle Ministerial meeting of the WTO in December 1999 may be traced in part to dissatisfaction on the part of many developing countries and non-governmental organizations (NGOs) with TRIPs. Developing countries are frustrated with the absence of effort by rich nations to transfer more technology. The commitment to make such transfers, though exhortatory, was nonetheless a promise that was written into the agreement itself.

Many countries are further concerned about other issues discussed at length above, most significantly prices of pharmaceutical products and new seed varieties, uncompensated exploitation of genetic resources, the patenting of life forms, and IPR-based limitations on their access to information on the internet. There is additional frustration that many of the TRIPs provisions were reached without adequate consideration of how developing countries could participate in them. For example, the evolving language in TRIPs on geographical indications remains largely remains confined to wines and spirits, while many developing countries point to food products that could be protected to their advantage, such as Basmati rice and Darjeeling tea.

It is conceivable, finally, that such frustrations and the inability to launch a new round of trade negotiations could weaken the resolve of WTO member states to finish implementing the more difficult TRIPs obligations.

The concerns expressed by NGOs share some of these features but extend further to the potential implications of TRIPs for the environment. There are reasons to think that better defined property rights could rationalize and improve exploitation of the environment, but this outcome is not assured. Thus, significant questions remain about the interplay between IPRs, the health implications of genetically modified organisms, and biodiversity. These issues will be at the forefront of the emerging global debate about TRIPs in particular and the WTO in general.

The point here is that if the considerable dynamic gains that TRIPs proffers are to be achieved, some costs must be absorbed by numerous developing and developed economies. Copying and imitative industries in many countries will be pressured to contract and restructure. Access to important therapies, inputs, and technologies will become more expensive. Costs of administration and enforcement will rise as standards are strengthened.

Yet a main theme of this book is that such costs can be accompanied by even larger benefits, though with a time lag. Stronger IPRs can usher in more certain contracts that raise the quality of technology acquired and permit tighter partnerships between domestic and foreign firms. They can set the stage for efficient generation of follow-on and adaptive technologies that help diffuse learning throughout the economy. They can provide incentives for significant investments to start up new firms, build product quality, and expand marketing networks. These gains are not merely theoretical. There is solid evidence to back up each of these claims.

However, to improve the prospects for realizing these benefits, many nations must engineer significant and broad reforms. The effectiveness of IPRs is maximized in an environment of open markets, competitive entry, and sound opportunities for taking risks and building skills. A basic policy prescription of this volume—that poor nations and industrializing countries should adopt procompetitive forms of IPRs—is meaningful only if competition remains effective. As IPRs change the terms of international competition, they also could alter the severity of international market failures. In some circumstances, stronger IPRs could improve the efficiency with which markets are served and the environment is used. In other circumstances, unfortunately, those processes could be worsened. Thus there is scope for international management of certain aspects of intellectual property protection. Technology developers in industrial countries should not expect to be exempt from international regulation, for they face it deeply in their own countries. Thus, it is important to think through definitions of practices that would constitute abuses at the international level. It is important also to consider circumstances under which adequately compensated compulsory licenses, issued by an international authority, could be beneficial in meeting problems of the global commons. Finally, it makes sense to use the concepts of IPRs, in the form of global market guarantees, to motivate firms to undertake research into critical medicines and vaccines for impoverished nations.

Further growth in the global IPRs system requires due concern for the needs of fair technology followers and flexibility to accommodate the evolution of technology leaders. Technical change always outstrips IPRs reform; IPRs change in response to the former. The newest technologies in information science, telecommunications, and biotechnology already have placed heavy stresses on the TRIPs system and on national regulatory regimes. Because dynamic evolution of demands for protection is thus inevitable, the global system will continue to evolve.

The advantage of the current system, as reflected in TRIPs, is that it establishes minimum standards that can be competitively applied to the benefit of follower countries, but does not prevent technology leaders from adopting higher standards. As I have explained in this volume, competitive application in the former group can be beneficial if it is accompanied with hard work. Ultimately, the ability of follower countries to experiment competitively could rein in the protective excesses of leading countries. If that equilibrium were to emerge, the designers of TRIPs would deserve significant praise.

References

Abbott, Frederick. 1998. First Report (Final) to the Committee on International Trade Law of the International Law Association on the Subject of Parallel Importation. *Journal of International Economic Law* 1: 607-36.

Aitken, Brian, and Ann Harrison. 1993. *Does Proximity to Foreign Firms Induce Technology Spillovers?* PRD Working Paper. Washington: World Bank.

Aitken, Brian, Ann Harrison, and Gordon Hanson. 1994. *Spillovers: Foreign Investment and Export Behavior.* NBER Working Papers 4967. Cambridge, MA: National Bureau of Economic Research.

Aitken, Brian, Ann Harrison, and Robert E. Lipsey. 1996. Wages and Foreign Ownership: A Comparative Study of Mexico, Venezuela, and the United States. *Journal of International Economics* 40: 345-71.

Anderson, Robert, and Nancy T. Gallini. 1998. *Competition Policy and Intellectual Property Rights in the Knowledge-Based Economy.* Calgary: University of Calgary Press.

Arora, Ashish. 1996. Contracting for Tacit Knowledge: The Provision of Technical Services in Technology Licensing Contracts. *Journal of Development Economics* 50: 233-56.

Bale, Harvey E., Jr. 1998. The Conflicts between Parallel Trade and Product Access and Innovation: The Case of Pharmaceuticals. *Journal of International Economic Law* 1: 637-53.

Barfield, Claude E., and Mark A. Groombridge. 1998. The Economic Case for Copyright Owner Control over Parallel Imports. *The Journal of World Intellectual Property* 1: 903-39.

Barro, Robert J., and J. H. Lee. 1994. Sources of Economic Growth. *Carnegie-Rochester Conference Series on Public Policy* 40: 1-46.

Barton, John H. 1993. Adapting the Intellectual Property System to New Technologies. In *Global Dimensions of Intellectual Property Rights in Science and Technology*, ed. by M. B. Wallerstein, M. E. Mogee, and R. A. Schoen. Washington: National Academy Press.

Barton, John H. 1995. Patent Scope in Biotechnology. *International Review of Industrial Property and Copyright Law* 26: 605-18.

Beier, Friedrich-Karl, and Gerhard Schricker. 1996. *From GATT to TRIPs—The Agreement on Trade-Related Aspects of Intellectual Property Rights.* IIC Studies 18. Munich: Max Planck Institute for Foreign and International Patent, Copyright and Competition Law.

Besen, Stanley M., and Leo J. Raskind. 1991. An Introduction to the Law and Economics of Intellectual Property. *Journal of Economic Perspectives* 5, no. 1 (Winter): 3-27.

Blomstrom, Magnus. 1989. *Foreign Investment and Spillovers*. London: Routledge Press.

Borensztein, E., J. De Gregorio, and J.-W. Lee. 1998. How Does Foreign Direct Investment Affect Economic Growth? *Journal of International Economics* 45: 115-35.

Bradley, A. Jane. 1987. Intellectual Property Rights, Investment, and Trade in Services in the Uruguay Round: Laying the Foundations. *Stanford Journal of International Law* 23: 57-87.

Braga, H., and L. Willmore. 1991. Technological Imports and Technological Effort: An Analysis of Their Determinants in Brazilian Firms. *Journal of Industrial Economics* 39: 421-32.

Brainard, S. Lael. 1993. *An Empirical Assessment of the Proximity Concentration Trade-off between Multinational Sales and Trade*. Working Paper No. 4583. National Bureau of Economic Research.

Bresnahan, Timothy F. 1986. Measuring the Spillovers from Technical Advance: Mainframe Computers in Financial Services. *American Economic Review* 76: 742-55.

Bronckers, Marco C. E. J. 1998. The Exhaustion of Patent Rights Under World Trade Organization Law. *Journal of World Trade* 32: 137-38.

Business Software Alliance and Software and Information Industry Association. 1999. *1998 Global Software Piracy Report*. http://www.bsa.org (May).

Carr, David L., James R. Markusen, and Keith E. Maskus. 2000. Estimating the Knowledge Capital Model of the Multinational Enterprise. *American Economic Review:* forthcoming.

Caves, Richard E. 1996. *Multinational Enterprise and Economic Analysis*. 2d Ed. London: Cambridge University Press.

Chard, J. S., and C. J. Mellor. 1989. Intellectual Property Rights and Parallel Imports. *The World Economy* 12: 69–83.

Cheung, Stephen. 1986. Property Rights and Invention. In *Research in Law and Economics, Volume 8: The Economics of Patents and Copyrights*, ed. J. P. Palmer and R. V. Zerbe, Jr. Greenwich, CT: JAI Press.

Coe, David T., and Elhanan Helpman. 1995. International R&D Spillovers. *European Economic Review* 39: 859–87.

Coe, David T., Elhanan Helpman, and Alexander W. Hoffmaister. 1997. North-South R&D Spillovers. *Economic Journal* 107: 134-49.

Coloma, F., A. Gabrielli, and C. Williamson. 1987. *Efectos de las Patentes de Medicamentos Sobre el Mercado Farmacéutico y su Impacto Sobre la Salud y el Gasto Fiscal*. Santiago: Instituto de Economía, Universidad Católica de Chile.

Contractor, Farok J. 1980. The Profitability of Technology Licensing by US Multinationals: A Framework for Analysis and an Empirical Study. *Journal of International Business Studies* 11: 40-63.

Correa, Carlos M. 1999. Reforming the Intellectual Property Rights System in Latin America. University of Buenos Aires. Photocopy.

Cottier, Thomas. 1998. The WTO System and Exhaustion of Rights. Paper presented at Conference on the Exhaustion of Intellectual Property Rights and Parallel Importation in World Trade, Committee on International Trade Law, Geneva (7 November).

Dahab, S. 1986. *Technological Change in the Brazilian Agricultural Implements Industry*. Unpublished Ph.D. dissertation. Yale University.

Danzon, Patricia M. 1997. *Pharmaceutical Price Regulation*. Washington: American Enterprise Institute Press.

Danzon, Patricia M., and Jeong D. Kim. 1995. International Price Comparisons for Pharmaceuticals. Leonard Davis Institute for Health Economics, University of Pennsylvania. Photocopy.

David, Paul A. 1993. Intellectual Property Institutions and the Panda's Thumb. In *Global Dimensions of Intellectual Property Rights in Science and Technology*, ed. by M. B. Wallerstein, M. E. Mogee, and R. A. Schoen. Washington: National Academy Press.

Davidson, William H., and Donald G. McFetridge. 1984. International Technology Transactions and the Theory of the Firm. *Journal of Industrial Economics* 32: 253-64.

Davies, H. 1977. Technology Transfer through Commercial Transactions. *Journal of Industrial Economics* 26: 161-75.

DiMasi, J. A., H. G. Grabowski, and L. Lasagna. 1991. The Costs of Innovation in the Pharmaceutical Industry. *Journal of Health Economics* 10: 107-42.

Diwan, Ishak, and Dani Rodrik. 1991. Patents, Appropriate Technology, and North-South Trade. *Journal of International Economics* 63: 79-90.

Dougherty, Sean M. 1997. The Role of Foreign Technology in Improving Chinese Productivity. MIT Science and Technology Initiative, Beijing, China. Photocopy.

Dunning, John H. 1981. *International Production and the Multinational Enterprise*. London: George Allen and Unwin.

Eaton, Jonathan, and Samuel J. Kortum. 1996. Trade in Ideas: Patenting and Productivity in the OECD. *Journal of International Economics* 40: 251-78.

Esty, Daniel C. 1994. *Greening the GATT: Trade, Environment, and the Future*. Washington: Institute for International Economics.

Evenson, Robert E. 1984. International Invention: Implications for Technology Market Analysis. In *R&D, Patents and Productivity*, ed. by Zvi Griliches. Chicago: University of Chicago Press.

Evenson, Robert E., and Larry E. Westphal. 1997. Technological Change and Technology Strategy. In *Handbook of Development Economics*. Vol. 3, ed. by Hollis Chenery and T. N. Srinivisan. Amsterdam: North-Holland.

Feenstra, Robert C., and Gordon H. Hanson. 1997. Foreign Direct Investment and Relative Wages: Evidence from Mexico's Maquiladoras. *Journal of International Economics* 42: 371-94.

Ferrantino, Michael J. 1993. The Effect of Intellectual Property Rights on International Trade and Investment. *Weltwirtschaftliches Archiv* 129: 300-31.

Finger, J. Michael, and Philip Schuler. 1999. Implementation of Uruguay Round Commitments: The Development Challenge. Washington: World Bank. Photocopy.

Fink, Carsten. 2000. Patent Protection, Transnational Corporations, and Market Structure: A Simulation Study of the Indian Pharmaceutical Industry. Photocopy. Washington: World Bank.

Fox, Eleanor M. 1995. Competition Law and the Agenda for the WTO: Forging the Links of Competition and Trade. *Pacific Rim Law and Policy Journal* 4: 1-36.

Frankel, Jeffrey A., and David Romer. 1999. Does Trade Cause Growth? *American Economic Review* 89: 379-99.

Friedman, David D., William M. Landes, and Richard A. Posner. 1991. Some Economics of Trade Secret Law. *Journal of Economic Perspectives* 5: 61-72.

Gadbaw, R. Michael, and Timothy J. Richards, eds. 1988. *Intellectual Property Rights: Global Consensus, Global Conflict?* Boulder, CO: Westview Press.

Gallini, Nancy T., and Michael Trebilcock. 1998. Intellectual Property Rights and Competition Policy: A Framework for Analysis of Economic and Legal Issues. In *Competition Policy and Intellectual Property Rights in the Knowledge-Based Economy*, ed. by Robert Anderson and Nancy T. Gallini. Calgary: University of Calgary Press.

Ginarte, Juan Carlos, and Walter G. Park. 1997. Determinants of Patent Rights: A Cross-National Study. *Research Policy* 26: 283-301.

Glass, Amy, and Kamal Saggi. 1995. Intellectual Property Rights, Foreign Direct Investment, and Innovation. Ohio State University. Photocopy.

Gould, David M., and William C. Gruben. 1996. The Role of Intellectual Property Rights in Economic Growth. *Journal of Development Economics* 48: 323-50.

Graham, Edward M., and J. David Richardson. 1997a. *Competition Policies for the Global Economy*. Policy Analyses in International Economics 51. Washington: Institute for International Economics.

Graham, Edward M., and J. David Richardson. 1997b. *Global Competition Policy*. Washington, DC: Institute for International Economics.

Griliches, Zvi, ed. 1984. *Research and Development, Patents, and Productivity*. Chicago: University of Chicago Press.

Grossman, Gene M., and Alan B. Krueger. 1993. Environmental Impacts of a North American Free Trade Agreement. In *The US-Mexico Free Trade Agreement*, ed. by Peter Garber. Cambridge: MIT Press.

Grubaugh, S. 1987. Determinants of Direct Foreign Investment. *Review of Economics and Statistics* 69: 149-51.

Hanson, Gordon H. 1996. Localization Economies, Vertical Organization, and Trade. *American Economic Review* 86: 1266-78.

Harris, Richard G. 1984. Applied General Equilibrium Analysis of Small Open Economies with Scale Economies and Imperfect Competition. *American Economic Review* 74: 1016-32.

Harris, Richard G. 1996. Conference Summary and Wrap–Up. In *Policy Frameworks for a Knowledge Economy*, ed. by Thomas J. Courchene. Kingston, ON: John Deutsch Institute for the Study of Economic Policy.

Harrison, Glenn A., Thomas F. Rutherford, and David G. Tarr. 1996. Quantifying the Uruguay Round. In *The Uruguay Round and the Developing Countries*, ed. by Will Martin and L. Alan Winters. Cambridge: Cambridge University Press.

Heath, C. 1997. Intellectual Property Rights in Asia: An Overview. *International Review of Industrial Property and Copyright Law* 28: 303-9.

Helpman, Elhanan. 1987. Imperfect Competition and International Trade: Evidence from Fourteen Industrial Countries. *Journal of the Japanese and International Economies* 1: 62-81.

Helpman, Elhanan. 1993. Innovation, Imitation, and Intellectual Property Rights. *Econometrica* 61: 1247-80.

Helpman, Elhanan, and Paul R. Krugman. 1985. *Market Structure and Foreign Trade: Increasing Returns, Imperfect Competition and the International Economy*. Cambridge, MA: MIT Press.

Hilke, John C. 1988. Free Trading or Free Riding: An Examination of the Theories and Available Evidence on Gray Market Imports. *World Competition* 32: 75-92.

Horstmann, Ignatius, and James R. Markusen. 1987. Licensing Versus Direct Investment: A Model of Internalization by the Multinational Enterprise. *Canadian Journal of Economics* 20: 464-81.

International Intellectual Property Association. 1998a. *Estimates of 1995 US Losses Due to Foreign Piracy and Levels of Piracy*. http://www.iipa.com/html/worldp_piracy_losses.html (3 August).

International Intellectual Property Association. 1998b. *Parallel Import Protection in 107 Selected Countries*. http://www.iipa.com.

International Intellectual Property Association. 1999. *IIPA 1999 "Special 301" Recommendations: Estimated Trade Losses Due to Piracy*. http://www.iipa.com/html (15 July).

International Monetary Fund. Various Years. *Balance of Payments Statistics Yearbook*. Washington: IMF.

International Monetary Fund. Various Years. *International Financial Statistics Yearbook*. Washington: IMF.

Jaffe, Walter, and Jeroen van Wijk. 1995. The Impact of Plant Breeders' Rights in Developing Countries. IICA-University of Amsterdam. Photocopy.

Jensen, Richard, and Marie Thursby. 1999. Proofs and Prototypes for Sale: The Licensing of University Inventions. Purdue University. Photocopy.

Johnson, B. T., and T. P. Sheehy. 1995. *The Index of Economic Freedom*. Washington: Heritage Foundation.

Katz, J., and S. Groisman. 1988. La Industria Farmacéutica en Argentina: Período 1983-1988. Paper presented at the conference Seminario Sobre el Uso Racional de los Medicamentos, Mexico City.

Kawaura, Akihiko, and Sumner J. LaCroix. 1995. Japan's Shift from Process to Product Patents in the Pharmaceutical Industry: An Event Study of the Impact on Japanese Firms. *Economic Inquiry* 33: 88-103.

Kirim, A. S. 1985. Reconsidering Patents and Economic Development: A Case Study of the Turkish Pharmaceutical Industry. *World Development* 13: 219-36.

Kitch, Edmund W. 1977. The Nature and Function of the Patent System. *Journal of Law and Economics* 20: 265-90.

Klemperer, Paul. 1990. How Broad Should the Scope of Patent Protection Be? *RAND Journal of Economics* 21: 113-30.

Kondo, Edson K. 1995. The Effect of Patent Protection on Foreign Direct Investment. *Journal of World Trade* 29: 97-122.

Korenko, George C. 1999. Intellectual Property Protection and Industrial Growth: A Case Study. *The Journal of World Intellectual Property* 2: 47-75.

Krugman, Paul R. 1987. The Narrow Moving Band, the Dutch Disease, and the Competitive Consequences of Mrs. Thatcher: Notes on Trade in the Presence of Dynamic Scale Economies. *Journal of Development Economics* 27: 41-55.

LaCroix, Sumner. 1992. The Political Economy of Intellectual Property Rights in Developing Countries. In *The Economics of Cooperation: East Asian Development and the Case for Pro–Market Intervention*, ed. by James A. Roumasset and Susan Barr. Boulder, CO: Westview Press.

LaCroix, Sumner J., and Denise Eby-Konan. 1998. Intellectual Property Rights in China: American Pressure and Chinese Resistance. University of Hawaii. Photocopy.

LaCroix, Sumner J., and Akihiko Kawaura. 1996. Product Patent Reform and Its Impact on Korea's Pharmaceutical Industry. *International Economic Journal* 10: 109-24.

Lai, Edwin L. C. 1998. International Intellectual Property Rights Protection and the Rate of Product Innovation. *Journal of Development Economics* 55: 115-30.

Landes, W. M., and Richard A. Posner. 1987. Trademark Law: An Economic Perspective. *Journal of Law and Economics* 30: 265-309.

Lanjouw, Jean O. 1997. The Introduction of Pharmaceutical Product Patents in India: Heartless Exploitation of the Poor and Suffering? Yale University, Economic Growth Center. Photocopy (August).

Lanjouw, Jean O. 1998. *The Introduction of Pharmaceutical Product Patents in India: "Heartless Exploitation of the Poor and Suffering"?* NBER Working Paper 6366. Cambridge, MA: National Bureau of Economic Research.

Lee, J.-Y. and Edwin Mansfield. 1996. Intellectual Property Protection and US Foreign Direct Investment. *Review of Economics and Statistics* 78: 181-86.

Levin, Richard C., Alvin K. Klevorick, Richard R. Nelson, and Sidney G. Winter. 1987. Appropriating the Returns from Industrial Research and Development. *Brookings Papers on Economic Activity* SP ISS: 783-820.

Malueg, David A., and Marius Schwartz. 1994. Parallel Imports, Demand Dispersion, and International Price Discrimination. *Journal of International Economics* 37: 167-96.

Mann, Catherine L., and Sarah C. Knight. 1999. Electronic Commerce in the World Trade Organization. Paper presented at Preparing for the Seattle Ministerial Conference, sponsored by the Institute for International Economics, Washington (26 October).

Mansfield, Edwin. 1985. How Rapidly Does Industrial Technology Leak Out? *Journal of Industrial Economics* 34: 217-23.

Mansfield, Edwin. 1986. Patents and Innovation: An Empirical Study. *Management Science* 32, no. 2: 173-81.

Mansfield, Edwin. 1988. Intellectual Property Rights, Technological Change, and Economic Growth. In *Intellectual Property Rights and Capital Formation in the Next Decade*, ed. by Charles E. Walker and Mark A. Bloomfield. Lanham, MD: University Press of America.

Mansfield, Edwin. 1993. Unauthorized Use of Intellectual Property: Effects on Investment, Technology Transfer, and Innovation. In *Global Dimensions of Intellectual Property Rights* in *Science and Technology*, ed. by M. B. Wallerstein, M. E. Mogee, and R. A. Schoen. Washington: National Academy Press.

Mansfield, Edwin. 1994. *Intellectual Property Protection, Foreign Direct Investment, and Technology Transfer.* International Finance Corporation, Discussion Paper 19.

Mansfield, Edwin. 1995. *Intellectual Property Protection, Direct Investment and Technology Transfer: Germany, Japan, and the United States.* International Finance Corporation, Discussion Paper 27.

Mansfield, Edwin, Mark Schwartz, and Samuel Wagner. 1981. Imitation Costs and Patents: An Empirical Study. *Economic Journal* 91: 907-18.

Marino, Poorti S. 1998. An Empirical Analysis of the Indian Pharmaceutical Industry. Boston University. Photocopy (December).

Markusen, James R. 1984. Multinationals, Multi-Plant Economics, and the Gains from International Trade. *Journal of International Economics* 16: 205-26.

Markusen, James R. 1995. The Boundaries of Multinational Enterprises and the Theory of International Trade. *Journal of Economic Perspectives* 9: 169-89.

Markusen, James R. 2000. Contracts, Intellectual Property Rights, and Multinational Investment in Developing Countries. *Journal of International Economics*, forthcoming.

Marron, Donald B., and David G. Steel. 2000. Which Countries Protect Intellectual Property? An Empirical Analysis of Software Piracy. *Economic Inquiry* 38: 159-74.

Maskus, Keith E. 1990. Normative Concerns in the International Protection of Intellectual Property Rights. *The World Economy* 13: 387-409.

Maskus, Keith E. 1993. The New Issues: Trade-Related Intellectual Property Rights and the European Community. *The European Economy* 52: 157-84.

Maskus, Keith E. 1997a. Implications of Regional and Multilateral Agreements for Intellectual Property Rights. *The World Economy* 20: 681-94.

Maskus, Keith E. 1997b. *Intellectual Property Rights in Lebanon.* International Trade Division, World Bank. Photocopy.

Maskus, Keith E. 1998a. The International Regulation of Intellectual Property. *Weltwirtschaftliches Archiv* 134: 186-208.

Maskus, Keith E. 1998b. The Role of Intellectual Property Rights in Encouraging Foreign Direct Investment and Technology Transfer. *Duke Journal of Comparative and International Law* 9: 109-61.

Maskus, Keith E. 1998c. Intellectual Property Rights in the World Trade Organization: Progress and Prospects. In *Launching New Global Trade Talks: An Action Agenda*, ed. Jeffrey J. Schott. Washington: Institute for International Economics.

Maskus, Keith E. 1998d. Strengthening Intellectual Property Rights in Asia: Implications for Australia. *Australian Economic Papers* 37: 346-61.

Maskus, Keith E. 1998e. Price Effects and Competition Aspects of Intellectual Property Rights in Developing Countries. Background paper for *World Development Report 1998/1999: Knowledge in Development.* Washington: World Bank. Photocopy. (12 January)

Maskus, Keith E. 1999. Evidence on Intellectual Property Rights and Economic Development: A Broader Policy Perspective for China. Paper presented at the Conference on Intellectual Property Rights and Economic Development in Shanghai and the Lower Yangzi Region, Shanghai (11 May).

Maskus, Keith E. 2000a. Strengthening Intellectual Property Rights in Lebanon. In *Catching Up with the Competition*, ed. by Bernard Hoekman and Jamel E. Zarrouk. Ann Arbor: University of Michigan Press.

Maskus, Keith E. 2000b. Regulatory Standards in the WTO: Comparing Intellectual Property Rights with Competition Policy, Environmental Protection, and Core Labor Standards. Working Paper 00-1. Washington, DC: Institute for International Economics.

Maskus, Keith E., and Yongmin Chen. 1999. Vertical Price Control and Parallel Imports. Paper presented at the International Seminar on International Trade. Cambridge, MA: National Bureau of Economic Research (5 June).

Maskus, Keith E., Sean M. Dougherty, and Andrew Mertha. 1998. Intellectual Property Rights and Economic Development in China. Paper presented at the Southwest China Regional Conference on Intellectual Property Rights and Economic Development, Chongqing (16 September).

Maskus, Keith E., and Denise Eby-Konan. 1994. Trade-Related Intellectual Property Rights: Issues and Exploratory Results. In *Analytical and Negotiating Issues in the Global Trading System*, ed. by Alan V. Deardorff and Robert M. Stern. Ann Arbor, MI: University of Michigan Press.

Maskus, Keith E., and Mohamed Lahouel. 2000. Competition Policy and Intellectual Property Rights in Developing Countries. *The World Economy* 23: 595-611.

Maskus, Keith E., and Christine McDaniel. 1999. Impacts of the Japanese Patent System on Productivity Growth. *Japan and the World Economy* 11: 557-74.

Maskus, Keith E., and Mohan Penubarti. 1995. How Trade–Related Are Intellectual Property Rights? *Journal of International Economics* 39: 227-48.

Maskus, Keith E., and Mohan Penubarti. 1997. Patents and International Trade: An Empirical Study. In *Quiet Pioneering: Robert M. Stern and His International Economic Legacy*, ed. by Keith E. Maskus, Peter M. Hooper, Edward E. Leamer, and J. David Richardson. Ann Arbor, MI: University of Michigan Press.

Mazzoleni, Roberto, and Richard R. Nelson. 1998. Economic Theories about the Benefits and Costs of Patents. *Journal of Economic Issues* 32: 1031-52.

McCalman, Phillip. 1999a. National Patents, Innovation and International Agreements. Canberra: Australian National University. Photocopy.

McCalman, Phillip. 1999b. *Reaping What You Sow: An Empirical Analysis of International Patent Harmonization*. Working Paper in Economics and Econometrics 374. Canberra: Australian National University.

Mikkelsen, K. W. 1984. *Inventive Activity in Philippines Industry*. Unpublished Ph.D. dissertation. Yale University.

Moran, Theodore H. 1999. *Foreign Direct Investment and Development: The New Policy Agenda for Developing Economies and Economies in Transition*. Washington: Institute for International Economics.

Morck, Randall, and Bernard Yeung. 1992. Internalization: An Event Study Test. *Journal of International Economics* 33: 41-56.

Mowery, David C., ed. 1996. *The International Computer Software Industry*. New York: Oxford University Press.

Mutti, John, and Bernard Yeung. 1997. Section 337 and the Protection of Intellectual Property in the US: The Impact on R&D Spending. In *Quiet Pioneering: Robert M. Stern and His International Economic Legacy*, ed. by Keith E. Maskus, Peter M. Hooper, Edward E. Leamer, and J. David Richardson. Ann Arbor, MI: University of Michigan Press.

National Economic Research Associates. 1999. *The Economic Consequences of the Choice of Regime of Exhaustion in the Area of Trademarks*. London: NERA.

Nelson, Richard R., and Howard Pack. 1999. The Asian Miracle and Modern Growth Theory. *Economic Journal* 109: 416-36.

Nogues, Julio J. 1990. Patents and Pharmaceutical Drugs: Understanding the Pressures on Developing Countries. *Journal of World Trade* 24, no. 6: 81-104.

Nogues, Julio J. 1993. Social Costs and Benefits of Introducing Patent Protection for Pharmaceutical Drugs in Developing Countries. *The Developing Economies* 31: 24-53.

North, Douglass C. 1981. *Structure and Change in Economic History*. New York: Norton.

Oddi, S. A. 1996. TRIPs—Natural Rights and a "Polite Form of Economic Imperialism." *Vanderbilt Journal of Transnational Law* 29: 415-570.

Ordover, Janusz A. 1991. A Patent System for Both Diffusion and Exclusion. *Journal of Economic Perspectives* 5: 43-60.

Organization for Economic Cooperation and Development. 1989. *Competition Policy and Intellectual Property Rights*. Paris: OECD.

Organization for Economic Cooperation and Development. 1996. *Trade, Employment, and Labor Standards: A Study of Core Workers' Rights and International Trade.* Paris: OECD.

Organization for Economic Cooperation and Development. Various years. *Basic Science and Technology Statistics.* Paris: OECD.

Organization for Economic Cooperation and Development. 1999. *The Economic and Social Impact of Electronic Commerce.* Paris: OECD.

Pakes, Ariel, and Mark Schankerman. 1984. The Rate of Obsolescence of Knowledge, Research Gestation Lags, and the Private Rate of Return to Research Resources. In *Research and Development, Patents, and Productivity,* ed. by Zvi Griliches. Chicago: University of Chicago Press.

Palia, A. P., and C. F. Keown. 1991. Combating Parallel Importing: Views of US Exporters to the Asia-Pacific Region. *International Marketing Review* 8: 47-56.

Panagariya, Arvind. 1999. *TRIPs and the WTO: An Uneasy Marriage.* University of Maryland. Photocopy.

Park, Walter G. 1997. Issues in International Patenting. Paper presented at a meeting of the OECD Working Group on Innovation and Technology Policy, Paris (April).

Park, Walter G., and Carlos Ginarte. 1997. Intellectual Property Rights and Economic Growth. *Contemporary Economic Policy* 15: 51-61.

Pharmaceutical Research and Manufacturers' Association. 1999a. *Pharmaceutical Industry Profile: 1999.* Washington: Pharmaceutical Research and Manufacturers' Association.

Pharmaceutical Research and Manufacturers' Association. 1999b. *Submission of PhRMA for the "Special 301" Report on Intellectual Property Barriers.* www.pharma.org/issues/nte (16 February).

Pollin, Michael. 1998. Playing God in the Garden. *New York Times Sunday Magazine* (25 October).

Post, David G. 1998. Some Thoughts on the Political Economy of Intellectual Property: A Brief Look at the International Copyright Relations of the United States. Paper presented at the Sino-US Conference on Intellectual Property Rights and Economic Development, Chongqing (17 September).

Powelson, John. 1994. *Centuries of Economic Endeavor: Parallel Paths in Japan and Europe and Their Contrast with the Third World.* Ann Arbor, MI: University of Michigan Press.

Priest, George L. 1986. What Economists Can Tell Lawyers about Intellectual Property. In *Research in Law and Economics, Volume 8: The Economics of Patents and Copyrights,* ed. by J. Palmer and R. V. Zerbe, Jr. Greenwich, CT: JAI Press.

Primo Braga, Carlos A. 1996. Trade-Related Intellectual Property Issues: The Uruguay Round Agreement and Its Economic Implications. In *The Uruguay Round and Developing Countries,* ed. by Will Martin and L. Alan Winters. Cambridge: Cambridge University Press.

Primo Braga, Carlos A., and Carsten Fink. 1998. The Relationship between Intellectual Property Rights and Foreign Direct Investment. *Duke Journal of Comparative and International Law* 9: 163-88.

Primo Braga, Carlos A., and Carsten Fink. International Transactions in Intellectual Property and Developing Countries. *Journal of International Technology Management* 14, 1999.

Primo Braga, Carlos A., Carsten Fink, and Claudia Sepulveda. 2000. *Intellectual Property Rights and Economic Development.* World Bank Discussion Paper no. 412.

Rapp, Richard T., and Richard P. Rozek. 1990. Benefits and Costs of Intellectual Property Protection in Developing Countries. *Journal of World Trade* 24: 75-102.

Rathmann, George B. 1993. Biotechnology Case Study. In *Global Dimensions of Intellectual Property Rights in Science and Technology,* ed. by M. B. Wallerstein, M. E. Mogee, and R. A. Schoen. Washington: National Academy Press.

Reichman, J. H. 1993. From Free Riders to Fair Followers: Global Competition Under the TRIPs Agreement. *New York University Journal of International Law and Politics* 29: 11-93.

Reichman, J. H. 1994. Legal Hybrids between the Patent and Copyright Regimes. *Columbia Law Review* 94: 2432-2558.

Reichman, J. H. 1995. Universal Minimum Standards of Intellectual Property Protection under the TRIPs Component of the WTO Agreement. *International Lawyer* 29: 345-88.

Reichman, J. H. 1998. Solving the Green Tulip Problem: Packaging Rights in Subpatentable Innovation. Paper presented at the New York University Conference on Intellectual Products. La Pierra, Italy (25-28 June).

Reichman, J. H., and Jonathan A. Franklin. 1999. Privately Legislated Intellectual Property Rights: Reconciling Freedom of Contract with Public Good Uses of Information. *University of Pennsylvania Law Review* 147: 875-970.

Reichman, J. H., and Pamela Samuelson. 1997. Intellectual Property Rights in Data? *Vanderbilt Law Review* 50: 51-166.

Reichman, J. H., and Paul F. Uhlir. 1999. Database Protection at the Crossroads: Recent Developments and Their Impact on Science and Technology. *Berkeley Technology Law Journal* 14: 793-838.

Rockett, Katharine. 1990. The Quality of Licensed Technology. *International Journal of Industrial Economics* 8: 559-74.

Rodrik, Dani. 1988. Imperfect Competition, Scale Economies, and Trade Policy in Developing Countries. In *Trade Policy Issues and Empirical Analysis*, ed. by Robert E. Baldwin. Chicago: University of Chicago Press.

Rodrik, Dani. 1994. Comments on Initial Draft of Chapter. In *Analytical and Negotiating Issues in the Global Trading System*, ed. by Alan V. Deardorff and Robert M. Stern. Ann Arbor, MI: University of Michigan Press.

Romer, Paul. 1993. Idea Gaps and Object Gaps in Economic Development. *Journal of Monetary Economics* 32: 543-73.

Ross, J. C., and J. A. Wasserman. 1993. *Trade-Related Aspects of Intellectual Property Rights*. Deventer: Kluwer Law and Taxation Publishers.

Rozek, Richard P., and Ruth Berkowitz. 1998. The Effects of Patent Protection on the Prices of Pharmaceutical Products: Is Intellectual Property Protection Raising the Drug Bill in Developing Countries? *Journal of World Intellectual Property* 1: 179-244.

Rugman, Alan M. 1986. New Theories of the Multinational Enterprise: An Assessment of Internalization Theory. *Bulletin of Economic Research* 38: 101-18.

Ryan, Michael P. 1998. *Knowledge Diplomacy: Global Competition and the Politics of Intellectual Property*. Washington: Brookings Institution Press.

Sachs, Jeffrey. 1999. Helping the World's Poorest. *The Economist*. 14 August: 17-20.

Sachs, Jeffrey, Michael Kremer, and Amar Hamoudi. 1999. The Case for a Vaccine Purchase Fund. Harvard University. Photocopy.

Sachs, Jeffrey, and Andrew Warner. 1995. Economic Reform and the Process of Global Integration. *Brookings Papers on Economic Activity* 1: 1-95.

Samuelson, Pamela, Randall Davis, Mitchell D. Kapor, and J. H. Reichman. 1994. A Manifesto Concerning the Legal Protection of Computer Programs. *Columbia Law Review* 94, no. 8: 2308-2431.

Scherer, F. M. 1980. *Industrial Market Structure and Economic Performance*. 2nd ed. Chicago: Rand-McNally.

Scherer, F. M., and Sandy Weisburst. 1995. Economic Effects of Strengthening Pharmaceutical Patent Protection in Italy. *International Review of Industrial Property and Copyright Law* 26: 1009-24.

Schmalensee, Richard. 1981. Output and Welfare Implications of Monopolistic Third-Degree Price Discrimination. *American Economic Review* 71: 242-47.

Schut, F. T., and P. A. G. Van Bergeijk. 1986. International Price Discrimination: The Pharmaceutical Industry. *World Development* 14: 1141-50.

Scotchmer, Suzanne. 1991. Standing on the Shoulders of Giants: Cumulative Research and the Patent Law. *Journal of Economic Perspectives* 5: 29-42.

Segerstrom, Paul S. 1998. Endogenous Growth without Scale Effects. *American Economic Review* 88: 1290-1310.

Segerstrom, Paul S., T. C. A. Anant, and Elias Dinopolous. 1990. A Schumpeterian Model of the Product Life Cycle. *American Economic Review* 80: 1077-91.

Sell, Susan K. 1998. *Power and Ideas: North-South Politics of Intellectual Property and Antitrust.* Albany: State University of New York Press.

Shapiro, Carl, and Hal R. Varian. 1999. *Information Rules.* Boston: Harvard Business School Press.

Sherwood, Robert M. 1990. *Intellectual Property and Economic Development.* Boulder, CO: Westview Press.

Sherwood, Robert M. 1995. Compulsory Licensing under the TRIPs Agreement. *Latin American Law and Business Report* 3: 25-29.

Sherwood, Robert M. 1997. The TRIPs Agreement: Implications for Developing Countries. *IDEA: The Journal of Law and Technology* 37: 491-544.

Smith, Pamela J. 1999. Are Weak Patent Rights a Barrier to US Exports? *Journal of International Economics* 48: 151–77.

Subramanian, Arvind. 1995. Putting Some Numbers on the TRIPs Pharmaceutical Debate. *International Journal of Technology Management* 10: 252-68.

Tarr, David G. 1985. *An Economic Analysis of Gray Market Imports.* Washington: United States Federal Trade Commission.

Taylor, C. T., and Z. A. Silbertson. 1973. *The Economic Impact of the Patent System.* Cambridge: Cambridge University Press.

Taylor, M. Scott. 1993. TRIPs, Trade, and Technology Transfer. *Canadian Journal of Economics* 26: 625-38.

Taylor, M. Scott. 1994. TRIPs, Trade, and Growth. *International Economic Review* 35: 361-82.

Teece, David J. 1977. Technology Transfer by Multinational Firms: The Resource Cost of Transferring Technological Know-how. *Economic Journal* 87: 242-61.

Teece, David J. 1986. *The Multinational Corporation and the Resource Cost of International Technology Transfer.* Cambridge: Ballinger Press.

United Nations Conference on Trade and Development. 1995a. *Compendium of Documents and Reports Relating to the Work of the UNCTAD Ad Hoc Working Group on the Interrelationship Between Investment and Technology Transfer.* Geneva: United Nations.

United Nations Conference on Trade and Development. 1995b. *Technological Capacity-Building and Technology Partnership: Field Findings, Country Experiences and Programmes.* Geneva: United Nations.

United Nations Conference on Trade and Development. 1996. *The TRIPs Agreement and Developing Countries.* Geneva: UNCTAD.

United Nations Conference on Trade and Development. 1998. *World Investment Report 1998.* Geneva: UNCTAD.

United States Chamber of Commerce. 1987. *Guidelines for Standards for the Protection and Enforcement of Intellectual Property Rights.* Washington: United States Chamber of Commerce.

United States Congressional Budget Office. 1994. *How Health Care Reform Affects Pharmaceutical R&D.* Washington: Government Printing Office.

United States Congressional Budget Office. 1998. *How Increased Competition from Genetic Drugs Has Affected Prices and Returns in the Pharmaceutical Industry.* Washington: Government Printing Office.

United States International Trade Commission. 1984. *The Effects of Foreign Product Counterfeiting on US Industry.* Washington: USITC.

United States International Trade Commission. 1988. *Foreign Protection of Intellectual Property Rights and the Effect on US Industry and Trade.* Washington: USITC.

United States Office of Technology Assessment. 1993. *Pharmaceutical R&D: Costs, Risks and Rewards.* Washington: OT-H-522.

United States Trade Representative. Various years. *National Trade Estimates Report on Foreign Trade Barriers.* Washington: USTR.

UPOV (The International Union for the Protection of New Varieties of Plants). 1999. *States Party to the International Convention for the Protection of New Varieties of Plants.* http://www.upov.int.eng/brief.htm (13 July).

Vaitsos, Constantine. 1972. Patents Revisited: Their Function in Developing Countries. *Journal of Development Studies* 9: 71-97.

Varian, Hal R. 1985. Price Discrimination and Social Welfare. *American Economic Review* 75: 870-75.

Vishwasrao, Sharmila. 1994. Intellectual Property Rights and the Mode of Technology Transfer. *Journal of Development Economics* 44: 381-402.

Watal, Jayashree. 1999. Introducing Product Patents in the Indian Pharmaceutical Sector: Implications for Prices and Welfare. *World Competition* 20: 5-21.

Watal, Jayashree. 2000a. Pharmaceutical Patents, Prices, and Welfare Losses: A Simulation Study of Policy Options for India under the WTO TRIPs Agreement. *The World Economy* 23: 733-52.

Watal, Jayashree. 2000b. *Intellectual Property Rights in the World Trade Organization: The Way Forward for Developing Countries.* New Delhi: Oxford University Press, India and London: Kluwer Law International.

World Bank. 1997. *World Development Report 1997.* Oxford: Oxford University Press.

World Economic Forum. 1995. *World Competitiveness Report.* Davos, Switzerland: World Economic Forum.

World Health Organization. 1996. *Investing in Health Research and Development: Report of the Ad Hoc Committee on Health Research Relating to Future Intervention Options.* Geneva: World Health Organization.

World Intellectual Property Organization. 1988. *Background Reading on Intellectual Property.* Geneva: WIPO.

World Intellectual Property Organization. 1993. *Questions Concerning Possible Protocol to the Berne Convention: Memorandum Prepared by the International Bureau, Part III, News Items.* Geneva: WIPO (March).

World Intellectual Property Organization. 1999. *Contracting Parties of Treaties Administered by WIPO.* http://www.wipo.int/eng/ratific/c-wipo.htm. (13 July).

World Trade Organization. 1998. *Electronic Commerce and the Role of the WTO.* Geneva: WTO.

Yang, Guifang, and Keith E. Maskus. 2000a. Intellectual Property Rights, Licensing, and Innovation in an Endogenous Product-Cycle Model. *Journal of International Economics,* forthcoming.

Yang, Guifang, and Keith E. Maskus. 2000b. Intellectual Property Rights, Licensing, and Innovation. University of Colorado. Photocopy.

Yang, Guifang, and Keith E. Maskus. 2000c. Intellectual Property Rights and Licensing: An Econometric Investigation. University of Colorado. Photocopy.

Zeile, William J. 1993. Merchandise Trade of US Affiliates of Foreign Companies. *Survey of Current Business* 73: 52-65.

Zhang, Kevin H. 1996. *Theory and Evidence Regarding Multinational Enterprises and International Trade.* Unpublished Ph.D. dissertation. University of Colorado.

Index

Brazil (*cont.*):
　trade, 79, 81
　trademark applications, 70
　utility models, 147-48
breeder's exemption, 57, 166, 179, 224
Bristol-Myers Squibb, 218
broadcasts, 46, 51, 83
BSA. *See* Business Software Alliance
Budapest Treaty, 90
businesses. *See* multinational enterprises
Business Software Alliance (BSA), 100

cable television systems, 46
Canada
　effects of TRIPs implementation, 185, 191
　intellectual property rights enforcement, 5
　investment flows, 83
　patent system, 69, 101, 175, 182, 185
　perceived strength of intellectual property
　　rights protection, 98
　pharmaceuticals, 35, 217, 221
　plant variety registration, 71
　publishing industry, 72
　trade, 79
　trademark applications, 70
　See also North American Free Trade
　　Agreement (NAFTA)
capital markets, 201-2
chemical industry
　foreign investment decisions, 127, 130
　importance of patents, 43, 52
　international trade, 78, 116
　test data, 65
Chile
　costs of TRIPs compliance, 173
　pharmaceutical prices, 161
　plant breeders' rights, 166
　plant variety registration, 71
China
　effects of improved intellectual property
　　rights enforcement, 190
　intellectual property rights laws, 4, 6, 16,
　　94
　investment flows, 83, 153
　patent applications, 69, 175
　patents, 78, 101, 151-52, 156, 177
　pharmaceutical prices, 162
　productivity growth, 153
　publishing industry, 72
　research and development, 32, 154-55, 203
　software industry, 149
　software piracy, 101, 149
　software prices, 166
　technology transfer to, 154-55, 203
　television sets, 73
　trade, 78, 79, 151
　trademark applications, 70
　trademark infringement, 149, 156
　WTO membership, 6, 94, 236

Clinton administration, 55
Collections of Information Antipiracy Act, 62
Community Plant Variety Office (CPVO), 71
competition, relationship to intellectual
　property rights, 36, 110
competition policy
　abuses of intellectual property rights, 41-42,
　　206-8, 238
　defining, 180
　in developing countries, 141, 208
　in European Union, 207
　links to intellectual property rights
　　protection, 110, 205
　market structures, 208
　multilateral accord, 226-27
　non-price predation, 207
　parallel imports as, 211-12, 213-14, 215
　regulating monopoly pricing, 205-6
　TRIPs provisions, 24-25
　in United States, 207
　See also market-power pricing
compulsory licenses, 21, 178-79, 232
computer and information services, 79-81
computer chips. *See* integrated circuits
computers
　numbers of, 73
　trade, 78-79
　See also database copyrights; electronic
　　commerce; Internet
computer software. *See* software
contracts
　costs, 123-24
　See also licensing
Convention on Biodiversity, 225
copyrights
　alternatives, 46
　benefits for developing countries, 180, 191
　database. *See* database copyrights
　demand for products, 72-73, 72*t*
　distinction from patents, 44
　economic effects, 167
　economic justification, 45-46
　enforcement, 58, 158-59, 175
　fair use doctrine, 6, 45, 62, 180
　history, 34-35
　industries involved, 57-63
　infringements, 58, 100-01, 102, 149, 175
　international trade, 78
　issues related to Internet, 6, 46-47, 51, 60-
　　61, 227, 228
　legal principles, 44-45
　market power resulting from, 159
　measuring number of, 71-73
　moral rights and, 17, 45
　NAFTA provisions, 195
　objectives, 44, 45
　recorded entertainment, 58
　registration, 45
　rental rights, 19, 172
　software, 46, 50-51, 59, 158-59, 167, 177, 180

vaccine fund proposal, 229-30
See also pharmaceutical industry
Helpman-Krugman trade model, 113
HIV, 229
Hong Kong, 166
horticulture. *See* plant varieties
human capital
   development policies, 200-201
   generation of knowledge-based assets, 121
   relationship to patent protection, 105, 107
   role in economic growth, 153-54
   skills, 133, 134, 135
Hungary, 164

IIPA. *See* International Intellectual Property
   Association
imports. *See* parallel imports; trade
incomes
   relationship to intellectual property rights
      protection, 99, 102, 144
   relationship to patent protection, 95-96,
      102-5, 104*f*, 107-9, 108*t*, 129
   types of foreign investment, 122
India
   copyright protection, 149
   effects of TRIPs implementation, 185, 188
   film industry, 149
   patent applications, 175
   patent laws, 53, 94, 101, 108, 127, 160, 164,
      215
   pharmaceutical industry, 78, 162-63, 164,
      185, 215, 220
   publishing industry, 72
   television sets, 73
   trade, 78, 79, 81
   trademark applications, 70
Indonesia
   intellectual property rights laws, 94
   patent applications, 69-70
   trade, 78
industrial designs, 39-40, 83
information technology. *See* computers;
   database copyrights; electronic
   commerce; Internet
innovation
   in developing countries, 34, 35
   effects of intellectual property rights, 43,
      193
   human capital development, 200, 201
   limited by inadequate intellectual property
      rights, 147, 148-49
   promoting, 35, 193-94, 202-3
   social costs and benefits, 31
   tradeoff with access to technology, 29-31,
      30*f*, 32-33
   See also research and development
input measures of intellectual property rights
   protection, 88
   discrepancies among, 99-100

GP index of patent protection, 96-97, 99-
   100, 105-6, 106*t*, 107, 182
indexes, 94, 95*t*
membership in international conventions,
   88-91, 89*t*
perceptions of foreign executives, 91-93,
   92*t*, 97-99, 98*t*, 125-27
RR index of patent protection, 94-96, 102-3,
   113, 169
instruments, trade in, 78-79
integrated circuits
   international trade, 78
   NAFTA provisions, 195
   protection of, 51
   TRIPs provisions, 22
intellectual property
   definition, 27
   ease of copying and imitating, 3, 29, 46, 47,
      83-84, 167-68
   economic value, 2-3, 193-94
   market characteristics, 32
   output measurements, 67-70
   as public good, 28-29
   use in international economy, 3, 16, 66-67
intellectual property creation (IPC), 196
intellectual property diversion (IPD), 196
intellectual property rights (IPRs)
   abuses, 41-42, 168, 206-8, 238
   definition, 27
   enforcement. *See* enforcement
   exhaustion, 208-9, 210*t*
   expansion, 1
   goals, 31
   history, 2, 34-35, 190
   hybrid forms, 50-51, 60
   legal basis, 3
   links to trade, 110-11
   natural-rights view, 27
   objectives, 36
   public-rights view, 27-28
   sectoral reliance on, 51-52, 78
   structures, 36
   utilitarian view, 28
   See also copyrights; economics of intellec-
      tual property rights; patents; plant
      breeders' rights; trademarks
intellectual property rights (IPRs) protection
   agreements, 37-38*t*
   benefits, 4, 6-7, 147-50, 190-91, 199, 240
   costs, 6, 7, 33-34, 173-74
   demand and supply, 235-36
   determinants of, 102, 109, 144
   in developed countries, 3, 237
   in developing countries, 3-4, 6, 144, 147-50
   differences among national systems, 3-4, 34,
      35, 87-88
   economic impact. *See* economics
   input measures. *See* input measures
   instruments, 37-38*t*
   international cooperation, 174, 240-41

intellectual property rights (IPRs) protection
(*cont.*):
measuring effects of variations, 87-88, 109-10
output measures, 100-102, 109
pressures for change, 4, 16, 35-36, 58, 83-84, 144
related policy reforms, 200
relationship to incomes. *See* incomes
weaknesses, 4, 15-16
International Copyright Act, 34
International Intellectual Property Association (IIPA), 58, 59, 100
International Rice Research Institute, 56
International Union for the Protection of New Plant Varieties (UPOV), 90-91, 172, 179
Internet
access to, 73
copyright issues, 6, 46-47, 51, 60-61, 227, 228
patented business methods, 65-66
piracy, 83
trademark registration databases, 174
TRIPs provisions, 60
See also database copyrights; electronic commerce
inventions. *See* innovation
investment. *See* foreign direct investment
IPC. *See* intellectual property creation
IPD. *See* intellectual property diversion
IPRs. *See* intellectual property rights
Ireland, 172
Italy
benefits from TRIPs, 183
pharmaceutical industry, 165
pharmaceutical patents, 35, 165
pharmaceutical price regulation, 217, 219

Japan
investment flows, 83
lack of pharmaceutical patents, 35
parallel imports, 211, 212
patent applications, 69
patent system, 35, 93, 101, 143, 148, 190
pharmaceutical industry, 165, 217
plant variety registration, 71
pressure for stronger intellectual property rights, 16
publishing industry, 79
software patents, 51, 60
as technology follower, 143
total factor productivity, 148
trade, 78, 79, 81
utility models, 148
joint ventures, 137, 151

KBAs. *See* knowledge-based assets
knowledge, 120-21, 152

knowledge-based assets (KBAs), 120-22, 124
knowledge capital model, 133-35, 134*t*

labor
employed in infringing activities, 157-59, 158*t*, 201
flexibility of market, 201
Lebanon
effects of improved enforcement of intellectual property rights, 157-59, 158*t*, 190
pharmaceutical industry, 165
weak enforcement of intellectual property rights laws, 148, 149
licensing
compulsory, 21, 178-79, 232
decision factors, 154-55
designing contracts, 137
effects of intellectual property rights strength, 109, 127-29, 154-55, 183
effects of patent protection, 87
effects of TRIPs implementation, 186-88, 187*t*, 189-90
exclusionary effects, 207
fees and royalties, 79-81, 80*t*
government reviews of contracts, 204
growth, 16
restrictions, 206-8
software, 60
technology transfer through, 137, 138, 142, 150, 154-55, 203, 207
literary and artistic works. *See* copyrights; intellectual property
living organisms
patents for, 55-56, 222-23
See also biotechnology
location advantages, 121-22, 125

Madrid Protocol (MP), 70
malaria, 229
Malaysia
intellectual property rights laws, 109
patent applications, 69-70
trade, 78
market freedom, 105
marketing, 155-56
market-power pricing
effects of copyright and patent enforcement, 159, 174-76, 206-8
factors in, 160
in pharmaceuticals, 159-65, 182
medical research, 156-57, 229-30
medicines. *See* pharmaceutical industry
Merck and Company, 218
Mercosur, 5, 16
Mexico
effects of TRIPs implementation, 185, 188
foreign investment, 153

intellectual property rights laws, 5, 93, 109, 195
investment flows, 83
manufacturing exports, 153
maquiladora plants, 153
measures of intellectual property rights strength, 99-100
patent applications, 69, 175
patent system, 154, 164, 190
pharmaceutical prices and patents, 164
research and development in, 196
television sets, 73
trade, 79, 81, 153, 188
trademark applications, 70
See also North American Free Trade Agreement (NAFTA)
microorganisms
patents for, 223
See also biotechnology
Microsoft, 59
MNEs. *See* multinational enterprises
monopolies
creation by intellectual property rights, 30, 215
regulation of, 205-6
See also competition policy
moral rights, 17, 45
MP. *See* Madrid Protocol
multinational enterprises (MNEs)
affiliate sales, 131, 132*t*, 135
benefits of TRIPs implementation, 181, 186
chemical industry, 78, 116, 127, 130
exclusive territorial rights, 213-14
internalization advantages, 123-24
investment decisions, 120-24, 131-33, 132*t*
licensing decisions, 154-55
outsourcing, 122
ownership advantage, 120-21, 125
pressure for stronger intellectual property rights protection, 4, 15
technology transfer decisions, 131-33, 132*t*, 151-55
technology transfer within, 137, 150
vertical integration, 213-14
See also foreign direct investment; pharmaceutical industry; surveys of US business executives
music industry
copyrights, 58
electronic transmissions, 60-61
international trade, 78, 79
piracy, 83, 100

NAFTA. *See* North American Free Trade Agreement
National Institutes of Health, 223
National Trade Estimates Reports, 91-93
natural resources, protection of, 216-17

natural-rights view of intellectual property rights, 27
Netherlands, 217
New Zealand
effects of TRIPs implementation, 191
pharmaceutical price regulation, 217
test data regulations, 23
NGOs. *See* nongovernmental organizations
Nigeria, 102-3, 108
nongovernmental organizations (NGOs), 239, 240
North American Free Trade Agreement (NAFTA)
effects on research and development, 196
intellectual property rights provisions, 1, 5, 16, 93, 195, 196
trade secrets protection, 23, 195

ownership-location-internalization (OLI) paradigm, 120-24, 125

parallel imports
arguments against, 212-15, 238
arguments for, 211-12
books and sound recordings, 79
definition, 208
lack of empirical data, 215-16
policies on, 208-11, 212, 218
regulation tradeoffs, 213
TRIPs provisions, 21
in United States, 34
vertical price control and, 213-14
Paris Convention, 2
incorporation in TRIPs, 90
membership, 89-90, 91
perceived problems with, 15-16, 91
trade secrets provisions, 22
Patent Cooperation Treaty (PCT), 67, 69, 90, 174
patents
applications, 67-70, 68*t*, 175
of biotechnological inventions, 6, 20-21, 55, 90, 222-24
breadth, 40
for business methods on Internet, 65-66
competition issues, 41-42
compulsory licenses and, 21, 178-79, 232
criteria, 39
criticism of US system, 65-66, 237-38
in developing countries, 69-70, 182
distinction from copyrights, 44
domestic and foreign applicants, 69, 175
economic justification, 40-42, 43-44
effectiveness, 42-44
effects of strengthened protection, 151-52
estimated effects of TRIPs, 114-16, 185-88, 187*t*, 189, 190

structure, 51, 57
TRIPs provisions, 57, 165, 179
plant varieties
    biodiversity, 216, 225, 231, 240
    genetically engineered, 56, 222, 223, 231, 240
    International Union for the Protection of New Plant Varieties (UPOV), 90-91, 172, 179
    potential impact of patents, 6, 230-31
    protection of, 56-57, 216-17, 224
    registration applications, 70-71, 71*t*
    research, 56-57
pneumonia, 156
preferential trade areas (PTAs)
    exemptions from international treaties, 17
    intellectual property rights provisions, 1, 5, 16, 93, 194-97
    regulatory integration, 195
    See also North American Free Trade Agreement (NAFTA)
Priceline.com, 66
productivity. *See* total factor productivity
property rights, 145-46
PTAs. *See* preferential trade areas
public health, 35, 216
public-rights view of intellectual property rights, 27-28
publishing industry
    book production, 72
    international trade, 78, 79
    in Lebanon, 159
    in United States, 34, 72, 79
    See also copyrights

quality
    reputation for, 124
    role of intellectual property rights in improving, 155-56
    trademarks and, 48, 49, 156

RCA. *See* revealed comparative advantage
recorded entertainment
    copyrights, 58
    electronic transmissions, 60-61
    international trade, 78, 79
    piracy, 58, 83, 100
    prices, 159
    trademarks, 58
    See also film industry
regional trade agreements. *See* preferential trade areas
regulation
    alternatives to price controls, 221
    international harmonization efforts, 2, 5, 195
    pharmaceutical price controls, 53-54, 206, 214, 217-21

price controls, 214-15, 218-21
    social objectives, 214-15, 216-17
rent transfers, 175, 181-85, 184*t*, 224-25
research and development
    agricultural, 56-57
    commercialization, 202-3
    costs, 52, 53, 54-55, 214
    in developing countries, 56-57, 118, 165, 203
    effects of regional agreements on intellectual property rights, 196
    effects of stronger patent protection, 193-94
    global allocation, 193
    government monopolies, 32
    imitative capacity and, 118
    importance of patent system for investment in, 154, 156-57
    medical, 156-57, 229-30
    pharmaceutical, 53, 54, 165, 219
    public funding, 32, 56, 156, 202-3
    social returns on, 193
revealed comparative advantage (RCA), 73, 78, 79
reverse engineering
    in biotechnology, 55
    of integrated circuits, 22
    legitimacy, 23, 179, 180
    of pharmaceuticals, 136
    of software, 35, 45, 51, 60, 136, 180
    of trade secrets, 23, 50, 179
RLF. *See* royalties and license fees
Rome Convention, 17, 19
royalties and license fees (RLF), 79-81, 80*t*
RR index of patent protection, 94-96, 102-3, 113, 169
Russia, 101, 236

scientists
    in labor force, 107
    use of electronic databases, 61, 62, 228
    See also research
semiconductors. *See* integrated circuits
service marks, 47, 70, 70*t*
    See also trademarks
services sensitive to intellectual property rights protection, 79-81
SIIA. *See* Software and Information Industry Association
Singapore, 223
socialist countries, 28
social objectives
    of intellectual property rights, 35, 231-32
    of regulation, 214-15, 216-17
software
    anti-piracy measures, 61
    copyrights, 46, 50-51, 59, 158-59, 167, 177, 180
    demand for, 73
    industry, 59

United States (*cont.*):
    test data regulations, 23
    trade, 79, 81
    trademark applications, 70
    trade policy, 4, 16, 58, 181
    trade secrets protection, 190
    TRIPs implementation, 172
    See also North American Free Trade
        Agreement (NAFTA)
US Chamber of Commerce, 94
US International Trade Commission, 15
US Patent and Trademark Office, 55, 65-66
US Supreme Court, 55, 210-11, 222-23
US Trade Representative, 91, 99, 100, 101,
    218
UPOV. *See* International Union for the
    Protection of New Plant Varieties
Uruguay, 166
Uruguay Round, 16, 110
utilitarian view of intellectual property rights,
    28
utility models, 39, 147-48, 177

vaccine fund proposal, 229-30
Venezuela, 152, 153
video recordings, 83, 159
    See also film industry

Walt Disney, 52
wines. *See* alcoholic beverages
WIPO. *See* World Intellectual Property
    Organization
World Competitiveness Report, 98, 100
World Economic Forum, 98
World Health Organization, 156
World Intellectual Property Organization
    (WIPO)
    conventions, 6, 15-16, 60-61, 89, 89*t*, 172
    parallel imports issue, 213
World Trade Organization (WTO)
    dispute settlement, 5-6, 26, 172
    information technology agreements, 204
    Seattle Ministerial meeting (1999), 239
    TRIPs as part of, 5-6, 192, 238-39

Other Publications from the Institute for International Economics

* = out of print

Toward Renewed Economic Growth in Latin America*   Bela Balassa, Gerardo M. Bueno, Pedro-Pablo Kuczynski, and Mario Henrique Simonsen
1986   ISBN 0-88132-045-5
Capital Flight and Third World Debt*
Donald R. Lessard and John Williamson, editors
1987   ISBN 0-88132-053-6
The Canada-United States Free Trade Agreement: The Global Impact*
Jeffrey J. Schott and Murray G. Smith, editors
1988   ISBN 0-88132-073-0
World Agricultural Trade: Building a Consensus*
William M. Miner and Dale E. Hathaway, editors
1988   ISBN 0-88132-071-3
Japan in the World Economy*
Bela Balassa and Marcus Noland
1988   ISBN 0-88132-041-2
America in the World Economy: A Strategy for the 1990s   C. Fred Bergsten
1988   ISBN 0-88132-089-7
Managing the Dollar: From the Plaza to the Louvre*   Yoichi Funabashi
1988, 2d ed. 1989   ISBN 0-88132-097-8
United States External Adjustment and the World Economy*   William R. Cline
May 1989   ISBN 0-88132-048-X
Free Trade Areas and U.S. Trade Policy*
Jeffrey J. Schott, editor
 May 1989   ISBN 0-88132-094-3
Dollar Politics: Exchange Rate Policymaking in the United States*
I.M. Destler and C. Randall Henning
September 1989   ISBN 0-88132-079-X
Latin American Adjustment: How Much Has Happened?*   John Williamson, editor
April 1990   ISBN 0-88132-125-7
The Future of World Trade in Textiles and Apparel*   William R. Cline
1987, 2d ed. June 1990   ISBN 0-88132-110-9
Completing the Uruguay Round: A Results-Oriented Approach to the GATT Trade Negotiations*   Jeffrey J. Schott, editor
September 1990   ISBN 0-88132-130-3
Economic Sanctions Reconsidered (2 volumes)
Economic Sanctions Reconsidered: Supplemental Case Histories
Gary Clyde Hufbauer, Jeffrey J. Schott, and Kimberly Ann Elliott
1985, 2d ed. Dec. 1990   ISBN cloth 0-88132-115-X
                           ISBN paper 0-88132-105-2
Economic Sanctions Reconsidered: History and Current Policy
Gary Clyde Hufbauer, Jeffrey J. Schott, and Kimberly Ann Elliott
December 1990   ISBN cloth 0-88132-140-0
                           ISBN paper 0-88132-136-2

Pacific Basin Developing Countries: Prospects for the Future*   Marcus Noland
January 1991   ISBN cloth 0-88132-141-9
                           ISBN 0-88132-081-1
Currency Convertibility in Eastern Europe*
John Williamson, editor
October 1991   ISBN 0-88132-128-1
International Adjustment and Financing: The Lessons of 1985-1991*   C. Fred Bergsten, editor
January 1992   ISBN 0-88132-112-5
North American Free Trade: Issues and Recommendations
Gary Clyde Hufbauer and Jeffrey J. Schott
April 1992   ISBN 0-88132-120-6
Narrowing the U.S. Current Account Deficit*
Allen J. Lenz
June 1992   ISBN 0-88132-103-6
The Economics of Global Warming
William R. Cline/June 1992   ISBN 0-88132-132-X
U.S. Taxation of International Income: Blueprint for Reform*   Gary Clyde Hufbauer, assisted by Joanna M. van Rooij
October 1992   ISBN 0-88132-134-6
Who's Bashing Whom? Trade Conflict in High-Technology Industries   Laura D'Andrea Tyson
November 1992   ISBN 0-88132-106-0
Korea in the World Economy   Il SaKong
January 1993   ISBN 0-88132-183-4
Pacific Dynamism and the International Economic System*
C. Fred Bergsten and Marcus Noland, editors
May 1993   ISBN 0-88132-196-6
Economic Consequences of Soviet Disintegration*
John Williamson, editor
May 1993   ISBN 0-88132-190-7
Reconcilable Differences? United States-Japan Economic Conflict
C. Fred Bergsten and Marcus Noland
June 1993   ISBN 0-88132-129-X
Does Foreign Exchange Intervention Work?
Kathryn M. Dominguez and Jeffrey A. Frankel
September 1993   ISBN 0-88132-104-4
Sizing Up U.S. Export Disincentives*
J. David Richardson
September 1993   ISBN 0-88132-107-9
NAFTA: An Assessment
Gary Clyde Hufbauer and Jeffrey J. Schott/rev. ed.
October 1993   ISBN 0-88132-199-0
Adjusting to Volatile Energy Prices
Philip K. Verleger, Jr.
November 1993   ISBN 0-88132-069-2
The Political Economy of Policy Reform
John Williamson, editor
January 1994   ISBN 0-88132-195-8

DISTRIBUTORS OUTSIDE THE UNITED STATES

Australia, New Zealand, and Papua New Guinea
D.A. INFORMATION SERVICES
648 Whitehorse Road
Mitcham, Victoria 3132, Australia
tel: 61-3-9210-7777
fax: 61-3-9210-7788
e-mail: service@dadirect.com.au
http://www.dadirect.com.au

Caribbean
SYSTEMATICS STUDIES LIMITED
St. Augustine Shopping Centre
Eastern Main Road, St. Augustine
Trinidad and Tobago, West Indies
tel: 868-645-8466
fax: 868-645-8467
e-mail: tobe@trinidad.net

United Kingdom and Europe (including Russia and Turkey)
The Eurospan Group
3 Henrietta Street, Covent Garden
London WC2E 8LU England
tel: 44-20-7240-0856
fax: 44-20-7379-0609
http://www.eurospan.co.uk

Northern Africa and the Middle East (Egypt, Algeria, Bahrain, Palestine, Jordan, Kuwait, Lebanon, Libya, Morocco, Oman, Qatar, Saudi Arabia, Syria, Tunisia, Yemen, and United Arab Emirates)
Middle East Readers Information Center (MERIC)
2 bahgat Aly Street
El-Masry Towers, Tower #D, Apt. #24, First Floor
Zamalek, Cairo EGYPT
tel: 202-341-3824/340 3818;
fax 202-341-9355
http://www.meric-co.com

Taiwan
Unifacmanu Trading Co., Ltd.
4F, No. 91, Ho-Ping East Rd, Sect. 1
Taipei 10609, Taiwan
tel: 886-2-23419646
fax: 886-2-23943103
e-mail: winjoin@ms12.hinet.net

Argentina
World Publications SA.
Av. Cordoba 1877
1120 Buenos Aires, Argentina
tel/fax: (54 11) 4815 8156
e-mail:
http://wpbooks@infovia.com.ar

People's Republic of China (including Hong Kong) **and Taiwan** (sales representatives):
Tom Cassidy
Cassidy & Associates
70 Battery Place, Ste 220
New York, NY 10280
tel: 212-706-2200   fax: 212-706-2254
e-mail: CHINACAS@Prodigy.net

India, Bangladesh, Nepal, and Sri Lanka
Viva Books Pvt.
Mr. Vinod Vasishtha
4325/3, Ansari Rd.
Daryaganj, New Delhi-110002
INDIA
tel: 91-11-327-9280
fax: 91-11-326-7224 ,
e-mail: vinod.viva@gndel.globalnet.
ems.vsnl.net.in

South Africa
Pat Bennink
Dryad Books
PO Box 11684
Vorna Valley 1686
South Africa
tel: +27 14 576 1332
fax: +27 82 899 9156
e-mail: dryad@hixnet.co.za

Thailand
Asia Books 5 Sukhumvit Rd. Soi 61
Bangkok 10110 Thailand
(phone 662-714-0740-2 Ext: 221, 222, 223
fax: (662) 391-2277)
e-mail: purchase@asiabooks.co.th
http://www.asiabooksonline.com

Canada
RENOUF BOOKSTORE
5369 Canotek Road, Unit 1,
Ottawa, Ontario K1J 9J3, Canada
tel: 613-745-2665
fax: 613-745-7660
http://www.renoufbooks.com

Colombia, Ecuador, and Peru
Infoenlace Ltda
Attn: Octavio Rojas
Calle 72 No. 13-23 Piso 3
Edificio Nueva Granada, Bogota, D.C.
Colombia
tel: (571) 255 8783 or 255 7969
fax: (571) 248 0808 or 217 6435

Japan and the Republic of Korea
United Publishers Services, Ltd.
Kenkyu-Sha Bldg.
9, Kanda Surugadai 2-Chome
Chiyoda-Ku, Tokyo 101
JAPAN
tel: 81-3-3291-4541;
fax: 81-3-3292-8610
e-mail: saito@ups.co.jp
For trade accounts only.
Individuals will find IIE books in leading Tokyo bookstores.

South America
Julio E. Emod
Publishers Marketing & Research
Associates, c/o HARBRA
Rua Joaquim Tavora, 629
04015-001 Sao Paulo, Brasil
tel: (55) 11-571-1122;
fax: (55) 11-575-6876
e-mail: emod@harbra.com.br

Visit our Web site at:
http://www.iie.com
E-mail orders to:
orders@iie.com